EXPATS GUIDE

MEXICO

Mikkel Thorup

ExpatMoney.com

Cover Design: Ceylan Sahin Eker

IG: @ceylanswatercolors

Some of the images: Pixabay.com

ISBN: 978-9962-17-485-1

To my beautiful wife, none of this would be possible without your unwavering support.

To my mother, who sacrificed countless hours to help me to bring these books to fruition.

CONTENTS

1. BEFORE YOU GET STARTED 7

2. SHOULD YOU MOVE TO MEXICO...................................19

3. WELCOME TO MEXICO..33

4. A BRIEF HISTORY...59

5. WEATHER AND CLIMATE..65

6. SAFETY...77

7. HOW TO GET TO MEXICO..87

8. STUFF THAT'S GOOD TO KNOW....................................95

9. RELIGION AND HOLIDAYS..119

10. MEXICO CITY..135

11. BEST CITIES FOR EXPAT LIVING................................161

12. PETS...201

13. LANGUAGE 213

14. CULINARY AND FOOD...227

15. COST OF LIVING...2375

16. HEALTH CARE..253

17. EDUCATION..275

18. IMMIGRATION..285

19. TRANSPORTATION...325

20. REAL ESTATE IN MEXICO............................353

21. YOUR HOME.......................................389

22. WORKING ABROAD...............................431

23. DOING BUSINESS IN MEXICO...................437

24. MEXICAN TAXES................................447

25.CONCLUSION....................................459

SOURCES...466

ABOUT THE AUTHOR................................472

CHAPTER 1

BEFORE YOU GET STARTED

ANTES DE EMPEZAR

For what it's worth: It's never too late, or in my case, too early, to be whoever you want to be. There's no time limit. Stop whenever you want. You can change or stay the same. There are no rules to this thing. We can make the best or the worst of it. I hope you make the best of it, and I hope you see things that startle you. I hope you feel things you have never felt before. I hope you meet people with different points of view. I hope you live a life you're proud of. If you find that you're not, I hope you have the courage to start all over again.

F. SCOTT FITZGERALD

WHY I'M WRITING THIS BOOK

Honestly, as I write this book, I realize that more and more people are waking up to the fact that for a minimal amount of money, you can get residency in a country like Mexico that offers more freedom. If you are immigrating to Mexico or looking to see if Mexico is the best country for you and your family, this book is for you. If done correctly, the immigration process to Mexico can be quick and efficient, allowing you to stay in the country for as long as you want. Mexico can be your new home; stay, enjoy, eat the fresh fruit and vegetables and enjoy the mountain breeze or the beautiful ocean view.

AFTER READING THIS BOOK, YOU WILL KNOW OR HAVE

- A thorough understanding of the types of visas to be able to move to Mexico and the specific requirements to get residencies

- The safest cities to live in as expats

- What cities, areas and neighbourhoods to consider when moving to Mexico

- A relocation checklist and cost of living analysis

- What you can bring into the country when you move to Mexico

- If you have children, how you can educate them as an expat

- What do you need to do as a pet owner so that they can live with you in Mexico

- What to know when buying/renting real estate if you want to live in Mexico or if you want a rental property and stay in your home country

- Your tax responsibilities in Mexico, how to open a bank account, and what structures to use to hold property legally

- How to acquire a Mexican passport quickly and efficiently

- The kinds of food you'll be enjoying in Mexico

...And so much more!

Ask Yourself, Is This Book For Me?

Many people dream of moving to Mexico but don't realize that the process can be complicated, confusing and stressful if you don't work with the right people.

Moving to another country is an exciting quest, but the journey involves risks. Many decide to move, only to encounter more problems along the way.

Others pick up and go without really understanding what they are getting into, only to return home.

Yet others do extensive research and planning on their own but still run into surprises and setbacks because they never reached out to people who have already moved or to experts who can lend assistance and provide valuable input.

And the last group of people who do their research and work with a professional like us here at ExpatMoney.com have very few headaches along the way and are quite happy and secure in their new lives abroad.

No matter your decision, this book will help guide you through the process and pitfalls that can happen to anyone when moving overseas.

You can make many choices, and there will not be just one right choice. You will likely read everything you can on 2 or 3 countries, narrow it down, and then go for it.

My first job as an author is to discuss mindset. Are you ready for a change, and how will you accomplish it? Throughout this book, we'll look into all the pieces that make up an international move. Whether you are moving from the USA, Canada, Europe, or elsewhere, all pieces will look fairly similar.

Next, my job is to present to you all the good, bad and ugly of the country of choice. And today, we're talking about Mexico.

Depending on your situation, there are many factors to consider when contemplating any move. Indeed, this is even more true when one is considering a move to a foreign country. Whether you are single or married, have children or don't, have an employment contract or will need to find employment or start a business.

These things will need to be considered as you evaluate whether or not Mexico could be a place you would want to call 'home'... either temporarily or permanently.

If you are interested in shortcutting the entire process and want expert assistance, I do work 1-on-1 with private clients; you can find out more about how we can help you on our website www.ExpatMoney.com

SHOULD I STAY OR SHOULD I GO?

Do I believe I must stay and live out the rest of my life in the country of my birth? OR, can I move to a country where potentially my life can be much better? Somewhere I can keep more of my hard-earned money, have a simpler life if I choose, and love life the way it was meant to be.

I was born and raised in London, Ontario, Canada. Canadians love being Canadians. We're told from a very young age that Canadians are happy, loving, and courteous people, and for the most part, they are correct. However, the brainwashing only goes so far.

I started writing this book in the Spring of 2021. It is now late in 2022, and look what is happening and has been happening for a long time in Canada.

The Canadian government is reaching into people's bank accounts and freezing their assets if they disagree with them.

Who could have ever imagined this would happen? Earlier in 2022, the Prime Minister of Canada mandated that you could not leave the country if you were not vaccinated. What is happening, and where will this end?

Every day people reach out to me, asking for my assistance in leaving Canada behind, a country they've lived their entire lives in, to find a more accessible country that believes in a free market. The citizens of Canada are afraid they will become the next Venezuela. Only time will tell.

Even before this nightmare with Covid and the mandated vaccines, Canadians lived with high taxes (really high). The crazy thing about the Canadian tax system is that you get taxed on after-taxed dollars. If you make $100,000, you will likely pay the government about 40% of that through federal and provincial taxes.

You're left with $60,000.

Then you have to pay tax on everything you purchase and, depending on the province you are in, it can be up to 15%. You have land taxes, gasoline taxes, food taxes, and entertainment taxes. Nothing is free of tax except fruits, vegetables and meat. Everything else is taxed. You can pay upwards of 80% of your income to taxes. And the more money you make, the higher the tax bracket you are placed in.

This is why I left Canada at 17 years old... okay, I didn't understand the depth of taxation then, but I knew I didn't want to spend the rest of my life in Canada.

Inherently I knew something was wrong with the system, and I wanted to see, feel and enjoy what the rest of the world had to offer. So I set out to find where the best countries were to live. Where was the safest, best countries to start a job, and a family, raise happy, healthy children, and optimally pay fewer taxes?

FEARS ABOUT BECOMING AN EXPAT

In our Private Group, https://ExpatMoneyForum.com, the question of the day:

What is your biggest fear in becoming a first-time Expat?

People opened up within the first 24 hours and talked about their fears. Here are some of the biggest ones:

• Being mugged in the wrong neighbourhoods

• The cost without commensurate reward

• The logistics of financial/taxes, particularly on the U.S. side

• Not knowing the language

• Mail service

- Healthcare

- Taxes

- Children and will they adapt

- Income

- What if I move my entire life somewhere else and don't like it?

These are real problems, and luckily enough, we have real answers. I'll discuss the topics in detail in this book and much more.

ARE YOU CRAZY FOR WANTING SOMETHING DIFFERENT?

No matter your age, background, ethnicity, gender, or whatever, at some point, you'll ask yourself, 'Am I crazy for wanting something different' and the simple answer is NO.

Many of us want something different from the gal or guy next door. What was fine and dandy for previous generations doesn't cut it for us. It's perfectly fine for your sister to want to stay in the city she was born in, raise a family and enjoy Sunday dinners with her friends, but maybe the thought of that for the rest of your life is too much to bear.

After 22+ years of continual travel around the world and living as an expat, I can tell you that many people just like us have asked themselves these difficult questions and decided that the path forward for them was living outside their country of birth.

KNOW YOUR WHY

Why do you want to move abroad? Are you finally saying enough? Enough interference by my government! Enough with the high taxes!

Is it for business, or are you being transferred?

Are you at retirement age and want to spend the rest of your days lounging around and going to the beach every day, or do you hate the winters and need the warmth and sunshine day in and day out? Or is it a second passport you're after to protect yourself, your family and your wealth?

Ask yourself:

- Why do I want to move?

- What sacrifices am I willing to make (or not make)?

- Am I good at making new friends?

- Is anything holding me back from making connections and learning about a new culture?

An essential part of moving abroad and starting over is having the courage to leave everything behind, the naysayers, those that don't support you and find new, courageous friends who do.

Moving abroad can be both exhilarating and terrifying for many. I hope the information you read in this book will help alleviate some of your issues. I want you to love the next chapter of your life, really go for it!

Regardless of where you currently call home, you will find that Mexico can offer you excellent quality of life, most likely for a lot less money than you are presently accustomed to.

Here is a study on 'Why People Move Overseas.' Some of the reasons may surprise you!

- Lower Cost of Living 86.6%

- A simpler, less stressful life 82.0%

- Better weather 73.8%

- A less materialistic or more meaningful life 55.8%

- A more romantic, exotic, or adventurous life 42.4%

- Be more engaged in charitable activities/help others 31.4%

- Better access to less expensive, quality healthcare 30.9%

- A fresh start 22.1%

- A job or a place to run a business 21.1%

I've discussed who this book IS for -the adventurous, can't wait to learn a second language, yearning to build character, change your life for the better, and meet new people kind of person.

BUT WHAT IF THIS BOOK ISN'T FOR YOU

Let's talk very quickly about who this book is NOT for.

Suppose you are the kind of person looking for a country that will adapt to YOU.

In that case, a country that only speaks English and you are not interested in learning a second language and being able to fit in nicely with the locals, plus you think you're entitled to have the government pay for you to sit on the couch, day in and day out.

This book is NOT for you. Please feel free to refund the book and go no further, I can't help you here.

Becoming an expat is a big step, and it's not always easy, but I can promise you it will be an adventure.

CHAPTER 1: QUICK SUMMARY

After reading this book, you will know or have:

- A thorough understanding of the types of visas to be able to move to Mexico and the specific requirements to get residencies

- The safest cities to live in as expats

- What cities, areas and neighbourhoods to consider when

moving to Mexico

- A relocation checklist and cost of living analysis

- What you can bring into the country when you move to Mexico

- If you have children, how you can educate them as an expat

- What do you need to do as a pet owner, so that they can live with you in Mexico

- What to know when buying/renting real estate if you want to live in Mexico or if you want a rental property and stay in your home country

- Your tax responsibilities in Mexico, how to open a bank account, and what structures to use to hold property legally

- How to acquire a Mexican passport quickly and efficiently

- The kinds of food you'll be enjoying in Mexico

...And so much more! In Chapter 2, we will discuss why Mexico might be the perfect place to live, get residency and possibly a second passport. If Mexico still sounds like an exciting place for you, continue reading; we have a lot to cover!

SHOULD YOU MOVE TO MEXICO?

¿DEBERÍAS MUDARTE A MÉXICO?

Not all those who wander are lost.

J.R.R. TOLKIEN, THE FELLOWSHIP OF THE RING

If the journey is just beginning for you and you're comparing different countries, let's see if Mexico is the right fit. As mentioned in Chapter 1, this book will give you all you need to know about Mexico to make an informed decision.

It's essential to ensure that Mexico is the right place for you and your family, considering the heat, sun and sand.

There is something special about every country and culture; you just have to find the best one for you.

And here's the best part, if you get to Mexico and hate it, you can leave and try again. Yes, it's work to pack everything back up, but it's your life. Don't let that bog down the decision to possibly have the best life ever.

You can make many choices, and there will not be just one right choice. You will likely read everything you can on two or three countries (I have books on several countries to help narrow it down), and then go for it.

As you well know, Mexico has had a bad rap over the years. You are not alone in your decision to move to Mexico as an estimated 1.5 million US citizens are living in Mexico, according to the US State Department, and Mexico is the top foreign destination for US travellers.

With a vibrant culture and an economy that is moving upward thanks to new socio-economic policies implemented by Mexican President Andres Manuel Lopez Obrador, Mexico is quite possibly on the verge of a long-overdue positive social transformation.

The weather, lifestyles and steadily increasing quality of life could make Mexico the perfect destination for you to settle down.

If you are from the US, Mexico is close enough to feel slightly familiar but different enough to feel like an adventure in another country and culture. Also, Mexico is the closest option to living in a sunny, temperate coastal community with perfect welcoming weather.

Mexico has a much cheaper standard of living than the US or Canada, as for several years, one US dollar has been worth just under 20 pesos. Labour is also cheaper, which makes the cost of goods more affordable. Here you can hire a maid, gardener and even a chef to cook you lunch and dinner, all for what you would pay a maid for one day a week in Toronto or New York.

Family and friends will be a short plane ride away, so frequent visits are quite doable and easy. In most of the larger cities, you will find many stores you are accustomed to seeing in the USA, such as Walmart, Sam's Club, Costco, Starbucks, and Home Depot. In metropolitan areas, roads are generally good, and the internet can be fast and reliable.

Regardless of where in the world you currently call home, you will find that Mexico can offer you excellent quality of life, most likely for a lot less money than you are presently accustomed. The Latin American region is currently brimming with economic opportunities and offers expats numerous chances to enhance their quality of life. Mexico is one of the fastest-growing economies in the region–coming in second after Brazil and beating all other countries in the region with its high income per capita of $9673 as of 2018.

The Mexican economy and society are characterized by political stability, consistent economic growth, and increasing global trade shares than the rest of its Latin American counterparts. In 2018, Mexico hosted 49.6 million visitors, including not just tourists and vacationers from all over the world but also retirees and 'snow birds' seeking to escape the brutal winters in Canada and the northern US.

Tourist visas only allow you to stay in the country for 180 days (for Americans, Canadians and Europeans), so if your move to Mexico will be long-term or permanent, you will need to educate yourself on the different legal residency options. Several visa options are available, and we will examine these carefully later in Chapter 18: Immigration.

Foreigners are not permitted to work in Mexico without a work permit. If you are planning to open a business or need to find employment, the necessary permit will need to be obtained. This prevents foreigners from taking jobs away from Mexicans and applies to professionals such as doctors and lawyers.

If you are being transferred to Mexico by your current employer, they will no doubt take care of this or help you, but you will want to double-check with them to be sure. A work permit is not required for those operating companies or services entirely online, and many expats with location-independent businesses, or 'digital nomads,' enjoy life in Mexico.

WHAT IS IT LIKE TO LIVE IN MEXICO?

Living in Mexico is very different from living in Canada, Europe or the United States.

English is spoken in most tourist centres, big hotels, resorts, and bigger cities. However, it is not common to expect that people will be able to converse with you in English. We will cover languages in chapter 13, but this cannot be stressed enough. It would help if you learned even a fraction of Spanish to have an enjoyable conversation and your life in Mexico. I always suggest to my clients to start working on learning Spanish before moving overseas. The best program I have found for learning Spanish is from my dear friend Olly Richards at https://StoryLearningCourses.com

Mexico's pace of life is considerably slower than in Canada, Europe and the US., especially when we talk about living outside of the bigger cities.

One common issue in Mexico and Central America is that when things are promised at a certain time or date, they don't mean it. This can be very frustrating. If a plumber says he will fix your toilet on Monday, you have to ask him, which Monday? Next Monday? Or the Monday after that? It's something that I still struggle with, even after living in Latin America for several years.

The people in Mexico are extremely warm and friendly. They genuinely love to hear your stories of living in another country, another world for most of them.

Integrating yourself into Mexican culture and communities is important if you want to enjoy your life in Mexico. If you stay within the expat community, you will never really understand and appreciate what Mexico is all about.

Mexico is laid back, with an emphasis on a cool, calm, and collected pace. You've heard the saying 'mañana'. That means tomorrow, and that's how most Mexicans lead their lives.

Mexico's culture has a rich history and is solidly based on tradition, family and people. Family is a central theme and a cornerstone of their culture. Often you will see 3 or 4 generations coming together for lunch or dinner, sitting around a big table and talking about their lives.

Religion is another big part of Mexican culture. They tend to be religious and fatalistic. Most Mexicans still go to church every Sunday.

REASONS TO MOVE TO MEXICO

People move to Mexico for various reasons: professional, personal, or a combination of both.

Some move to Mexico to retire, especially for the climate. Thousands of foreign professionals arrive in Mexico annually as part of a temporary assignment with their company. American, Canadian, European and Asian corporations have offices and manufacturing facilities in Mexico, and it's common for managers and specialists to be allowed to work in Mexico.

Although the reasons that people make a conscious decision and choose to live in Mexico are many, here are some common reasons.

GROWING ECONOMY

If we go back to recent years, Mexico was becoming one of the fastest-growing economies in the world. The state system offered incentives for people to invest in the country and drew in vast amounts of foreign investments responsible for the economic growth spurt Mexico was experiencing. The country had a GDP of $244 billion as of the first quarter of 2019 and is expected to grow higher as time passes.

With these considerations in mind, there's still plenty of reason for people to move to Mexico. I am highlighting the advantages of moving to Mexico so that more people understand why it's essential to branch out and get multiple passports and how that ties into their financial interests.

Before Covid-19, Mexico was one of the largest growing economies in the world; owing to the development of the tech sector, you can even cash in on these nascent organizations.

Do you remember that boom of start-ups around the early 2000s? Mexico was going through one at the close of 2019. Speculating that life will return to somewhat normal activity for the tech industry, I would certainly be looking into investing in Mexico.

AVAIL OF THE ADVANTAGES OF DUAL NATIONALITIES

Whenever my clients come to me for advice, I've always supported the idea of dual nationality. There are plenty of reasons for my stance on multiple passports.

Most of them are of a financial nature, such as tax considerations, ease of doing business, and opening bank accounts and companies, but also because it becomes easier to travel the world visa-free.

Even if you need a visa, you can send one passport away for a visa and still travel on the backup passport.

The Mexican government has recently promoted dual nationalities in light of improvements in foreign relations with the US.

They've eliminated many barriers to immigration that people face, and the process has become a lot easier over the past few years.

With a Mexican nationality, you get access to investment opportunities unique to Mexico. The tax system is very convenient (I'll discuss that in a bit), and the country is one of the cheapest places to live.

CLOSE PROXIMITY TO THE UNITED STATES

Travelling to and from almost anywhere in the United States is pretty easy if you are living in Mexico.

Flights only take a couple of hours at max before you land in the country, and if you're managing your businesses in the United States, it's pretty easy to do it from Mexico.

There's no reason why moving to Mexico should hold back your business interests even in the slightest. As a Canadian, Toronto, Montreal and Vancouver have direct flights to Mexico City. All can be accomplished within 4-6 hours at the most.

MEXICO IS PRETTY CHEAP

If we're judging living standards by the number of goods and services you can buy, then there's no better place to live than Mexico. The housing is pretty cheap, the healthcare system is great, and services like home care and travel are equally as affordable compared to other countries worldwide. If you're earning in dollars or the euro, the exchange rate differences enable you to buy many things at a fraction of their actual cost.

Research indicates that Mexico has a purchasing power index rating of 30.8, which means that prices in Mexico are about 70% lower than those of the United States.

When you consider the differences in the exchange rates between the US dollar and the Mexican Peso (roughly $1 to 20 Pesos), you'll live like a king or queen in the country.

The fact that Mexico isn't as wealthy a nation as the United States has its advantages because of the lower inflationary pressures in the economy and is, therefore, so much cheaper than the United States.

THE TAX ADVANTAGES

Mexico also has a very convenient tax system, making it incredibly easy for people to buy property in the country and run a business there as a resident.

Whenever you're thinking of moving to a new country, I advise that you always check their tax profiles to see how much of your money you can retain while living there.

As time passes, tax burdens can take up much of your money, and it pays to minimize your tax liabilities. You can read more about taxation in Chapter 24.

Mexico, fortunately, is one of those countries that offer really low tax rates—not a tax haven, but pretty decent nonetheless.

Here are a few of the benefits:

• 10% tax on dividends

• No capital duty

- No payroll taxes

- Transfer taxes of 2%-5%

- No stamp duty

- Non-residents are taxed only on their income derived in Mexico

- No capital acquisition tax

CULTURALLY VIBRANT SOCIETY

If there's one thing I can promise you, it's that Mexico is one of the most culturally vibrant countries in the world. It's so appealing to people that entire food chains commercialize Mexican cuisine, and Americans celebrate Mexican holidays.

The country offers a lot to people from a cultural aspect. Whether you're thinking about the food, holidays, people or the beaches, there's a lot to experience in the country.

REAL ESTATE IS PRETTY CHEAP IN MEXICO

One thing I love about Mexico is the real estate markets in the country. In recent years, the real estate industry has been growing consistently. The latest figures for 2019 show that real estate prices rose by nearly 10% over the last quarter, and even today, with Covid-19, when we go back to 'normal,' the real estate prices will continue to be competitive especially compared to the US.

For someone looking to move to Mexico, the average home price is $90,591 compared to a median-priced, middle-class home in the United States, priced at $248,857.

The exact amount of money can get you a far more luxurious house in Mexico, with more amenities and a team of gardeners, housekeepers, and other services.

GETTING A RETIREMENT VISA IS SIMPLE

If you want to settle down in an exotic location—Mexico is pretty simple, offers plenty of investment opportunities, and it's straightforward to get a retirement visa. I'll outline the basics of the process in Chapter 18 – Immigration.

You should make note that your income can come from any of the following sources:

• Rental income

• Pensions

• Interest income, and returns on cash deposits in banks

I believe that Mexico has yet to manifest its full economic potential. These countries that were once celebrated for their cultural value are finally settling down the path of economic development and prosperity, which will bode well for everyone.

For one thing, their growth will take away the economic hegemony of the leading economic nations which have been coercing the world for centuries. For another, this financial growth comes hand in hand with an immense cultural value you won't find anywhere else in the world.

Even with governments' responses worldwide to covid, the best financial decision is one that factors in the economic and political circumstances and how these affect your financial well-being.

Mexico may have been in the United States' bad books over the past few years, but things are finally looking up. Considering the country's recent political stability and economic prosperity, you should consider Mexico as one of your retirement destinations. It can be done for those who aren't looking to retire but are considering getting dual nationalities. It may not be the easiest country, but as long as you work with a professional and put the time in, you will have a new passport.

CHAPTER 2: QUICK SUMMARY

Some popular reasons to move to Mexico:

- Growing economy

- Avail the advantages of dual nationality

- Close proximity to the United States

- Mexico is easier on the pocket

- The tax advantages

- The new technological hub of the Americas

- Culturally vibrant society

- Real Estate is pretty cheap in Mexico

- Getting a retirement visa Is simple

In Chapter 3, we'll look closely at Mexico, the country, the people and their culture

WELCOME TO MEXICO

BIENVENIDO A MÉXICO

The real voyage of discovery consists not in seeking new landscapes but in having new eyes.

MARCEL PROUST

Mexico is a vast country, and living in Mexico City is nothing like living in Mazatlan or Puerto Vallarta. It's a beautiful country with so many unique living experiences.

Mexico, officially the United Mexican States, is a country in the southern portion of North America between the USA and Central America. Mexico borders the USA to the north and Guatemala and Belize to the south.

The western border of Mexico is a coastline of the Pacific Ocean, except for the inward jutting Gulf of California that separates the Baja Region from the rest of the country. On the eastern coast, you will find the Gulf of Mexico.

Mexico has 32 autonomous federal states and 2,456 municipalities. As of this writing, the current population is 132,061,307 million, 83.8% concentrated in urban areas and covers 761,610 sq mi (1,972,550 sq km), making it the world's 13th-largest country by area; it is the 10th-most-populous country and has the most Spanish-speaking population.

The population grew 48.4% between 1990 and 2015, with greater aging and a reduction in its expansive structure, especially in groups under 20. 7.2% are 65 years of age or older. Life expectancy in 2022 is 72.6 years for men and 78.2 for women.

The Intercensal Survey revealed that 21.5% of the population thinks of itself as indigenous and 1.2% as Afro-descendant.

With a nominal gross domestic product (GDP) of $1076.16 billion USD in 2020, the country's economy is one of the 20 most extensive in the world. In 2020, the services sector represented around 60.16% of the GDP.

Mexico is a land of extremes, with high mountains and deep canyons in the country's center, sweeping deserts in the north, and dense rain forests in the south and east.

The Sierra Madre Oriental mountain range in the east and the Sierra Madre Occidental in the west lie small mountain ranges on the Central Plateau. These regions are rich in valuable metals like silver and copper.

The stretch of land called the Yucatán Peninsula juts into the Gulf of Mexico from Mexico's southeastern tip. It was once the home of the Maya civilization, an ancient culture whose impressive buildings can still be seen today.

From its tiny pueblos and villages reminiscent of old Mexico to massive urban areas with every modern convenience, Mexico truly has something for everyone. According to 2020 census numbers, Mexico's ten largest cities (by population) are

- Mexico City, states of Mexico (District Federal) and Hidalgo, pop. 21,804,515

- Guadalajara, state of Jalisco, pop. 5,179,000

- Monterrey, state of Nuevo Leon, pop. 4,874,000

- Puebla, State of Puebla, Tlaxcala, pop. 3,244,710

- Toluca, State of Mexico, pop. 2,467,000

- Tijuana, state of Baja California, pop. 2,157,853

- Leon, state of Guanajuato, pop. 1,768,193

- Juarez, state of Chihuahua, pop. 1,391,180

- Torreon, states of Coahuila and Durango, pop. 1,283,835

- Queretaro, states of Queretaro and Guanajuato, pop. 1,255,185

PROVINCES AND STATES

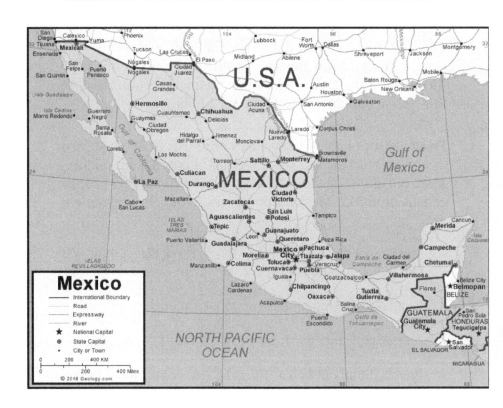

Mexico is divided into 31 states, with its capital, Mexico City, being a federal entity.Chihuahua is the largest state by land area, and Tlaxcala is the smallest.

- Aguascalientes
- Baja California
- Baja California Sur
- Campeche
- Chiapas
- Chihuahua
- Coahuila
- Colima
- Durango
- Guanajuato
- Guerrero
- Hidalgo
- Jalisco
- México (State of)
- Mexico City (former Mexico D.F.)
- Michoacán
- Morelos
- Nayarit
- Nuevo León
- Oaxaca
- Puebla
- Queretaro
- Quintana Roo
- San Luis Potosí
- Sinaloa
- Sonora
- Tabasco
- Tamaulipas
- Tlaxcala
- Veracruz
- Yucatán
- Zacatecas

PEOPLE & CULTURE

Mexico is the product of a rich Native American heritage, three centuries of Spanish rule, and a shared border with the world's richest country, the US. Today, many Mexicans are mestizos, which means they have a mix of Native American and Spanish blood.

Throughout its history, Mexico has been home to many great artists. To name a few: Frida Kahlo, born in Coyoacan, Mexico; Diego Rivera; Jose Clemente Orozco; Rufino Tamayo; Maria Izquierdo, and so many more.

The Maya and other Native Americans made impressive murals, sculptures, and jewelry. Modern Mexican artists include great painters, photographers, sculptors, and muralists.

More than half of the Mexican people live in the country's centre, whereas vast areas of the arid north and the tropical south are sparsely settled.

Migrants from impoverished rural areas have poured into Mexico's cities, and nearly four-fifths of Mexicans now live in urban areas. Mexico City, the capital, is one of the most populated cities and metropolitan areas.

Mexico has experienced a series of economic booms leading to periods of impressive social gains, followed by busts, with significant declines in living standards for the middle and lower classes. The country remains strong due to stronger ties with the United States and Canada through the North American Free Trade Agreement (NAFTA).

Mexico is more than 1,850 miles (3,000 km) across from northwest to southeast; its width varies from less than 135 miles (217 km) at the Isthmus of Tehuantepec to more than 1,200 miles (1,900 km) in the north.

NATIONAL BIRD OF MEXICO

The Golden Eagle (Aquila chrysaetos)

TIME ZONES IN MEXICO

If you are considering a move to Mexico and you are an

American, time zones are one thing you won't have to worry about too much. Mexico has four standard time zones, the same as the time zones in the 48 contiguous United States.

Coming from Europe, Asia, Australia or elsewhere in the world, keeping up with time zones will be much like adjusting to US time zones. Mexico observes Daylight Savings Time, which begins at 2:00 am local time on the first Sunday in April and ends at 2:00 am on the last Sunday in October.

The switch to and from Daylight Savings Time can get a little tricky as the switch in Mexico does not necessarily occur simultaneously in the US. Keep this in mind if you work online or have business dealings in the US. If you plan to travel to or live in the Mexican states of Sonora and Quintana Roo, these states do not observe Daylight Savings Time.

CURRENCY

WHERE AND HOW TO EXCHANGE CURRENCY

Generally speaking, do not exchange money at the airport. This will not be the place to get the best exchange rate. If possible, go to an ATM and withdraw money from your account in your home country in the local currency. Once you have set up a local bank account, this will not be such an issue.

The official currency of Mexico is the peso (sign: $, code: MXN). The Mexican Peso is the 10th most traded currency in the world, the most traded Latin American currency, and the third most traded currency in the Americas behind the US Dollar and the Canadian Dollar.

MEXICO HAS 35 UNESCO WORLD HERITAGE SITES

CULTURAL (27)

- Agave Landscape and Ancient Industrial Facilities of Tequila (2006)

- Aqueduct of Padre Tembleque Hydraulic System (2015)

- Archaeological Monuments Zone of Xochicalco (1999)

- Archaeological Zone of Paquimé, Casas Grandes (1998)

- Camino Real de Tierra Adentro (2010)

- Central University City Campus of the Universidad Nacional Autónoma de México (UNAM) (2007) (See Chapter 10: Best Cities For Expat Living)

- Earliest 16th-Century Monasteries on the Slopes of Popocatepetl (1994,2021)

- El Tajin, Pre-Hispanic City (1992)

- Franciscan Missions in the Sierra Gorda of Querétaro (2003)

- Historic Centre of Mexico City and Xochimilco (1987) (See Chapter 10: Best Cities For Expat Living)

- Historic Centre of Morelia (1991)

- Historic Centre of Oaxaca and Archaeological Site of Monte Albán (1987)

- Historic Centre of Puebla (1987)

- Historic Centre of Zacatecas (1993)

- Historic Fortified Town of Campeche (1999)

- Historic Monuments Zone of Querétaro (1996)

- Historic Monuments Zone of Tlacotalpan (1998)

- Historic Town of Guanajuato and Adjacent Mines (1988)

- Hospicio Cabañas, Guadalajara (1997)

- Luis Barragán House and Studio (2004)

- Pre-Hispanic City and National Park of Palenque (1987)

- Pre-Hispanic City of Chichen-Itza (1988)

- Pre-Hispanic City of Teotihuacan (1987) (See Chapter 10: Best Cities For Expat Living)

- Pre-Hispanic Town of Uxmal (1996)

- Prehistoric Caves of Yagul and Mitla in the Central Valley of Oaxaca (2010)

- Protective town of San Miguel and the Sanctuary of Jesús Nazareno de Atotonilco (2008) (See Chapter 10: Best Cities For Expat Living)

- Rock Paintings of the Sierra de San Francisco (1993)

NATURAL (6)

- Archipiélago de Revillagigedo (2016)

- El Pinacate and Gran Desierto de Altar Biosphere Reserve (2013)

- Islands and Protected Areas of the Gulf of California (2005)

- Monarch Butterfly Biosphere Reserve (2008)

- Sian Ka'an (1987)

- Whale Sanctuary of El Vizcaino (1993)

MIXED (2)

- Ancient Maya City and Protected Tropical Forests of Calakmul, Campeche (2002,2014)

- Tehuacán-Cuicatlán Valley: originary habitat of Mesoamerica (2018)

TOP PLACES TO VISIT IN MEXICO

Mexico is a big country. It has miles and miles of shoreline, all of it beautiful. If you're coming for a visit, then it's likely where you'll stay. But you can't go to Mexico without seeing a few of the most spectacular sites on earth.

Here are a few things to do and see when you're in Mexico. It depends on what part of the country you are staying in, but if you can find the time, then these are well worth the trip.

TULUM, QUINTANA ROO

Tulum is a small town with approximately 46,000 residents; however, don't let that deter you from visiting. There is so much to see and do here.

Today, Tulum is one of the most visited places in Mexico. It offers beautiful beachfront living, cenotes, Mayan ruins that you can spend days and days wandering through and surprisingly, active nightlife—something for everyone.

TEOTIHUACAN RUINS

The ancient Teotihuacan Pyramids (pronounced tay-oh-tee-wok-on), are located an hour outside Mexico City and is one of the UNESCO Sites in Mexico. Built thousands of years ago by the mysterious Teotihuacanos, the Pyramid of the Sun is the third-largest pyramid in the world, and temples and palaces flank the mile-long Avenue of the Dead.

Although taller, the Pyramid of the Sun is more accessible to climb than the Pyramid of the Moon because it has shorter steps. Much of Teotihuacan's culture and history remain a mystery as the city was abandoned around 750 AD, and no one knows why. Extensive ruins were left, but very little is known about its inhabitants.

MONTE ALBAN RUINS

The ancient city of Monte Alban is located just 30 minutes outside Oaxaca City Centre. It is the most-visited of all archeological sites and ancient ruins in Oaxaca, making it a UNESCO World Heritage Site.

GREAT PYRAMID OF CHOLULA

Located underneath the Iglesia de Nuestra Señora de los Remedios Cholula church, you'll find the Great Pyramid of Cholula. It is the largest pyramid on Earth by volume and the largest archeological site that has a pyramid in the New World.

COPPER CANYON (BARRANCA DEL COBRE)

Copper Canyon is the eighth largest canyon on Earth, the second largest in North America (after the Grand Canyon), and a UNESCO World Heritage Site.

The best way to see the Mexico Copper Canyon is on the El Chepe Train. This famous Mexico train goes through the canyon and the deserts in Northern Mexico. For the best views, board in Los Mochis, Sinaloa, and travel 220 miles (354 km) northeast to the city of Creel in Chihuahua, Mexico.

CHICHEN ITZA MAYAN RUINS, YUCATAN

With two million visitors a year, Chichen Itza Mayan Ruins are the most visited of all Mexico tourist attractions. Chichen Itza is one of the New Seven Wonders of the World and one of Mexico's UNESCO World Heritage Sites in Yucatan. Chichen Itza is located 3-hours from all the top Yucatan Mexico destinations, like Cancun, Tulum, Merida and Playa del Carmen.

AKUMAL, QUINTANA ROO

The beach town of Akumal is located in the Yucatan Peninsula, between Tulum and Playa del Carmen and is known as one of the best Mexico resort areas, as it is famous for its turtles. Swimming with the turtles in Akumal is quite an experience, and the only way to have this experience is to book a tour with one of the local agencies, for the safety of the turtles. Akumal Bay restricts the number of people on the beach daily. The best time to see the Akumal turtles is from May to November.

TRADITIONAL DRESS

Each area in Mexico has their traditions and customs. Each has a unique dress for the woman.

In Jalisco, the typical dress has a striking design and is a skirt and matching blouse. It consists of a very wide skirt with ribbon stripes in the middle that form a star and more ribbon stripes at the bottom. The blouse has a high collar and matching stripes on the sleeves. It is very similar to the so-called Escaramuza dress. (Escaramuza Charra is the name given to the female participating in the sport of Charreria).

In Tabasco, the typical dress is very different. It is usually a skirt using a flower print fabric, a white blouse, and embroidery figures in the collar and sleeves. They also like to wear sophisticated hairstyles with flowers.

Their clothing has evolved through history; in the past, before the Spanish arrived, they had a simpler apron and top. With the textile industry developing, they started to create their textile designs. Michoacán is the state of Mexico where Purepechas have lived for a long time, in the land around Lake Patzcuaro.

Women use sophisticated clothing: A skirt with a pattern, a long blouse with embroidery at the bottom and around the neck, a belt strapped on the back, and usually a rebozo.

Blouses with more embroidery are used in special celebrations. Aprons are also typically used and have nice cross-stitch embroidery decoration.

SPORTS

FÚTBOL

They call it fútbol in Mexico, soccer in the United States, and football in the rest of the world. But no matter what you call it, it's the most popular sport in Mexico and the rest of the world.

Football was a pastime sporting activity introduced by English miners in the late 1900s, which did not go professional until 1943. Mexico successfully hosted two FIFA World Cup matches in 1970 and 1986. The Mexican National Soccer team has performed well in Pan America, CONCACAF and NAFC

BASEBALL

There are two leagues in Mexico. A 16-team Summer League (Mexican League of Baseball) and an 8-team Winter League (Mexican Pacific League) bring laurels to the country.

While baseball has had its glorious moments in the past (Monterrey Little League team and outstanding players from Negro Leagues and American Leagues), it remains a regional sport today.

BULLFIGHTING

Although animal rights advocates criticize bullfighting worldwide as cruel and inhumane for the animals, bullfighting is still popular in places like Spain and Mexico.

Apart from being a blood sport, it includes auxiliary events of folkloric dances and rodeo. Mexican bullfighting is one of the profitable sports as well as a popular tourist attraction.

CHARRERÍA

Charrería or Charreada is a national sport of Mexico similar to an American rodeo. This competitive equestrian event evolved from the ranch work activities followed by Old Mexico's haciendas (estates).

Today, the Charrería comprises several events involving both horses and cattle. The charros display their horse-lassoing skills and are garbed in traditional charro clothing, often with a live Mariachi band accompaniment. Winners of the Charrería do not receive any monetary rewards but saddles and horse trailers.

GEOGRAPHY

Mexico is incredibly diverse in terms of not only people but climates and landscapes. It has the 4th highest biodiversity in the world, with about 10% of all the world's species living somewhere in Mexico.

This large country is covered in mountains, deserts, and rainforests, but the most significant division may be the Tropic of Cancer, which cuts right through the middle of Mexico. This is important because Mexico's climate is different on either side. To the north, the weather is temperate and relatively dry.

Temperatures can reach extreme heat in summer and much colder in winter. South of the Tropic of Cancer, Mexico is much more tropical, with consistent yearly temperatures and more rainfall.

Another defining feature of Mexico's overall geography is that it sits over not one, not two, but three tectonic plates. As a result, Mexico is among the most seismically active places in the Western Hemisphere, and earthquakes have caused significant damage in the past.

This seismic activity is also one reason that Mexico is predominantly mountainous in terms of geological history.

NORTHERN MEXICO

You can divide Mexico into three loose regions, each of which has unique geographic features.

Northern Mexico, the part above the Tropic of Cancer, is defined by a mixture of deserts and mountains. There are two main mountain ranges in northern Mexico. To the west is the Sierra Madre Occidental, and to the east is the Sierra Madre Oriental. These twin ranges run parallel to each other from north to south, extending into central Mexico. The

Sierra Madre Oriental mountains are also a continuation of the same mountains that make up the Rockies in the United States.

Between these ranges is a high-elevation plain called the Mexican Altiplano, or Mexican Plateau. The Altiplano region is predominantly an arid desert, including the expansive Chihuahuan Desert.

There are a few other things that make northern Mexico notable. On its western side, it contains the world's longest peninsula, a 775-mile (1247 km) stretch of land called the Baja California Peninsula.

The northern state of Chihuahua also has Mexico's largest canyon, Copper Canyon, which is seven times the area of the Grand Canyon and over 1,400 feet (426 m) deeper. Major cities of northern Mexico include Ciudad Juárez, Tijuana, and Chihuahua.

CENTRAL MEXICO

The Sierra Madre Occidental range runs north to south for 683 miles (1,100 km), which joins the southern mountain range of Sierra Madre del Sur. This primarily volcanic range runs through the centre of Mexico and forms the western border of the Mexican Plateau. The elevation of the range averages 7478 – 8858 ft (2,400-2,700 m).

One of the most spectacular areas in the Sierra Madre Occidental is the Copper Canyon (Barranca del Cobre) in the north. The Copper Canyon is a series of six canyons formed by six rivers that merge into the Rio Fuerte and drain into the Gulf of California. And why is it called the Copper Canyon? The reason is that the canyon walls are copper/green in colour.

YUCATAN PENINSULA

The Yucatan Peninsula is in the southeast of Mexico. It separates the Caribbean Sea from the Gulf of Mexico and is the exposed portion of the Yucatan Platform. The region features many caves, sinkholes (cenotes), and tropical rainforests.

The Ring of Fire is a 25,000-mile (40,000 km) horseshoe-shaped line of volcanoes, earthquakes and other seismic activity, plus deep ocean trenches and high mountain ranges formed around the edges of the Pacific Ocean. Mexico lies in the Ring of Fire. Popocatepetl is one of Mexico's most active volcanoes and one of the most dangerous volcanoes in the Ring of Fire. This is also Mexico's second-highest peak at 17,800 ft (5,426 m). Colima, also known as Volcan de Fuego, is another of Mexico's most active volcanoes. Volcano Pico de Orizaba is, in fact, Mexico's highest point at 18,700 ft (5,700 m).

TOURISM

Tourism is one of Mexico's most influential businesses, and they are blessed to contain all the key ingredients of the perfect tourist destination. Since the 1960s, it has been heavily promoted by the Mexican government as "an industry without smokestacks."

According to the World Tourism Organization, Mexico has traditionally been among the most visited countries in the world. It is the second-most visited country in the Americas after the United States. Mexico attracted foreign visitors in the early nineteenth century for its cultural festivals, colonial cities, nature reserves and beach resorts. The nation's temperate climate and unique culture – a fusion of the European and Mesoamerican attract tourists.

The peak tourism seasons in the country are during December and the mid-Summer, with brief surges during the week before Easter and Spring break, when many beach resort sites become popular destinations for college students from the United States. The majority of tourists come to Mexico from the United States and Canada. Other visitors come from other Latin American countries. A small number of tourists also come from Europe and Asia.

LANGUAGES

Spanish is Mexico's official language; however, many languages are spoken in Mexico.

The indigenous languages are from 11 language families, including four isolates from the US. The Mexican government recognizes 68 national languages. 63 are indigenous.

FREQUENTLY ASKED QUESTIONS

Do I Need A Visa To Go To Mexico?

If you are from Canada, the USA, the United Kingdom or the EU, you can visit visa-free for 180 days.

Is There A Direct Phone Line That I Can Use In Case I Have An Emergency During My Trip To Mexico?

Dial 911 for the police, ambulance or fire.

Do I Need A Yellow Fever Vaccine?

You do not need a yellow fever vaccine to travel to Mexico if from Canada, the US, or Europe; however, you will require a yellow fever vaccination certificate if you are from certain South American countries.

Is Mexico A Safe Country?

Yes and no. We go into more depth on safety later in the book. Check out Chapter 6: Safety

Does Mexico Have An Army?

Yes, Mexico does have a standing army. They are ranked 17th in the world with 277,150 active military personnel.

What Is The Best Food In Mexico?

There are many excellent dishes here in Mexico. Many you would have had back home, like tacos and quesadillas. Dishes you need to taste are tamales, gorditas, and enfrijoladas, to name just a few.

What Are The Best Beaches In Mexico?

There are hundreds of fantastic beautiful beaches, in fact, almost 500. I'll list more later, but here are a few of my favourites: Tulum, Riviera Maya, Yucatan Peninsula; Playa del Amor, Cabo San Lucas and Cancun Beach, Riviera Maya.

What Places Should I Visit In Mexico?

Like beaches, there are dozens of fun and exciting places to visit. While in Tulum, you can't miss the Tulum Ruins, a Mayan archaeological site perched on a cliff that overlooks the Caribbean Sea, and the lesser-known Palenque ruins tucked deep in the jungle of Chiapas.

What is Mexico's Drinking Age?

18

How Old Do You Have To Be To Drive?

To drive in Mexico, you should be a minimum of 15 years old with adult supervision or 18 without.

Is Gambling and Prostitution Legal In Mexico?

Gambling is permitted in Mexico, although the local government imposes restrictions on these activities to protect citizens. Prostitution is legal under federal law in Mexico. The country's 31 states each enact their prostitution policies, and 13 of those states allow and regulate prostitution. Some cities have "tolerance zones," which act as red-light districts and enable regulated prostitution. Pimping is illegal in most parts of Mexico.

Does Mexico use the Metric System?

Like most countries, Mexico uses the metric system with temperatures in degrees Celsius and distances in kilometres, measurements in metres and weights in kilograms.

CHAPTER 3: QUICK SUMMARY

Concepts to help move you to Mexico;

- Rich native heritage with three centuries of Spanish rule

- Mexico is divided into 31 states, with its capital, Mexico City, being a federal entity

- Four standard time zones

- Currency is the peso

- Mexico has 35 Unesco World Heritage Sites

- Fútbol is the most popular sport in Mexico

- Tourism is one of Mexico's most influential businesses

- Spanish is the official language of Mexico

In Chapter 4, we discuss the history of Mexico and how it came to be under Spanish rule.

A
BRIEF
HISTORY

UNA BREVE HISTORIAE

If you don't know history, then you don't know anything. You are a leaf that doesn't know it is part of a tree.

MICHAEL CRICHTON

Pre-Columbian Mexico traces its origins to 8,000 BC and is identified as one of the six cradles of civilization. It was home to many advanced Mesoamerican civilizations, most notably the Maya and the Aztecs.

Just north of Mexico City are Teotihuacan's ruins, considered by most historians the most important of the pre-Columbian archaeological sites.

The origins of Teotihuacan are uncertain. It's thought that some of the inhabitants arrived from the Valley of Mexico to the south as refugees from the eruption of the Xitle volcano. Construction of the city probably started in the first two centuries BC, and the civilization reached its high point between 350 and 650 AD.

From there, and for centuries, there were invasions from the north. The Purepecha, or Tarascos, settled in the state of Michoacan, and the Toltecs settled at Tula and ended up being destroyed by invaders.

The Aztecs, known as the Mexica, were nomadic, warlike people who arrived in central Mexico from the north in the late 13th century.

By 1400, the Aztecs dominated the Valley of Mexico. Within 70 years, they had expanded their territory to be the largest empire in Mesoamerica's history, now known as Mexico City.

"In 1521, the Spanish Empire conquered and colonized the region from its base in Mexico City, establishing the colony of New Spain. The Catholic Church played an important role in spreading Christianity and the Spanish language while also preserving some indigenous elements.

Native populations were subjugated and heavily exploited to mine rich deposits of precious metals, which contributed to Spain's status as a major world power for the next three centuries, and to a massive influx of wealth and a price revolution in Western Europe. Over time, a distinct Mexican identity formed, based on a fusion of European and indigenous customs; this contributed to the successful Mexican War of Independence against Spain in 1821."

"Mexico's early history as a nation-state was marked by political and socio-economic upheaval. The Texas Revolution and the Mexican–American War in the mid-19th century led to huge territorial losses to the United States. Liberal reforms were enshrined in the Constitution of 1857, which sought to integrate indigenous communities and curtail the power of the church and the military. This triggered an internal war of Reform and intervention by France, in which conservatives installed Maximilian Habsburg as emperor against the Republican resistance led by Benito Juárez.

The last decades of the 19th century were marked by the dictatorship of Porfirio Díaz, who sought to modernize Mexico and restore order. The Porfiriato era ended in 1910 with the decade-long Mexican civil war, which killed approximately 10% of the population and after which the victorious Constitutionalist faction drafted a new 1917 Constitution, which remains in effect to this day. The revolutionary generals ruled as a succession of presidents until the assassination of Alvaro Obregón in 1928. This led to the formation of the Institutional Revolutionary Party the following year, which governed Mexico until 2000.

HISTORY OF THE MEXICAN FLAG

About 700 years ago, the "Aztecs lived in the arid desert in northern Mexico. They were looking for the ideal place to build their new city. In the legend, the Aztec god Huitzilopochtli (we-see-low-PōCH-tlee) told the Aztecs to build their city where they find an eagle carrying a snake that lands on a nopal (cactus).

As was predicted in the ancient prophecy, they spotted the eagle with a snake in its beak on a cactus – in a huge swampy

area. Despite the challenging conditions, they built their city, Tenochtitlán, on a small swampy island in Lake Texcoco. It was this area that eventually became Mexico City. This scene that the Aztecs first saw is displayed in the centre" of the Mexican flag as the Mexican Coat of Arms.

Over the years, the current crest and colours of the Mexican nation have undergone several changes.

Today, the coat of arms is in the centre of the flag, with a laurel branch symbolizing victory. The image was added to the flag for the Olympics in Mexico City in 1968. Before this date, the flag was presented without the emblem.

THE THREE-COLORED DESIGN

"The flag of Mexico has three vertical stripes - green, white, and red. The design dates back to 1821 when Mexico finally gained its independence from Spain. The colour green was chosen to represent independence from Spain. The red stood for union between the native peoples of Mexico and the elites of European heritage, a union that was key to the independence movement. The colour white was adopted to represent the purity of Roman Catholicism.

Today, no official explanation is given for the flag's colours, partly because the original meanings have little relevance to modern Mexican society. Yet many Mexicans have taken up this popular explanation: "Green represents hope for the nation, white represents unity, and red symbolizes the blood of those who died fighting for the nation's independence."

FLAG DAY IN MEXICO

The flag is so central to Mexican identity and culture that it has its own national day, celebrated on the 24th of February each year.

CHAPTER 4: QUICK SUMMARY

- History of Mexico.

- Officially the United Mexican States.

- It covers 761,610 sq miles, making it the 13th largest country by area.

- 131,378,356 inhabitants; 10th most populous country and has the most Spanish-speaking population.

- Pre-Columbian Mexico traces its origins to 8,000 BC.

- In 1521, the Spanish Empire conquered and colonized the region from its base in Mexico City, establishing the colony of New Spain.

- Mexico is a developing country, ranking 74th on the Human Development Index.

- The Mexican flag was created about 700 years ago by the Aztecs, who lived in the arid desert in what is now northern Mexico.

In Chapter 5, we talk about Mexico's weather and climate. Each month brings different weather conditions, and you can see the best month to travel.

WEATHER AND CLIMATE

TIEMPO Y CLIMA

The sun did not shine. It was too wet to play. So we sat in the house. All that cold, cold, wet day.

DR. SEUSS, THE CAT IN THE HAT

Each region in Mexico has a different climate and weather pattern. If you think about it, it makes sense. You have Northern Mexico, near the border of California and Arizona, where it's hot, scorching hot.

The weather there is usually arid except in January, when the temperatures drop to near freezing, with the occasional snowfall. So be prepared! Then as you move down, you have Baja California, where the temperatures are much more enjoyable at 80°F (27°C) most of the time. Central Mexico also has lovely weather, but as you go towards the Gulf Coast and Southern Mexico, the temperatures rise an additional 10°F (6°C).

Hottest of all is the Yucatan Peninsula, where 90°F (32°C) seems to be the sweet spot. That's really hot, and the average low is only 70°F (21°C). Hot during the day **and** hot at night. As I look at it, you will love these hot spots if you come from anywhere in Canada or the Northern States in the US.

High Season: December – April – The best time for outdoor activities

Shoulder Season: July & August – The best time for surfing and exploring the stunning Northern Central Highlands

Low Season: May & June, September – November – Great for inland explorations

JANUARY

It's warm in coastal and lowland areas, cool in the highlands and dry everywhere. The first week is the Mexican holiday season.

January is also the peak season for migratory birds along Mexico's Pacific coast. Lagoons and rivers at places like Laguna Manialtepec and Lagunas de Chacahua are packed with fowl, and San Blas even holds an International Migratory Bird Festival.

FEBRUARY

Temperatures are marginally higher than in January, but it remains dry, making this a great month to be in much of Mexico, though it can still be cold in the north and at high altitudes.

This is when the magnificent grey whales calve in bays and lagoons around the Baja Peninsula. They tend to arrive any time from mid-December and stay until mid-April. Whales can also be spotted along the whole Pacific coast during this period. The best months for Baja whale-watching are February and March..

MARCH

It's getting steadily warmer all over Mexico, but it's still dry and is classified as still the winter season.

March is also the Vernal Equinox when visitors mob Chichén Itzá to see shadows resembling a serpent ascending or descending the El Castillo pyramid. Almost the same effect occurs for a week preceding and following each equinox.

APRIL

Temperatures continue to increase, but it stays dry. Semana Santa (Easter Week), which can be in March or April, is Mexico's major holiday week of the year. Semana Santa is the week from Palm Sunday to Easter Sunday, and many things shut down in inland cities. Good Friday sees solemn processions in many places, and enormous crowds attend a re-enactment of the Crucifixion in Iztapalapa, Mexico City.

MAY

Temperatures reach annual peaks in cities such as Mérida (average daily high 95°F (35°C), Guadalajara (87°F (35°C)), Oaxaca (86°C) and Mexico City (79°C). Surf starts to be steady along the Pacific Coast.

JUNE

The rainy season begins, bringing heavy downpours in the southeast and some places along the Pacific coast and the central highlands. Countless spots along the Pacific coast, including Puerto Escondido with its legendary Mexican Pipeline, enjoy superb swells from April/May to October/

November. June to August generally sees the biggest waves. Beginners can learn to surf almost year-round.

JULY

It's rainy in the southeast, central highlands and along the Pacific coast, but this is a summer vacation month for both foreigners and Mexicans. Massive whale sharks congregate to feed on plankton off Isla Contoy, north of Cancún, between mid-May and mid-September. The best time to swim with these gentle giants is mid-June to July.

AUGUST

The summer holiday season continues, as do the rains, although they're less intense in most areas. June to August is brutally hot in the north.

SEPTEMBER

It's the height of the hurricane season on the Yucatán Peninsula and Mexico's coasts. It's also rainy in most places, with poor visibility for Caribbean divers.

The weather inland, especially in Mexico City, starts to cool, and there isn't nearly as much rain. This is the start of a beautiful season in the higher elevations. The water in Baja is crystal clear.

OCTOBER

There are possible hurricanes, but the rains ease off everywhere except the Yucatán Peninsula.

October, along with November and March, is one of the best months to visit northwest Mexico's spectacular canyon country, with temperatures not too hot at the bottom of the canyons nor too cold at the top.

Guanajuato hosts the Festival Internacional Cervantino, a two to three-week arts festival dedicated to Spanish writer Miguel de Cervantes, one of the biggest cultural happenings in Latin America, with performances by worldwide music, dance and theatre groups. It is most certainly worth a trip to this charming city for this incredible event.

NOVEMBER

The weather is mostly dry, and hot temperatures are subsiding. Snow tops the high peaks of the central volcanic belt. On the Día de Muertos (November 2), cemeteries come alive as families decorate graves and commune with their dead, some holding all-night vigils.

Special altars appear in homes and public buildings.

Associated events start days before, notably around Pátzcuaro, Uruapan, Mexico City and Oaxaca.

DECEMBER

A dry month almost everywhere and as cool as it gets. Christmas–New Year period is Mexican holiday time. From late October to mid–March, the forests of the Reserva de la Biosfera Santuario Mariposa Monarca (Monarch Butterfly Biosphere Reserve) turn orange as millions of large monarch butterflies winter here.

The best time to watch them is on a warm, sunny afternoon in December.

MEXICO'S SEVEN CLIMATE REGIONS

Given that Mexico has many mountains with rapid changes in elevation, temperature and rainfall, weather in Mexico can become extremely complicated. A relatively small area of Mexico may include several climate categories.

TWO TROPICAL CLIMATES

Mexico has two tropical climates, with average temperatures of over 64°F (18°C) for all twelve months of the year.

The first, tropical wet, has at least 2.4 inches (60 mm) of rain every month. This is the same climate as the Amazon and Indonesian rainforests.

In Mexico, this is the climate of the Gulf Coast Plain in southern Veracruz and Tabasco. It also occurs in the Oaxaca and Chiapas highlands. The rains fall all year, varying from about 4–5 inches (120–150 mm) in April to 15 inches (380 mm) in September.

The tropical wet-and-dry has a pronounced dry season. The dry winter months typically get less than 1 in (40 mm) of rain, compared to over 6 inches (150 mm) in each summer month.

Parts of West Africa, Brazil and India have a similar climate. Much of coastal Mexico, stretching from Nayarit along the Pacific coast to Guatemala, is in this category. It also covers many inland areas along the Pacific coast. Central and northern Veracruz and most of the Yucatán Peninsula also have this tropical climate with summer rains.

TWO DRY CLIMATES

Areas with an arid (desert) climate usually receive less than 10 inches (250 mm) of rain a year. This is the climate of the Sahara Desert and Central Australia.

In Mexico, dry desert areas include most of Baja California, western Sonora, and the northern section of the Central Plateau. These areas can experience frost and freezing during the winter.

Areas with the second type of arid climate, semi-arid (dry steppe), receive 10–30 in (250–750 mm) of rain annually. This is the climate of the African savanna lands and much of central Asia.

In Mexico, this climate region includes most of the Central Plateau and western sections of the Western Sierra Madre, northern Yucatán and scattered inland areas as far south as Oaxaca. The rains in this region fall mainly in the summer, and localized heavy thunderstorms are pretty common. The southern parts of this climatic region are warmer than the northern parts.

THREE TEMPERATE ZONES

Temperate climates typically have average temperatures above 50°F (10°C) in their warmest months, and the coldest month average between 27-64°F (3°C-18°C). Moisture characteristics distinguish between the three temperate climates.

Mild temperatures and low humidity characterize the temperate climate with dry winters and summer rainfall ranging from about 25-45 in (600-1200 mm) per year. This is classic Tierra templada country.

The low nighttime temperatures in winter are typically around 41°F (5°C). Of course, higher elevations have lower temperatures with occasional frost. The highest temperatures usually reach about 95°F (35°C), though temperatures may reach as high as 104°F (40°C). This climate is similar to that of the Kenyan Highlands.

In Mexico, this climate includes parts of Nuevo León and Tamaulipas, most of the Western Sierra Madre and many mountainous areas in western, central and southern Mexico. Most of the Volcanic Axis is in this temperate zone with dry winters. Here, the major control as far as temperatures are concerned is altitude. This directly affects precise rainfall amounts and seasonality, resulting in a mosaic of microclimates and natural vegetation regions.

Compared with the temperate climate with dry winters, the humid subtropical zone gets more rainfall, is more humid and gets rain throughout the year.

The only areas of Mexico with this climate are the eastern slopes of the Eastern Sierra Madre and some parts of the southern mountain systems.

The Mediterranean climate is the mild climate associated with Europe's Mediterranean coast and the California coast. The area around Tijuana is the only part of Mexico with this climate.

This area is relatively arid and gets less than 15 inches (400 mm) of rain a year; it is unique in Mexico, the only place that is dry in summer and gets rain only in winter.

Considering the vast geographic variations in landscape, the weather in Mexico varies wildly, depending on which region you are at the time.

If you don't like a hot, tropical climate, you'll find areas and cities inland to be much cooler than the coastal areas, which can be warm year-round and extremely hot in summer.

Cities in the central highlands, such as San Miguel de Allende and Guanajuato, are much more temperate than the low-lying coastal cities like Puerto Vallarta or Mazatlan.

The desert areas in the northern part of the country and the Baja Peninsula are predictably hot and dry, with the climate becoming more temperate as you travel southward.

Highland mountainous areas in the southern part of Mexico can have winter temperatures that may even reach freezing.

Temperatures in the flat, central Yucatan peninsula can be brutally hot in summer, with a more tropical climate in the Yucatan's coastal tourist cities like Cancun and Tulum.

Mexico does have approximately 77 volcanoes, some of which are active, and in some areas, earthquakes are not uncommon. Mexico City suffered a devastating earthquake in 1985 that killed thousands, but most earthquakes are minor and not damaging to life or property.

By and large, extreme weather events in Mexico are quite rare. If you like warm, exotic, tropical climates, Mexico's beautiful coastal areas await you.

If you like year-round spring-like temperatures, head inland to beautiful San Miguel de Allende, the Lake Chapala area, or the wine-growing region of Queretaro. All in all, Mexico's weather is just as diverse as she is, and there is pretty much something for everyone.

CHAPTER 5: QUICK SUMMARY

The Weather and Climate in Mexico

- Each region in Mexico has a different climate and weather pattern

- Hottest of all is the Yucatan Peninsula, where 90°F (32°C) seems to be the sweet spot

- Mexico has seven climate regions – two tropical climates, two dry climates and 3 temperate zones

In Chapter 6, we discuss safety in Mexico. Each city and region has their own difficulties. If you are not a drug dealer or an arms dealer, you will likely be safe anywhere you go inside Mexico..

SAFETY

SEGURIDAD

COMPARISON OF MEXICO & MEXICO CITY
HOMICIDE RATES
TO POPULAR CITIES IN THE UNITED STATES

49.1 NEW ORLEANS
40.5 SAINT LOUIS
34.8 BALTIMORE
21 WASHINGTON D.C.
20.7 BUFFALO
19.6 PHILADELPHIA
19 CLEVELAND
17.6 ATLANTA
15.4 MIAMI
15.2 CHICAGO
14 MEXICO
11.3 DALLAS
11.3 BOSTON
9 MEXICO CITY
6.4 NEW YORK

RATES PER 100,000. SOURCE FBI.

HowSafeIsMexico.com

An ounce of prevention is worth a pound of cure.

BENJAMIN FRANKLIN

In my 22+ years of travel, one thing has always stayed constant; people believe Mexico is possibly the most dangerous country in the world.

They've not travelled much because there are many, many countries that are far more dangerous.

This is what people think when you tell them you're moving to Mexico. You will be,

- Murdered,

- Robbed,

- Kidnapped,

- Raped,

- Stabbed, or, most likely,

- All of the above.

They watch their local news channel or check out 'State Department Travel Advisory', which says you shouldn't travel to Mexico, never mind leaving the USA and moving there.

Your friends have also watched programs on Netflix like El Chapo and Narcos, and you can see why they think this is all there is to the country.

The truth is, due to the voracious appetite for illicit, illegal drugs in the U.S. and beyond, the drug trade is unfortunately alive and well in Mexico. And that brings with it a host of horrors that neither the Mexican nor United States governments have been able to get under control.

The U.S. shares a vast border with her neighbour to the south, and incessant rival cartel fighting over entry points for drugs and transport routes through Mexico is a terrible and constant reality.

The vast majority of violent crimes, including homicides, occur between and among people involved in criminal activity. Tourists and expats are rarely targeted, and, other than occasional pickpocketing and petty theft in the big cities, generally, nothing need to worry you.

There are areas in every country that are less safe than others, but Mexico is a big country. There are many places that are quite safe, perhaps even safer than wherever you call home.

There will be areas to avoid, and it is always recommended to exercise situational awareness wherever in the world one is. Use the same common-sense safety precautions and awareness that you would anywhere else.

You wouldn't walk home alone late at night after consuming copious amounts of tequila, would you? Well, you shouldn't do that in Mexico either. You wouldn't flash wads of cash and expensive jewelry in a convenience store at home, right? Well, you get the idea.

In 2017, Mexico had an overall murder rate of 20.5 per 100,000. As a national average, that is relatively high, but it's pulled up because of cities like Acapulco at 106 and Tijuana at 101.

Ciudad Juárez, on the border with El Paso, Texas, had 56. And funny enough, St. Louis, Missouri, came in at just under 68. Dangerous??

Another good idea is to listen to others who have been to Mexico, find out if they felt unsafe, what they did to prepare and what you should do to prepare. One useful tip I got while I was in Acapulco was, 'don't go into the hills.' So, follow the advice of those who have probably done something stupid like going into the hills.

People who move to Mexico often report feeling safer than they ever did at home. It has often been said that some parts of Mexico are reminiscent of 1950s America. Children still play in the streets. Mexican neighbours are warm, helpful, and friendly. Family, faith and courtesy are still important.

In the United States, crime varies widely by location, as in Mexico. No matter which country you reside in, your greatest concern will always be about the specific area where you live.

In general, the impression advocated by most of the US media is utterly false. It can be distressing that so many people have come to believe it simply because of its constant repetition.

I've heard that the popular tourist destinations in the Mexican States that have been deemed dangerous, by and large, are relatively safe. For example, in Mazatlan; Morelia, Patzcuaro and the Monarch Butterfly sanctuaries in the state of Michoacán; and Taxco, Acapulco and Ixtapa-Zihuatanejo in the state of Guerrero, there has been very little reported violence.

Waves of drug-related violence flare-ups have been in the

states of Chihuahua, Sinaloa, Sonora, Coahuila, Nuevo Leon, Tamaulipas, Durango, Baja California, Zacatecas in the north of the country.

I'm not saying that once you get outside the tourist areas there is a lot of violence, but just be very wary of traveling there unaccompanied. If you have a driver, they will know and understand the areas to visit and not to visit. Be safe, as you would in any other country, maybe more so in Mexico.

I'm going to be discussing taxis and Uber's in my chapter on Transportation, but I want to discuss safety here in this chapter. My suggestion: if you are in Mexico City, call an Uber or Cabify, don't hail a taxi, and if you do need to call a taxi, use only the authorized taxis.

Make sure you understand the price prior to entering the vehicle if the taxi is not metered. Poke your head in and see if the car has a meter, and make sure it is turned on when the car starts to your destination. Mexico City has what is called taxi ranks (Sitios). They can be a little more expensive than street taxis, but still relatively inexpensive to use. You will find them at many hotels, and if you don't speak Spanish very well, you may be able to find someone that can help you.

If you are on the street, and need a taxi and don't speak Spanish, the best phrase you can learn is ¿Cuánto? (How Much?) or '¿Cuánto es?' 'How much is it?' then listen very carefully for the answer.

They may realize that Spanish is not your native language and answer in English, or hold up two fingers to tell you the price. If you agree, jump in the back of the taxi and everything should be good to go. They may also tell you in pesos, you will have to figure out the conversion and what the price is.

The other thing to understand is that taxis can sometimes give you the price based on who you are and what you look like.

They'll start high in price and if you are not satisfied with the price, barter with them and be willing to walk away. Just make sure you can catch another taxi and are not left stranded in an area all for an extra $2.

If you are arriving at Mexico City airport, the taxi companies have booths in the terminal.

Tell them where you are going and they will share with you the set price for the destination. Most often you cannot haggle wth them unless you know what you are talking about or your Spanish is of native level.

THEFT AND ROBBERY

FINANCIAL CRIMES

Financial crimes include mostly overcharging on credit/ debit cards. This occurs when a store or street vendor overcharges your credit card and does not present you with a receipt. To avoid this, always verify the amount to be charged on the credit card machine before accepting the charges. In addition, a paper receipt should be requested when you make a purchase. It would help if you turn on account notifications on your phone, so you can immediately verify each charge that you make. This also lets you see your exchange rate conversion, which is handy for keeping track.

When using ATMs, give preference to machines inside banks, hotels, airports, and other locations with secure surroundings. At night, I would not do it, I actually wouldn't do it in any country unless there is a posted guard and your car is right outside of the machine, even then, just think ahead and pull money out during the day or wait until the next day.

You won't look like a Mexican citizen, so the chances of you becoming a target for petty theft is likely a lot higher. Use precaution, don't wear big flashy jewellery, a big wallet hanging out of your back pocket and keep your valuables close to your body, don't flaunt your $1,000 iPhone and try not to look like you have valuables on you. If possible, have a cross bag that is closed and not easily snatched from your body. Be cautious, just as if you were home in downtown Toronto or Seattle.

Here are the U.S., Canadian, and British travel advisory sites:

- U.S. State Department (http://travel.state.gov/)

- Canadian Foreign Affairs Office (http://www.voyage.gc.ca/)

- British Foreign Office (https://www.gov.uk/foreign-travel-advice/mexico)

Here are some great rules to live by, no matter where you live:

- Never leave any bags in the car.

- Do not walk around with expensive jewelery.

- Always lock the doors to your house and car. Always lock important items (cameras, laptops, purses, luggage, etc.) in the trunk or stow them in a location where they cannot be seen from outside the vehicle, even when a guard is present.

- Do not sleep with windows or doors open.

- Do not go out alone at night; be careful if you do go out. Don't stay out until the middle of the night.

- Always give the appearance that you are alert and aware of your surroundings. If you look lost, you become a sure-fire target.

- Do not visit areas known to be higher crime neighbourhoods.

- Do not expose cameras, laptops, cell phones, etc., except to use them.

- Do not hike or explore remote areas alone; always go with an adult 'buddy'.

- Do not visit remote beaches, no matter how inviting they may appear.

- Do not park in remote areas at beaches.

- At the beach, do not leave items (passports, wallets, bags, cell phones, etc.) unguarded anytime. You should always keep money, passports, and vehicle keys under constant, close watch.

- When walking in a crowded area, men should carry wallets in a front pocket; women should wear purses with the strap over their heads.

- Do not roll down car windows at a stoplight if someone taps on the window or tries to talk to you.

- At restaurants, do not give your credit card to the server to pay the bill; if the server does not have a remote credit card terminal to process the bill at the table, pay at the counter.

- Do not sign a credit card receipt without reviewing the charges and total.

LAW ENFORCEMENT IN MEXICO

The Secretariat of Public Security of Mexico City manages a combined force of over 90,000 officers in Mexico City. The SSP is charged with maintaining public order and safety in the heart of Mexico City. The historic district is also manned by tourist police, aiming to orient and serve tourists. These horse-mounted agents are dressed in traditional uniforms.

Between 2000 and 2004, an average of 478 crimes were reported daily in Mexico City; however, the actual crime rate is thought to be much higher "since most people are reluctant to report a crime."

Under policies enacted by Mayor Marcelo Ebrard between 2009 and 2011, Mexico City underwent a major security upgrade, with violent and petty crime rates falling significantly despite the rise in violent crime in other parts of the country.

Some of the policies enacted included the installation of 11,000 security cameras around the city and an enormous expansion of the police force. Mexico City has one of the world's highest police officer-to-resident ratios, with one uniformed officer per 100 citizens.

CHAPTER 6: QUICK SUMMARY

- Mexico, like any other country, has areas that you need to stay away from, Seedy bars, strip clubs, dark alleys

- Don't get involved with drugs

- The homicide rate in 2017 was 20.5 per 100,000

- Talk to your friends that have been or live in Mexico and see how they feel about their safety

- Law Enforcement in Mexico is improving, with a combined force of over 90,000 officers in Mexico City

In Chapter 7, we'll talk about how you get to Mexico, what airlines will take you there, and why it's vitally important to never drive at night.

HOW TO GET TO MEXICO

CÓMO LLEGAR A MÉXICO

The journey of a thousand miles begins with a single step.

LAO TZU

Mexico is straightforward to get to from the US or Canada, with frequent and regular flights from many major cities and hubs in either country. Airfare fluctuates depending on the time of year and other factors, so try to purchase your tickets as far in advance as possible. Flights between the US or Canada and Mexico are usually relatively inexpensive. All major US cities will have abundant choices of flights, often direct, to major Mexican cities.

These American Airlines all offer services between the US to Mexico:

- American

- Delta

- United

- Southwest

- Alaska Airlines

- Interjet

- JetBlue

- Spirit Airlines

- Frontier Airlines

- Canadian airlines, Air Canada And WestJet, offer services between Canada and Mexico.

These Mexican airlines fly between Mexico and the US, and Canada.

- Aeromexico

- Volaris

- VivaAerobus

- Aeromar

These international airlines fly or connect between many major hubs in the world to Mexico:

- Copa

- KLM

- British Airways

- Virgin Atlantic

Flights on Mexican airlines within Mexico can be inexpensive and are a great way to visit different parts of the country. We will go into more detail in Chapter 19: Transportation on local flights within Mexico. Airports in Mexico's major cities and tourist destinations are modern and easy to navigate.

Driving, one can enter Mexico by crossing at any of the US border crossings in Texas, New Mexico, Arizona or California.

Some of these are safer, but the more significant crossings are generally best. The crossings at Eagle Pass, Del Rio, Laredo, Nogales, or San Diego are widely used by 'snowbirds' and others driving from the US or Canada into Mexico.

Travel from these crossings will be on modern 4-lane highways, and these roadways, along with all other highways and toll roads in Mexico, are patrolled by the famous 'Green Angels.'

The Green Angels are Federally funded and offer free bilingual roadside assistance, except for needed parts. Tips are appreciated. If you have a problem, pull over to the side of the road and call 078 from your cell phone or Telmex booth. Green Angels patrol the highways from dawn to dusk in easily identifiable green trucks.

Check out our Facebook Group:https://www.facebook.com/groups/expatmoneyforum, where you can ask questions regarding planning a trip to Mexico by car. We have expats who live all over the world; someone will be able to help you.

If you are traveling overland, you will also be responsible for finding the border office once you've crossed into Mexico and filling out the necessary paperwork to obtain a tourist visa.

Many Canadians and Americans drive from their homes down through Mexico every year on the run from the harsh winters. If you promise not to tell anyone, we will share a great secret truth that not many people know: there is no living being on this planet as fearless as the Canadian and American Snowbird.

snow•bird snō′bûrd″

Noun – One who moves from a cold to a warm place in the winter. (The American Heritage Dictionary of the English Language, 5th Edition)

These people will do almost anything to escape the snow, continuing snow, shovelling snow, driving in snow, and dressing for snow.

Driving across the North American continent isn't a deterrent to them. There is much debate on the safety of driving to and in Mexico, as your friends and family may well remind you, should you suggest it. But as a point of reference, snowbirds have and continue to do it year after year, time after time, and the great majority do so without incident.

Road signs may be challenging when driving if you don't speak Spanish. Make sure you have good maps or directions when you start your road trip. GPS and navigation devices are not always accurate for Mexico, so make sure you are prepared.

Many excellent toll roads and highways crisscrossing Mexico make road travel easy to navigate and safe. Toll roads involve some extra expense, but the superior streets make it worth using them if possible.

Regarding overland travel in Mexico in general, one major caveat you will often hear repeated: It is never advisable to drive after dark. There are many valid reasons for this.

- Smaller and even some not-so-small highways are dotted with the infamous 'topes.' Topes are large speed bumps that may pop up when you least expect them and are extremely hard to see at night. They can wreak havoc on your vehicle if hit at high speed. You must watch them on the roads through smaller towns and villages.

- Livestock, small animals, people, potholes, and many other obstacles can often appear unexpectedly on roadways and, likewise, can be difficult or impossible to see in the dark.

- As previously stated, road travel in Mexico can be, and usually is, quite safe. Being on the road after dark on unfamiliar roads, large highways or small back roads, which may or may not be well-travelled or well-lit, is just generally not a good idea.

- If vehicles or other problems arise, it is better to face them in the daylight, where reliable help may be more readily available.

It is always best to plan your route such that you have secured a place to stay for the night and can stop there well before nightfall. If you are traveling with household goods or pets in tow, either in a trailer, pickup, or car, you might want to consider stopping for the night in a 'No-Tell Motel'.

We can't guarantee what the original intent of these establishments was. Partial motivation could have been that Mexican households are often multi-generational; consequently, marriage couples' privacy is sometimes non-existent. No-Tell Motels, or 'Love Motels' as they are often called, rent by the hour and offer privacy to these couples who live in close quarters with extended family at home.

Of course, married couples are not the only ones availing themselves of these establishments. Couples other than married couples looking for privacy use these by-the-hour establishments, giving them a bit of a tarnished reputation.

In any event, No-Tell Motels are usually inexpensive, and many of them are clean and well-kept. They often have gated entry and enclosed garages attached to the rooms, which offer security for your vehicle. They can also be a great option if you travel with your furry buddies, as most regular hotels do not allow pets.

If flying or driving doesn't work for you, luxury buses are an often overlooked method for traveling to or within Mexico. Bus companies offer cross-border services between the US and Mexico as far north as Chicago and as south as Mexico City from the US.border. Purchase tickets on First Class buses, if possible, as these are more comfortable. Executive and Luxury service is available at the cost of approximately 60% more than first class, comparable to business class on a plane.

Cities with a large migration of Snowbirds tend to have much higher security rates and are heavily guarded by Mexican police. That is to say, the Mexican government focuses on the safety and security of these "high-value residents." Most know not to mess with the gringos in Mexico!

The Snowbirds prefer cities located in the south and east of Mexico because of their warm climate and cheap travel expenses. These cities are big hits with the Snowbirds, and we'll discuss them in the following chapter.

CHAPTER 7: QUICK SUMMARY

How easy is it to get to Mexico from Canada or the USA?

- Several American Airlines offer daily service to Mexico

- Air Canada and WestJet fly direct from many cities in Canada

- If you want to travel nationally, fly Aeromexico, Volaris,

VivaAerobus or Aeromar.

- Outside North America, Copa, KLM, British Airways, and Virgin Atlantic make daily flights.

- You can drive and enter Mexico in several locations along the border of the USA and Belize.

- For great information on being an expat, check out our FB group: https://ExpatMoneyForum.com.

- Once you pass the border, you must have Mexican car insurance

- Foreign-plated vehicles will need a Temporary Importation Permit

- If you are driving to Mexico, plan, pre-book hotels, and have pesos readily available

Chapter 8 talks about everything you need to know once you get to Mexico, like the drinking water, how much of a tip you should leave, electricity voltage, appropriate dress and more.

STUFF THAT'S GOOD TO KNOW

COSAS QUE ES BUENO SABER

Education is the most powerful weapon which you can use to change the world.

NELSON MANDELA

As you will learn, doing things in Mexico is different than doing something in your home country. If you want line-ups to move quickly, people answering the phone, and stores to be open when they say they are supposed to be open, you will be frustrated in all of Latin America, for that matter. That being said, here are some guidelines to make moving to Mexico a little easier.

DRINKING-WATER

Mexico has long had a bad rep regarding tap water, which may not be entirely unwarranted, at least in some areas. This is not entirely universal, however. For example, Puerto Vallarta's water agency has been the only one in Mexico certified as safe by the Federal Ministry of Health for the last 28 years.

While the water may be fine, it sometimes flows through old pipes, depending on where one is staying, allowing the water to pick up stuff you'd rather not drink.

I always suggest that my private clients pick up a high-quality water filter. This is the one my family uses, and after extensive research on the subject, I would argue it is the best option for all expats https://expatmoneyshow.com/water-filter

GRATUITY

If you live in Canada or the USA, you are probably accustomed to tipping at a restaurant or hair salon.

In Mexico, tipping (la propina) is also a common practice in all situations, similar to Canada and the USA.

- Bars – 10 pesos per drink

- Tour Guides – 10 – 20% of the total cost of the tour

- Luggage Delivery – 25-50 pesos

- Housekeeping 20-50 pesos

- Restaurants – 10 – 20%

- Hair Salon – 10 – 20%

- Taxis – tip only if they help with luggage – 10 pesos per bag

ELECTRICITY VOLTAGE

The standard voltage in Mexico is 127 V, and the frequency is 60 Hz. If the standard voltage in your country is 110 – 127 V (which is the case in the U.S., Canada and most of South America), your electrical appliances will work in Mexico.

If your devices do not run on 127 volts, you will need a Type B plug adapter, allowing you to use any 127-volt appliance or device.

APPROPRIATE CLOTHING

Mexican culture may be slightly more formal than you are accustomed to, influencing how people dress. Appropriate business attire will be expected in most office or business environments. People often dress up for dinner or other outings with their families.

Churches and cathedrals may have signs requesting that tourists not wear shorts or overly casual clothing. Bear this in mind when you schedule your tour of that beautiful cathedral.

DRESS CODE

Mexico City is relatively formal. Mexican business people wear suits.

Guadalajara, and Monterrey are different in that a collared shirt with pants is acceptable. Except for use in a beach resort, shorts are not part of the dress code anywhere.

If you are invited to a picnic or a tour of the countryside, dress casually but elegantly. Polo-style shirts, a sweater and sports slacks are best.

SALARIES

Salaries are considerably lower in Mexico, and some jobs are reserved for Mexican citizens.

The average wage is around 33,200 MXN ($1,624.00 USD). Salaries range from 8,410 MXN (lowest average) to 148,000 MXN (highest average, the actual maximum salary is higher).

The average monthly salary includes housing, transport, and other benefits. Salaries vary drastically between different careers.

Here, from Teleport.org https://teleport.org/cities/mexico-city/salaries/ are some typical salaries for 2022 in USD.

- IT Manager $31,965

- Nurse $29,173

- Sales Manager $27,825

- Dentist $24,750

- Attorney $23,691

- Chef $17,822

- Accountant $17,376

- Teacher $13,678

BANKING

When working and living in Mexico, investing in real estate or running your own business, you need to open a bank account. Opening a bank account in Mexico is relatively straightforward when you hold a residency visa (temporary or permanent).

Expect to have minimum balances for current and savings accounts with penalties for not conforming to the rules. Note that you must have a residency permit (temporary or permanent) to open a bank account in Mexico.

In Mexico, as an individual, you will not be able to have an overdraft on your account; this service is only offered on business accounts. Charges for cashiers' cheques and ATMs are made on certain personal accounts, so check with your bank to make sure you open an account that is right for your needs.

There are currently 48 different banks working in Mexico, with seven banks holding about 78% of the total market share. Within these 48 different banks, plenty of international financial institutions will extend world-class banking services, and it usually takes a few minutes to set up an account.

You'll need the following documents when you go to a bank for your account:

- Immigration card

- Passport

- Proof of address

- At least MXN 5000 to deposit in the account

CREDIT INTEREST AND BANK CHARGES

The amount of interest you pay at a Mexican bank will depend on many factors. They take into account the rate of interest and the means of repayment. There are several different charges and fees to consider when working with the actual cost of the credit.

You don't necessarily have to be a Mexican citizen to apply for a bank loan; you can be a legal resident of Mexico. The bank will likely do a credit check from your home country and ensure you are an upstanding citizen. If you were not an exemplary citizen, chances are you won't get credit in Mexico.

Don't be surprised if the bank official doesn't try to sell you an insurance policy or take out credit to buy a new car while applying for a credit card.

SALES TAX ON INTEREST AND CHARGES

All bank charges, aperture fees, commissions, and credit interest are subject to sales tax in Mexico.

MORTGAGES & CAR LOANS

All major banks offer mortgage products and car loans. The interest rates vary, as you would expect.

You Need To Know Spanish

Some financial institutions provide English translations of contracts (for example, mortgage products), although the official version will always be in Spanish. If you enter a credit agreement in Mexico, be sure you understand the terms offered. Even if there is an English translation of your credit agreement, only the Spanish contract will have a basis in law in case of a dispute with the credit institution.

El Buró: Mexico's Credit Agency

Like in Canada or the US, Mexico has a system of credit ratings. This is great if you want to buy a car or a home. Credit agencies share their information with financial institutions, and sometimes you will find employers who also use this system to check on their new employees.

GETTING A NEW CREDIT CARD

Much like Mexican mortgages, you can get a Mexican credit card, but the fees will be high, and the terms will not be as good as those of your home country.

Most Mexican credit cards have an annual fee, which may be as low as MXN 200.00 annually, and very high-interest rates (possibly as high as 50% APR).

Credit Card From Home

Make sure you have copies of the front and back of your

credit and debit cards stored securely. All credit cards have an international phone number to call during this kind of crisis. If you lose or your card is stolen, start the process immediately to cancel your card and have a new one issued.

Suppose you do end up needing to have a replacement mailed to you. In that case, receiving DHL and possibly FedEx deliveries in Mexico is possible, but check with your credit card company to see if they will send a replacement internationally. If possible, have a US or Canadian address on file so that a new card can be sent there, and then use DHL or FedEx to deliver to Mexico. Have backup credit cards, if possible, so that you are not entirely dependent on one card.

DEBIT CARDS

Before you have your residency, you will need to have access to funds. In Mexico, the ATMs charge fees, and possibly your bank will too.

When I moved to Panama, the ATMs here charged $5, and my Canadian bank also charged $5, so for every $500 I withdrew, it cost me $10. Charles Schwab High Yield checking account for US citizens refunds ATM fees.

Capital One and Charles Schwab offer credit cards with no international transaction fees. Canadians may be more familiar with Scotiabank and HSBC. Scotiabank Passport Visa, Scotiabank Gold American Express and HSBC World Elite Mastercard offer credit cards with no foreign transaction fees.

Canadians will find Scotiabank branches in Mexico City, Guadalajara, Monterrey, Puerto Vallarta and other Mexican cities. HSBC also has banks in Mexico. While your Canadian account may not offer you the same bank privileges, it is possible that your debit card might not incur foreign fees. Check with your bank to find out their policies about using your card for international purchases.

Once you have residency, most banks will offer a debit card with their checking accounts, which will function much like the debit card you have from your home country.

BBVA has banks all over Mexico and several other countries worldwide and might offer you debit card availability with no foreign fees. Check with them to find out.

COMMUNICATIONS

Communication in Mexico has evolved. Not so very long ago, a trip or relocation to Mexico was sure to turn communication with anyone back home into a nightmare, complete with plenty of conversations that included 'Can you hear me now?', texts that never arrived and dropped calls. Thankfully, this is no longer the case.

The major US carriers now include all of North America (Canada, the US and Mexico), and many US expats who are not relocating permanently opt to keep their US cell phone plans. It is easy to get a cell phone, and it's extremely inexpensive to use, about $40 - $50 USD a month, and that gives you nationwide calling coverage in Mexico with unlimited data and calls to North American numbers.

AT&T, T-Mobile (which has now merged with Sprint), Verizon and the new Google Fi are available and fully functional without additional fees in Mexico.

If you are going to be in Mexico permanently or for an extended period, you may want to drop your current plan and get a Mexican one. This may well offer significant savings over what you pay for your plan from your home country.

AT&T, Telcel, Movistar and Virgin Mobile offer Mexican plans and have storefront offices where you can sign up. As long as your phone is 'unlocked,' you can keep your current phone. You will just need a new sim card or 'chip.'

WhatsApp is a free messaging app that allows you to call and text anywhere in the world. Although not my favourite, I prefer Signal, WhatsApp is widely used in Mexico, even by business people, so you may want to install and set up the app on your cell phone before you arrive in Mexico. Facebook is also widely used in Mexico and is often used as an alternate method of communication.

WHAT TO BRING WHEN MOVING TO MEXICO

- Birth Certificate

- Marriage Certificate

- Medical Records

- School Records

- Social Security Card

You should make plenty of copies of these vital documents and leave a copy with a trusted person in your home country.

GETTING MARRIED IN MEXICO

Two Marriages: Civil And Religious

THE CIVIL MARRIAGE

Only a civil marriage is recognized as legal in Mexico. You don't need to engage in a religious ceremony, but if you omit the civil ceremony, the marriage will not be considered legal. Most Mexicans have two marriages: a civil (legal) marriage and a church (religious) one.

THE RELIGIOUS MARRIAGE

This can be arranged if you want to get married in a church in Mexico, although additional planning and fees will be required.

PREVIOUSLY MARRIED

Divorced

All states in Mexico have slightly different laws regarding when previously married couples can remarry.

Most places require the bride and groom to be divorced (starting from the date of the final divorce decree) at least one full calendar year before remarrying.

For example, in Quintana Roo, the state where Cancun is located (one of the most popular venues), only women (not men) who have been previously married may not remarry there for 300 calendar days following the date of the final decree of divorce.

The exception is if, during that time, they have given birth or can prove "by medical dictate" that they are pregnant. You'll need to check with the local authorities in the State where you plan to get remarried if you have not been divorced for at least a year.

Widowed

If either party is widowed, the deceased spouse's death certificate will be needed as part of the documentation requirements.

DOCUMENTS REQUIRED TO GET MARRIED IN MEXICO

The couple getting married must present the following documentation and requisites. Some requirements differ from state to state; check locally, but be prepared to gather all of the documents listed below.

Important! Foreign documents listed below (except for your passport and travel permit) will need to be:

• Translated into Spanish;

• Notarized by your nearest Mexican Consulate and;

• Be 'Apostilled' in the country where you live by the appropriate organization/authorities (see next section about Apostilles)

Documents required

Marriage Application Forms

These forms are attained from the local registry office in Mexico. On this form, you must specify whether you will get married under joint or separate property.

Passport – must be valid for at least six months and a copy of the same (both the bride and groom).

Travel visa or resident permits – Original and copies of Your Visitor's Permit (FMM), completed at the port of entry or, if you are resident in Mexico, your resident permit.

Birth certificates – Apostilled and translated by an approved translator

Divorce decree/Death certificate – If either spouse was previously married or either partner is widowed, copies of the divorce decree or death certificate, if applicable, will be required for presentation.

Chest X-rays – The plates from the chest x-rays, if required in the State where you get married. (Always get these in Mexico).

Blood test results – Written results (in Spanish) of the blood test. Get the blood test done in Mexico.

LEGALIZATION PROCEDURE – THE 'APOSTILLE'

Before the Mexican authorities receive foreign-issued legal documents for processing, it's necessary to get them Apostilled.

In the **USA**, this service is undertaken by the Office of Authentication (https://travel.state.gov/content/travel/en/legal-considerations/judicial/authentication-of-documents/office-of-authentications.html) at the State Department, although every state has its own requirements, and you need to Apostille documents in the State that they were issued.

Note for Canadians: Canada is not a signatory to the international Apostille convention, and the procedures do not apply there. Canada has a notarization procedure https://

travel.gc.ca/travelling/documents/notarial-services for legal documents instead.

In the **UK**, the Foreign Office undertakes this task; connect to the Legalization page https://www.gov.uk/government/organisations/foreign-commonwealth-office on the Foreign Office's website for details about obtaining this service.

In **Australia**, the Authentication and Apostilles https://www.dfat.gov.au/ section of the Department of Foreign Affairs takes care of the legalizing documents.

THE MARRIAGE

Once you have gathered all your paperwork and official documents, you will need to pay your Marriage License fee of approximately 30 USD and allow the waiting period to go by (anything from 30 minutes to a few days, depending on the state in Mexico where you get married).

The ceremony may then take place, and the marriage will be legal.

The least expensive option is to have the ceremony performed at the Local Registry Office. For a further fee, you can arrange for the ceremony to take place elsewhere (hotel, beach, colonial mansion, etc.). You will need to make further arrangements with all parties involved.

Once the civil ceremony has been completed, you will need to obtain a certified copy of the marriage certificate (Acta de Matrimonio). This will prove that you have been legally wed under Mexican law, and the marriage will be recognized everywhere in the world where it can be, including the US, Canada, the UK/European Union, Australia, etc.

Important Note! You should get your Mexican marriage certificate apostilled in Mexico to ensure that it will be accepted as a genuine document back in your home country.

This is the reverse process of having your home-country documents legalized by your home country; ask the local registry office for details about how you can go about this.

MARRYING A MEXICAN NATIONAL (IN MEXICO)

So far, the above requirements have assumed that a foreigner is marrying a foreigner in Mexico.

If you plan to marry a Mexican national in Mexico, you may need to apply for a permit to marry a Mexican national.

Most districts have done away with the requirement for a foreign marriage permit. It might still be necessary for the district where you plan to get married—check with the local Municipality for the latest policy.

In addition to all of the documentation listed above, depending on the state in which you plan to get married, you may need to obtain permission from the local immigration office, where, for a fee of around 200 USD, you'll need to acquire a permit to marry a Mexican national. The document is known as *"Permiso para contraer matrimonio con un nacional"*.

The office issuing this permit must be the same office that has jurisdiction over the area where the marriage is to take place; i.e. you cannot get the permit from one state, e.g. Mexico City, and then go to, e.g. Acapulco (in the State of Guerrero) to get married.

This process can take from two days to two weeks, depending on the state and the people at the local government office.

DOMESTIC HELP

Hiring help for domestic tasks like cooking, cleaning, and housekeeping is a common practice in Mexico. Even the middle-income population often hires domestic help to get chores done around the house, and very few laws regulate who can hire domestic help. There are, however, extensive rules and regulations regarding benefits for domestic employees, especially full-time employees.

If you plan on securing full-time, in-home child care, for example, you will need to consult an attorney to determine what benefits you are required to pay your employee.

Some required employee benefits may include Severance pay, annual Prima de antigüedad (Seniority Premium), Aguinaldo (something akin to a 'Christmas bonus') and Vacation pay.

Don't be discouraged by the possibility of having to pay employee benefits. Chances are that even if you were required to pay these benefits, though the cost to you would be minimal, the financial implications for your employee would be great and much appreciated.

Many people who hire occasional hourly employees for yard work or cleaning do not pay all of these benefits, but if you are in doubt, check with a local attorney to be sure.

You can often find domestic workers through word of mouth. The average wage in Mexico for domestic workers is $25 USD a day, but these rates will likely vary depending on where you live.

It is critical to have an employment contract. At some point, you may need to prove when an employee commenced employment, the wage you are paying, the number of hours worked, the days worked, the duties of the employee and any other specifics.

Mexican government labour boards, where employees can file disputes, are usually very pro-employee. Settlements of tens of thousands of pesos are not uncommon.

This is why employment contracts are so important in identifying hours, days of work, duties, expectations and more. You must have this in place before work begins.

Paid vacation must be made in cash either before the vacation or by the end of the year if no vacation has been taken. To calculate, divide the number of days worked during the past year by 365. Multiply that figure by the number of vacation days due x 1.25 x daily pay to determine the amount of vacation pay due. For example, you have an employee that has worked for you for 1 year, 1 day a week, making $10 USD: 52 days worked / 365 x 6 days due x 1.25 x 10.52 USD daily pay = $11 USD pay.

TERMINATION PAY

Unless termination is voluntary or justified as per the list below, termination pay includes three months' salary, 20 days for each year worked and prorated vacation and Christmas pay. Termination pay must be paid at the time of termination, or regular salary shall continue until the termination is settled in full.

GROUNDS FOR TERMINATION

Employees in Mexico can only be terminated if there is a cause for the termination (Article 47, Federal Labour Law). Document any of these instances, and have the employee sign the notes. Cause of termination:

- Use of false documentation to secure employment (this only applies within the first 30 days of employment)

- Dishonest or violent behaviour on the job

- Dishonest or violent behaviour against co-workers that disrupts work discipline

- Threatening, insulting or abusing the employer or his/her family, unless provoked or acting in self-defence

- Intentionally damaging the employer's property

- Negligently causing serious damage to the employer's property.

- Carelessly threatening workplace safety

- Immoral behaviour in the workplace

- Disclosure of trade secrets or confidential information

- More than three unjustified absences in 30 days

- Disobeying the employer without justification

- Failure to follow safety procedures

- Reporting to work under the influence of alcohol or non-prescription drugs

- Prison sentence that makes it impossible for the employee to render the services he or she was supposed to render

- The commission of any other acts of similar severity

The notice of termination must be delivered to the employee at the moment of dismissal. The notice must set out the precise causes by which the employee is being terminated.

MAIL DELIVERY

Mail delivery is extremely unreliable in Mexico. If you are in the US, US Priority mail is a good way to send a package to Mexico, or DHL, & FedEx. The other thing you may want to look at is if you are selling your home and will not have a mailing address, look at services that do it well. Here are some examples:

- SBI Mail Service

- UPS Store, which is not a PO box but a physical address, as your bank will not like you to have a PO box.

- iPostal1 is $10 USD monthly, and the bank and IRS accept it.

- Mailboxes Etc.

- Pay a friend $100 USD per year for using their address.

PAYING BILLS IN MEXICO

With today's technology, you can pay all of your bills online. For companies like Xoom, a PayPal Service, you just have to provide the account number, and your bills are paid securely within two business days.

The other service is SimplePay, a web and mobile app created to simplify life for expats and foreigners in Mexico.

LGBT RIGHTS

Mexico is quickly becoming one of Latin America's most LGBT and gay-friendly countries. Most other cities have followed, with the country's capital and biggest city legalizing gay marriage.

Mexico, like the United States, has an increasingly varied culture from state to state. Many Mexican states have become more accepting of LGBT communities than others.

On December 21, 2009, Mexico City became the first Latin American jurisdiction to legalize same-sex marriages. The law became effective on March 4, 2010.

On August 5, 2010, the Supreme Court voted 8-2 to uphold the constitutionality of Mexico City's same-sex marriage law. An amendment to the constitution in 2011 prohibits discrimination based on sexual orientation.

A 2015 Supreme Court thesis' changed the legal definition of marriage to include same-sex unions. Consequently, every judge in the country must recognize same-sex marriages. However, same-sex couples must request an injunction (Amparo) from a judge, which is a lengthy process that opposite-sex couples do not have to endure.

The most popular gay neighbourhood in Mexico City is called Zona Rosa.

This city, one of the largest in the world, is the most progressive in Latin America.

The Zona Rosa began in the late 1800s and consisted of affluent families who wanted to live like Europeans. In the 1950's Zona Rosa changed from a neighbourhood where the rich could build lavish European homes to a bohemian chic zone where coffee shops, boutiques, and discos started to open. Hence Zona Rosa was positioned as one of the most exciting places to visit in Mexico City.

In 1974 "El Nueve" the first gay nightclub in Mexico City, opened in Zona Rosa. El Nueve became very popular and inspired the gay community to build and plant roots around the club.

Zona Rosa soon became the first gay neighbourhood in Mexico and a symbol of freedom for the LGBT community

CHAPTER 8: QUICK SUMMARY

You need to be familiar with many essential items when you move to Mexico. Here are some that we discuss that will help you.

- You cannot drink the water.

- You must leave a tip at the bar for your tour guide, luggage delivery, etc.

- The electricity voltage is 127 V, and the frequency is 60 Hz

- Mexico has a dress code very different from Canada or the USA

- Listed are several jobs and their salaries if you are working in Mexico

- Banking and the rules in Mexico

- Communications

- Documents required when moving to Mexico

- Can you get married? What are the rules?

- LGBT Rights

In Chapter 9, we detail the most famous and important holidays of the year and how important they are when it comes to the Catholic religion practised by most Mexicans.

RELIGION AND HOLIDAYS

RELIGIÓN Y FIESTAS

Kindness is like snow. It beautifies everything it covers.

KAHLIL GIBRAN

RELIGION

Even though it's been centuries since the Spanish left the Mexican people to themselves, the occupation had long-lasting impacts on the country. To this day, you'll find that Mexico has retained much of its colonial traditions, including the population's religious leanings. Roughly 80% of the population is Catholic Christian. According to 2010 census numbers, religious demographics in Mexico were broken down as follows:

- 82.7% Roman Catholic

- 5% of other Evangelical churches

- 4.7% None

- 2.7% Unspecified

- 1.9% Other

- 1.6% Pentecostal Christian

- 1.4% Jehovah's Witnesses

Mexico is divided into 88 Catholic Dioceses, with something like 13,700 priests and 36,000 men and women in religious orders, according to http://mexico-landmarks.com/religion.html. Some Catholics with indigenous heritage mix Catholicism with elements of Mayan or Aztec religions.

There are many Mormons (Church of Jesus Christ of Latter-day Saints) in Mexico, with over a million followers. Show reverence in cathedrals and other religious sites, and appropriate dress is expected. If you are touring a cathedral, do not wear shorts.

HOLIDAYS

Mexican people have a vibrant and loud culture with plenty of yearly celebrations. These require plenty of parades and merrymaking with music and dancing in the streets. It's all quite pleasant once you get used to it, and they don't miss an opportunity to have fun. Some notable cultural festivals include:

Three Kings Day (El Dia de los Reyes) Also known as Epiphany, Three Kings Day is celebrated 12 days after Christmas on January 6th. This holiday is a Christian feast day to celebrate the incarnation of Jesus Christ by remembering the gifts of the Magi (the three kings or wise men) to the baby Jesus.

Christians believe that the three kings (or wise men) Melchor, Gaspar and Baltazar visited the child Jesus and presented him with gifts of gold, frankincense, and myrrh.

The person who finds the baby Jesus figurine inside his or her share of the sweet bread, Rosca de Reyes, symbolically "becomes" Jesus' godparent.

Day of the Holy Kings is an Observance type of holiday. Stores are open, and people work today.

Constitution Day – February 5-7 – Constitution Day (Día de la Constitución) is an official holiday celebrating the anniversary of Mexico's current constitution, promulgated on February 5, 1917.

Constitution Day is a public holiday. The general population has a day off, and schools and most businesses are closed.

Benito Juarez's Birthday Memorial – March 15 – 21 – The birthday of Benito Juárez is celebrated as a public holiday in Mexico on the third Monday in March. This national hero is known for making reforms to create the Democratic Federal Republic.

Benito Juárez's Birthday Memorial is a public holiday. The general population has a day off, and schools and most businesses are closed.

Benito Juárez was born in San Pablo Guelatao,Oaxaca, on March 21,1806. He was a lawyer who later held many public offices, including as a state legislator, civil judge, government secretary, and governor.

In 1853 he was exiled to the United States due to political conflict. The following year he helped publish the Plan de Ayutla, which ended the dictatorship of political leader Antonio Lopez de Santa Anna, thus convening a new Constitutional Congress.

In 1857 Juárez was elected president of the Supreme Court of Justice, a position he held until December of that year when he became president.

From then until he died in 1872, he led the government during historically significant events, including the Reform War, the French Intervention, the Second Empire and the republic's restoration.

Labour Day/May Day – May 1 - is a public holiday. The general population has a day off, and schools and most businesses are closed.

Some businesses may follow Saturday opening hours if it falls on a Saturday.

Mexico's labour movement was repressed in places such as Cananea in the north. However, the Constitution of 1917 instigated significant social reforms to labour laws. According to some sources, a Labour Day parade was held in Mexico as early as 1913, but the holiday was first officially commemorated on May 1, 1923. Labour Day is not exclusive to Mexico – many other countries also celebrate Workers' Day.

Battle of Puebla (Cinco de Mayo) – May 5 – celebrates the defeat of the French army during the Battle of Puebla (Batalla de Puebla) in Mexico on May 5, 1862. Contrary to popular belief, it is not the anniversary of the defeat and expulsion of the French forces by the Mexicans, which occurred in 1867. The battle in Puebla did, however, lift the confidence of the Mexican army and people. It helped boost national unity at the time.

It is a public holiday and a day off for the general population, and schools and most businesses are closed and is not to be confused with the country's Independence Day.

Mexican Independence Day – Mexico celebrates its independence on September 16. This holiday is observed with feasting and parades to commemorate the day in 1810 when Father Miguel Hidalgo Costilla rang his church bell in Dolores, Mexico, giving the call to arms which began the war for Mexican independence from Spain.

Often banks, as well as government and other offices, will be closed for some of these holidays, so make plans accordingly.

Dia De Los Muertos—(The Day of the Dead), or more correctly, Night of the Dead (Noche de Muertos), dates back to pre-Hispanic times. Indigenous Mexican peoples held many strong beliefs connected with death; for example, the dead needed the same things as the living; hence their bodies should be buried with their possessions, sandals and other objects.

The arrival of the Spanish gradually assimilated the Indians' pagan ideas and customs into the official Catholic calendar. Dead children (angelitos) are remembered on **November 1, All Saints' Day**, while deceased adults are honoured on **November 2, All Souls' Day**. Most of the activity occurs in the local cemetery on both days.

In many locations, festivities (processions, altars, concerts, meals, dancing, etc.) now last several days before the main days of November 1st and 2nd.

It is a time when Mexican people celebrate those who have passed on by decorating graves and organizing feasts with their families to remember their loved ones. Halloween, which falls on October 31, immediately before The Day of the Dead, is not widely celebrated. However, in areas with many American expats, the custom of 'Trick-or-Treat' is beginning to catch on. So it is advisable to ensure you are prepared with plenty of candy for the children, just in case.

UNESCO designated the Day of the Dead an "intangible world heritage" in 2008. The official UNESCO description of Mexico's "Indigenous Festivity dedicated to the Dead" summarizes its significance:

"This period also marks the completion of the annual cultivation cycle of maize, the country's predominant food crop."

"Families facilitate the return of the souls to Earth by laying flower petals, candles and offerings along the path leading from the cemetery to their homes. The deceased's favourite dishes are prepared and placed around the home shrine and the tomb alongside flowers and typical handicrafts, such as paper cut-outs. Great care is taken with all aspects of the preparations.

It is believed that the dead can bring prosperity (e.g. an abundant maize harvest) or misfortune (e.g. illness, accidents, financial difficulties) upon their families depending on how satisfactorily the rituals are executed.

The dead are divided into several categories according to the cause of death, age, sex and, in some cases, profession. A specific day of worship, determined by these categories, is designated for each deceased person. This encounter between the living and the dead affirms the role of the individual within society and contributes to reinforcing the political and social status of Mexico's indigenous communities."

The Day of the Dead celebration holds great significance in the life of Mexico's indigenous communities.

The fusion of pre-Hispanic religious rites and Catholic feasts brings together two universes, one marked by indigenous belief systems, the other by worldviews introduced by the Europeans in the sixteenth century."

Here, in no particular order, are 8 of the best places to visit for Mexico's Day of the Dead:

1. MICHOACÁN

The best-known location for the Day of the Dead in the country is the Island of Janitzio in Lake Pátzcuaro, Michoacán. This is one of Mexico's most famous major annual spectacles. Thousands of visitors worldwide watch the indigenous Purepecha people perform elaborate rituals in the local cemetery late into the night. Yes, it has become commercialized, but it remains a memorable experience and offers the opportunity to sample the local cuisine, which was declared an "intangible world heritage" by UNESCO in 2010!

Several other locations in the Lake Pátzcuaro area, including Ihuatzio, Tzintzuntzan, Arocutín and Jarácuaro, offer their own equally memorable (but less visited) festivities and rituals. Interesting observances of the Day of the Dead also occur in many other places in Michoacán, including Angahuan (near Paricutin Volcano) and Cuanajo.

2. MEXICO CITY

Two locations in the southern part of the city are well worth visiting for the Day of the Dead.

In San Andrés Mixquic, which has strong indigenous roots, graves are decorated with Mexican marigolds in a cemetery lit by hundreds and hundreds of candles. Street stalls, household altars and processions attract thousands of capitalinos each year.

In Xochimilco, the canals and chinampas are the backgrounds for special night-time Day of the Dead excursions by boat (trajinera).

3. VERACRUZ

Xico, one of Mexico's Magic Towns, has colourful Day of the Dead celebrations, including a flower petal carpet along the road to the graveyard. Don't miss sampling the numerous tamales that are a mainstay of the local cuisine.

4. SAN LUIS POTOSÍ AND HIDALGO

In the indigenous Huastec settlements of the mountainous area shared by the states of San Luis Potosí and Hidalgo, the Day of the Dead celebrations are known as Xantolo.

Multi-tiered altars are elaborately decorated as part of the festivities.

5. CHIAPAS

Several indigenous communities in Chiapas celebrate the

Day of the Dead in style. For example, in San Juan Chamula, the festival is known as Kin Anima and is based on the indigenous Tzotzil tradition.

6. YUCATÁN AND QUINTANA ROO

Day of the Dead celebrations are known in the Maya region as Hanal Pixan, a "feast for the souls." Families prepare elaborate food for the annual return of their dearly departed.

The cemeteries in the Yucatán capital Mérida are well worth seeing, as are the graveyards in many smaller communities. See, for example, this account of the festivities in Pac Chen, Quintana Roo: Hanal Pixan, Maya Day of the Dead in Pac Chen, Quintana Roo. Tourist locations offer their versions of Day of the Dead celebrations. For example, the Xcaret theme park in the Riviera Maya is the scene of the Festival of Life and Death (Festival de la Vida y la Muerte), featuring parades, rituals, concerts, theatre performances and dancing.

7. OAXACA

There are rich and varied observances of the Day of the Dead in the state of Oaxaca. Visitors to Oaxaca City can witness vigils in several of the city's cemeteries and night-time processions called comparsas.

The celebrations are very different on the Oaxacan coast, as evidenced by this account of the Day of the Dead in Santiago Pinotepa Nacional.

8. GUANAJUATO

The city of San Miguel de Allende in Guanajuato holds an annual four-day festival known as "La Calaca," with artistic and cultural events that are "integrated into the vibrant celebration of life and death known as "Dia de Muertos." In Mexico, the age-old cultural traditions of the Day of the Dead are still very much alive!

Note for armchair travellers.

Besides the usual travel accounts describing the Day of the Dead, numerous children's and adult novels include vivid accounts of typical Day of the Dead activities. There are also various novels entitled Day of the Dead, though not all focus on Mexican traditions. One of the earliest novels entitled Day of the Dead is Bart Spicer's 1955 spy novel, Day of the Dead, which has several scenes in Chapala, Guadalajara and Mexico City.

Revolution Day Memorial – November 15 – 20 – Mexico's Revolution Day (Dia de la Revolucion) is a national public holiday celebrating a 10-year revolution that began in 1910 to end the struggle against dictator José de la Cruz Porfirio Diaz Mori. It is on the third Monday in November, near the official day on November 20. Revolution Day Memorial is a public holiday. The general population has a day off, and schools and most businesses are closed.

The Mexican revolution started in 1910 to get rid of president Porfirio Díaz. He initially tried to revolt against Benito Juárez in 1871 but did not come into power until 1876, when he was president for one month. He was also president from 1877 to 1880 and from 1884 to 1911. While economic growth and modernization occurred, this progress did not filter through to many Mexicans, including labour workers and people in the poorer parts of Mexico. Several key players, including Francisco Madero, organized the revolt against Díaz. Madero was then elected as president in 1911.

November 20 was the original public holiday date for Revolution Day until 2005. A change in Mexico's labour law instituted that Revolution Day would be a public holiday across the country on the third Monday of November 2006.

Christmas – December 25 – Widely observed by Christians worldwide on December 25 to celebrate the birth of Jesus Christ.

Christmas Day is a public holiday. The general population has a day off, and schools and most businesses are closed. Some businesses may follow Saturday opening hours if it falls on a Saturday. Christmas celebrates the birth of Jesus Christ. His birth date is unknown because there is little public information about his early life. Many Christians celebrate Jesus' birthday on December 25. Orthodox Christians celebrate Christmas Day on or near January 7.

Other notable holidays to be aware of,

Guelaguetza Festival—This festival is held in Oaxaca from the 22—27 of July. Different indigenous people groups come out to celebrate their heritage, traditions and culture. Tickets are sold in advance, so you should prepare beforehand for this festival.

Dia de la Virgen de Guadalupe— It is widely believed that the Virgin Mary appeared to Juan Diego, one of Mexico's most revered patron saints. The festival pays respect to this occasion, and you will hear retellings of religious legends unique to Mexico.

Carnival in Veracruz & Mazatlan—While Carnival is associated with Brazil, some coastal areas in Mexico also celebrate the event. Carnival takes place between the Friday afternoon before Ash Wednesday and Ash Wednesday at noon, which is the beginning of Lent.

Lent is the 40 days before Easter observed by Roman Catholics and some Christians as a period of sacrifice, exhibited by abstaining from meat consumption. Consequently, the word 'Carnival' comes from the Latin 'Carne vale,' which means 'farewell to meat.'

CHAPTER 9: QUICK SUMMARY

Religion and holidays seem to go hand in hand in Mexico. Here are some statistics:

- 82.7% Roman Catholic

- 5% of other Evangelical churches,

- 4.7% None,

- 2.7% Unspecified,

- 1.9% Other,

- 1.6% Pentecostal Christian,

- 1.4% Jehovah's Witnesses

Holidays are a big deal in Mexico, with the biggest being Day of The Dead celebrated by all Mexican's. Top cities or areas to visit to celebrate Dia De Los Muertos are

- Michoacan

- Mexico City

- Veracruz

- San Luis Potosi and Hidalgo

- Chiapas

- Yucatan and Quintana Roo

- Oaxaca

- Guanajuato

In Chapter 10, we delve into Mexico City. If you are looking for a fast-paced, busy city with just a ton to see and do, Mexico City could be for you.

MEXICO CITY

CIUDAD DE MÉXICO

I was taken in by the bravado and the sounds of Mexico...not so much the music, but the spirit.

HERB ALPERT, AMERICAN TRUMPETER

Mexico's capital is Mexico City, the largest city and the most populous city in North America. In 2022 Mexico City's population was estimated to be 22,085,140, which makes it the second-largest metropolitan area in the Western Hemisphere (behind Sao Paulo, Brazil), the eleventh-largest agglomeration, and the largest Spanish-speaking city in the world. It is estimated that as many as 700,000 Americans live in Mexico City, the largest population of Americans living outside of the United States.

Mexico City is the oldest capital city in the Americas and one of two founded by indigenous people. The city was originally built on a group of islands in Lake Texcoco by the Mexica (Azteca) in 1325 as Tenochtitlan. It was almost destroyed in the 1521 Siege of Tenochtitlan and subsequently redesigned and rebuilt following the Spanish urban standards.

In 1524, the municipality of Mexico City was established, known as México Tenochtitlán, and as of 1585, it was officially known as Ciudad de México (Mexico City). Mexico City was the political, administrative, and financial centre of a significant part of the Spanish colonial empire. The federal district was created in 1824 after independence from Spain was achieved,

The vastness and diversity of Mexico City are impossible to describe adequately. According to the Secretariat of Tourism, the city has more than 1,500 historic buildings, 170 museums, over 100 art galleries, and some 30 concert halls, all of which maintain a constant cultural activity throughout the year. Lively music and art scene and a whopping 53,000 restaurants.

In addition, several haciendas are now restaurants, such as the San Ángel Inn, the Hacienda de Tlalpan, Hacienda de Cortés and the Hacienda de los Morales.

CULTURAL CENTRES

Mexico City is a cosmopolitan city with a thriving nightlife and an endless array of things to do, places to see, and foods to experience. You can feel the history alongside the modern skyscrapers and Mexico City's urban sprawl.

Mexico City is one of the world's most important cultural and financial centres.

It is located in the Valley of Mexico (Valle de México), a large valley in the high plateaus in the centre of Mexico, at an altitude of 7,350 ft (2,240 m). Travellers to Mexico City will need to beware of altitude sickness. If fatigue, shortness of breath, and lightheadedness crash your Mexico City visit, you might want to postpone your sightseeing until after you've had a couple of bottles of water and a nap.

Greater Mexico City had a GDP of $411 billion in 2011, which makes it one of the most productive urban areas in the world. The city was responsible for generating 15.8% of Mexico's GDP, and the metropolitan area accounted for about 22% of the country's GDP. If it were an independent country in 2013, Mexico City would be the fifth-largest economy in Latin America.

After years of demanding greater political autonomy, residents were finally given the right to elect both a head of government and the representatives of the unicameral Legislative Assembly by election in 1997. Since then, left-wing parties (first the Party of the Democratic Revolution and later the National Regeneration Movement) have controlled both. The city has several progressive policies, including abortion on demand, a limited form of euthanasia, no-fault divorce, and same-sex marriage.

On 29 January 2016, it ceased to be the Federal District (Spanish: Distrito Federal or D.F.) and is now officially known as Ciudad de México (or CDMX), with a greater degree of autonomy. However, a clause in the Constitution of Mexico prevents it from becoming a state within the Mexican federation, as it is the seat of power in the country unless its capital is relocated elsewhere.

Mexico City has a subtropical highland climate due to its tropical location but high elevation. The lower region of the valley receives less rainfall than the upper regions of the south; the lower boroughs and the east portion are usually drier and warmer than the upper southern boroughs of a mountainous region of pine and oak trees.

The average annual temperature varies from 54 to 61°F (12 to 16°C), depending on the altitude of the borough. The temperature is rarely below 37°F (3°C) or above 86°F (30°C).

Overall, precipitation is heavily concentrated in the summer months and includes dense hail. Snow falls in the city very rarely, although more often on nearby mountain tops.

The area receives about 32 in (820 mm) of annual rainfall,

concentrated from May through October, with little or no precipitation for the remainder of the year. The area has two main seasons.

The wet, humid summer runs from May to October when winds bring in tropical moisture from the sea, the wettest month being July. The cool sunny winter runs from November to April, when the air is relatively drier, the driest month being December. This season is divided into a cold winter period and a warm spring period.

The cold period spans from November to February, when polar air masses push down from the north and keep the air relatively dry. The warm period extends from March to May, when subtropical winds dominate but do not yet carry enough moisture for the rain to form.

POLLUTION

By the 1990s, Mexico City had become infamous as one of the world's most polluted cities; however, the city has become a model for drastically lowering pollution levels.

By 2014 carbon monoxide pollution had dropped drastically, while sulphur dioxide and nitrogen dioxide were at levels about a third of those in 1992.

The levels of signature pollutants in Mexico City are similar to those of Los Angeles. Despite the cleanup, the metropolitan area is still the most ozone-polluted part of the country,

To clean up pollution, the federal and local governments

implemented numerous plans, including the constant monitoring and reporting of environmental conditions, such as ozone and nitrogen oxides.

When these two pollutants reached critical levels, contingency actions were implemented, including closing factories, changing school hours, and extending the one-day without-a-car program to two days of the week.

The government also instituted industrial technology improvements, a strict biannual vehicle emission inspection and the reformulation of gasoline and diesel fuels. The introduction of Metrobús bus rapid transit and the Ecobici bike-sharing was among efforts to encourage alternate, greener forms of transportation.

BOROUGHS AND NEIGHBOURHOODS

The boroughs of Mexico City 2020 populations are

- Álvaro Obregón (pop. 759,137)

- Iztapalapa (pop. 1,835,486)

- Azcapotzalco (pop. 432,205)

- Magdalena Contreras (pop. 247,622)

- Benito Juárez (pop. 434,153)

- Miguel Hidalgo (pop. 414,470)

- Coyoacán (pop. 614,447)

- Milpa Alta (pop. 152,685)

- Cuajimalpa (pop. 217,686)

- Tláhuac (pop. 392,313)

- Cuauhtémoc (pop. 545,884)

- Tlalpan (pop. 699,928)

- Gustavo A. Madero (pop. 1,173,351)

- Venustiano Carranza (pop. 443,704)

- Iztacalco (pop. 404,695)

- Xochimilco (pop. 442,178)

METROPOLITAN AREA

Greater Mexico City is formed by Mexico City, 60 munici-palities from the State of Mexico and one from the state of Hidalgo. Greater Mexico City is the largest metropolitan area in Mexico and the area with the highest population density.

As mentioned earlier, 22,085,140 people live in this urban agglomeration, of which 9,209,944 live in Mexico City proper. In terms of population, the biggest municipalities that are part of Greater Mexico City (excluding Mexico City proper) are in the State of Mexico:

- Ecatepec de Morelos (pop. 1,645,352)

- Nezahualcóyotl (pop. 1,077,208)

- Naucalpan (pop. 834,434)

- Chimalhuacán (pop. 705,193)

- Tlalnepantla de Baz (pop. 672,202)

Approximately 75% (10 million) of the State of México's population live in municipalities that are part of Greater Mexico City.

Greater Mexico City was the fastest-growing metropolitan area in the country until the late 1980s. Since then, and through a decentralization policy to reduce the environmental pollutants of the growing conurbation, the annual growth rate of the agglomeration has decreased. It is lower than that of the other four largest metropolitan areas (namely Greater Guadalajara, Greater Monterrey, Greater Puebla and Greater Toluca) even though it is still positive.

TOURISM

The Historic centre of Mexico City and the "floating gardens" of Xochimilco in the southern borough have been declared World Heritage Sites by UNESCO. Landmarks in the historic centre include the Plaza de la Constitución (Zócalo), the main central square with its epoch-contrasting Spanish-era Metropolitan Cathedral.

The National Palace, ancient Aztec temple ruins Templo Mayor ("Major Temple"), and modern structures are all within a few steps of one another. (The Templo Mayor was discovered in 1978 while workers were digging to place underground electric cables).

The most recognizable icon of Mexico City is the golden Angel of Independence on the wide, elegant avenue Paseo de la Reforma, modelled by order of the Emperor Maximilian of Mexico after the Champs-Élysées in Paris. This avenue was designed over the Americas' oldest known major roadway in the 19th century to connect the National Palace (seat of government) with the Castle of Chapultepec, the Imperial Residence.

Today, this avenue is an important financial district in which the Mexican Stock Exchange and several corporate headquarters are located. Another important avenue is the Avenida de los Insurgentes, which extends 17.9 mi (28.8 km) and is one of the longest single avenues in the world.

Chapultepec Park houses the Chapultepec Castle, now a museum on a hill that overlooks the park and its numerous museums, monuments, the National Zoo and the National Museum of Anthropology (which houses the Aztec Calendar Stone).

Another piece of architecture is the Palacio de Bellas Artes, a white marble theatre/museum whose weight is such that it has gradually been sinking into the soft ground below. Its construction began during the presidency of Porfirio Díaz and, after being interrupted by the Mexican Revolution in the 1920s, ended in 1934.

The Plaza de las Tres Culturas, in this square, is located at the College of Santa Cruz de Tlatelolco. This is the first and oldest European school of higher learning in the Americas, and the archeological site of the city-state of Tlatelolco, the shrine and the Basilica of Our Lady of Guadalupe are also important sites.

A double-decker bus, known as the "Turibus", circles most of these sites and has timed audio describing the sites in multiple languages as they are passed.

UNESCO SITES IN MEXICO CITY

As we discussed earlier in the book, Mexico is home to 35 UNESCO (United Nations Educational, Scientific and Cultural Organization) World Heritage Sites.

XOCHIMILCO

Xochimilco was built in the 16th century by the Spanish on the ruins of Tenochtitlan, the old Aztec capital. Mexico City has five Aztec temples.

The ruins of which have been identified, a cathedral (the largest on the continent) and some fine 19th – and 20th-century public buildings such as the Palacio de las Bellas Artes.

Xochimilco lies 17 miles (28 km) south of Mexico City. With its network of canals and artificial islands, it testifies to the efforts of the Aztec people to build a habitat in the midst of an unfavourable environment.

Its characteristic urban and rural structures, built since the 16th century and during the colonial period, have been preserved in an exceptional manner.

CENTRAL UNIVERSITY CITY CAMPUS OF THE UNIVERSIDAD NACIONAL AUTÓNOMA DE MÉXICO (UNAM)

The ensemble of buildings, sports facilities and open spaces of the Central University City Campus of the Universidad Nacional Autónoma de México (UNAM) was built from 1949 to 1952 by more than 60 architects, engineers and artists who were involved in the project.

As a result, the campus constitutes a unique example of 20th-century modernism integrating urbanism, architecture, engineering, landscape design and fine arts with references to local traditions, especially to Mexico's pre-Hispanic past.

The ensemble embodies social and cultural values of universal significance and is one of Latin America's most significant icons of modernity.

PUEBLA

Situated at the foot of the Popocatepetl volcano, Puebla has preserved its many 16th and 17th-century churches, chapels and monasteries. The fusion of European and American styles is unique to Puebla's Baroque District.

A unique feature of Puebla, "the true capital of Mexican Baroque," is the Talavera tile. These brightly coloured hand-painted tiles adorn the facades of many of the local buildings.

This feature has led to a distinctly personal and localized style evolution with a pronounced Indian flavour.

You can observe the modern-day production of these exquisite tiles and other traditional Mexican pottery at the Talavera de la Reyna Factory outside Puebla in nearby Cholula.

THE GREAT PYRAMID OF CHOLULA

A quick Google search will reveal, perhaps not entirely accurately, that not Egypt but Sudan is purportedly the country in the world boasting the most pyramids. In reality, although no one knows how many pyramids there are in Mexico, it is estimated to be in the hundreds and may quite possibly be more than there are in Egypt and Sudan combined.

Mexico is home to the largest pyramid on earth, the Great Pyramid of Cholula, built by the Aztecs in Puebla around 300 BC and largely overlooked until the early 1900s as it is covered by vegetation and appears to be a mountain.

This incredible structure is so well hidden and looks so much like a mountain that Spanish explorer Hernan Cortes never even saw it at all and, in fact, built a church right on top of it. The Great Pyramid of Cholula is about four times the size of the Great Pyramid of Giza in Egypt.

Even today, it's understandable how this came to pass, thanks to the old Spanish chapel perched at its summit.

Originally constructed over 2000 years ago, the Great Pyramid of Tepanapa (often referred to as the Great Pyramid of

Cholula) boasts a larger volume than any other ancient man-made structure, including the Egyptian pyramids. Stylistically, the pyramid is an oddity, puzzling archeologists to this day by incorporating architectural elements of both the Teotihuacan and El Tajin civilizations.

During the many pre-Columbian power shifts in Mexico, the pyramid itself fell out of use. Other structures, such as one of the many sacrificial altars on the ten-acre site, were favoured.

It is unclear whether it was through disuse that the pyramid became overgrown with shrubbery or if, when the Aztecs caught wind of the impending Spanish arrival, the Cholulans buried the pyramid in a last-ditch, communal effort to preserve the massive temple, an important piece of their culture.

Either way, when the Spanish arrived at Cholula in 1519, Cortes and his men were so occupied with the decimation of the indigenous people and their more conspicuous holy sites that they failed to recognize the pyramid.

They mistakenly thought it the perfect hill site for one of their countless new churches! Within the year, La Iglesia de los Remedios was constructed, where it remains to this day.

As the dirt began to fall away, the pyramid revealed itself to archeologists, who have excavated the pyramid's stairways, platforms, altars, and over five miles of tunnels snaking through the structure's innards.

TOP EXPAT BOROUGHS TO LIVE IN MEXICO CITY

Here, we will look at cities that are safe for you and your family to live in. Some of these cities are also great for retirement.

I mentioned earlier that an estimated 700,000 Americans were living in Mexico City. There are 2 million expats in this region from around the world. I don't think you'll pick an area in the city that doesn't have a ton of expats.

There are some fantastic cities to move to in Mexico. There is something for everyone.

CENTRO HISTORICO

Centro Historico is the heart of Mexico City with its massive Zócalo plaza. Many cool spots surround the area, and although it is generally safe here, it is still advised to walk the streets more during the daytime rather than at night.

This large area occupies 668 blocks and is a living organism of non-stop transformation and renovation.

What's amazing is that you can go back in time until the Aztec era and also see where the Spaniards began building what is now modern Mexico City. You can find iconic and historical landmarks such as Metropolitan Cathedral and the art nouveau Palacio De Bellas Artes.

The street market is very active and has high-end restaurants that await patrons and visitors at the pedestrianized Calle Madero. The affluent historic district bustles with activities and cultural events all year round.

There are more than 1,500 historic buildings, ancient Aztec ruins, and vibrant and some of the nation's most absorbing museums.

Living here and homeschooling your children would be a dream for many families. There is much to see and do, with culture abounding and food for every taste. Centro would make an excellent home for everyone!

COYOACAN

Coyoacan is south of the city centre and was one of the first neighbourhoods in Mexico City.

It has plenty of historical architecture that you will love if this is your idea of the perfect place to set down roots. Rents are less here than, let's say, Condesa.

You will find cobblestone streets and countless colonial buildings. Here too, the crime rate is low. This area is known to be family-friendly and has a laid-back feel to it.

Coyoacan is a bit off the beaten path, and there are two great markets here: Mercado Coyoacan and Mercado de Antojitos.

Real Estate

At any given time, you will find hundreds of listings in this area, both for rent and sale. As this area is upscale, you can rent a beautiful 7 bedroom, 6 bath, 6,000 sq ft home for just under $7,000 USD per month. Or, a quaint 2 bedroom apartment, 2 baths, 1100 sq ft for as low as $689 USD per month. And everything in between.

LA CONDESA

The first owner of the lands here was Maria de la Campa y Cos, Countess of San Mateo de Valparaíso. She married Miguel de Berrio y Zaldívar Ortíz de Landáuzari, who would later acquire the title of Marquis of Jaral de Berrio.

For the first two-thirds of the 20th century, the Colonia grew, becoming popular with the middle and upper classes and many foreigners.

Today, Condesa is an ideal place to live and call home as it is considered by most to be the safest neighbourhood in Mexico City, hence making it a top pick for expats alike.

The medians of Avenida Ámsterdam, which runs as an oval around Parque México, and the medians of Avenidas Campeche, Benjamín Hill and Alfonso Reyes, are lined with trees and plants on either side of pedestrian paths that run down the middle.

It is European-inspired, with stately Art Nouveau mansions on tree-lined avenues and world-class fashion boutiques throughout the neighbourhood.

The trolleybuses of Roma Condesa have permanently parked trolleybuses donated to Mexico by the Japanese government in 2000, with the idea of creating educational centres.

They sat abandoned until 2005 when the "Galería Trolebús" (Trolleybus Gallery) began to promote non-traditional art projects. The gallery ceased operations in 2009 due to financial problems, but the buses are still used for theatre and other art projects.

Stroll through the neighbourhood, enjoy the scenery and feel safe. Parks here always have a police officer or two. Their presence helps if anything goes wrong and helps to curb the likelihood of crime.

One can argue that the trendy Condesa hood has taken a back seat to ultra-hip Roma. However, it's still one of the city's most attractive places to live for its convivial bars and highly diverse culinary offerings.

ROMA

Colonia Roma, also called Roma, is a neighbourhood just west of the city's historic centre of Cuauhtemoc borough. It is extremely safe here and has one of the lowest crime rates in the city.

The Colonia was planned as an upper-class Porfirian neighbourhood in the early twentieth century. By the 1940s, it had become a middle-class neighbourhood in slow decline, with the downswing being worsened by the 1985 Mexico City earthquake. Since the 2000s, the area has seen increasing gentrification.

Roma and neighbouring Condesa are known for being the epicentre of hipster subculture in the city and rival Polanco as the centre of the city's culinary scene.

Besides residential buildings, the neighbourhood streets are lined with restaurants, bars, clubs, shops, cultural centres, churches and galleries.

Many are housed in former Art Nouveau and Neo-Classical buildings dating from the Porfiriato period at the beginning of the 20th century. Roma was designated as a "Barrio Mágico" ("magical neighbourhood") by the city in 2011.

This area was designated as a "Barrio Magico" by the city, and the magic of this place will be instantly apparent when you see the art deco. This is what makes this neighbourhood so spectacular. Writers and artists flock here, and dining here is second to none.

Roma's borders are: Avenida Chapultepec to the north, across which is the Zona Rosa, Colonia Juárez area

- Avenida de los Insurgentes to the west, across which is the Condesa district

- Eje 4 Sur Benjamin Franklin, Antonio M. Anza and Viaducto Miguel Alemán to the south, across which are Colonia del Valle and Colonia Narvarte Avenidas Cuauhtémoc and Jalapa to the east, across which is Colonia Doctores.

- In addition, a section (Roma Norte I) lies west of Insurgentes, whose borders are Chapultepec (N), Av.

Veracruz (W), Parque España/Avenida Álvaro Obregón (S)

Avenida Coahuila divides Roma into the officially recognized neighbourhoods of Roma Norte and Roma Sur.

POLANCO

Polanco is one of the most upscale neighbourhoods in Mexico City. It is the city's business centre, and many companies have headquarters here. There are lots of fine-dining restaurants and tons of places to shop.

This area is quieter and less crowded than La Condesa, so if you are moving with your family, this is a great option.

One of the reasons I like this area is that it has some of the best parks in all of Mexico City for your children to enjoy. Similar to Condesa and Roma, Polanco is very safe for expats.

Polanco also has some of Mexico City's best places to go. You can see the brilliant Museo Soumaya and the amazing Museo Nacional de Antropologia.

The borders of Polanco are:

- On the north, Avenida Ejército Nacional and the Nuevo Polanco area as well as Colonia Irrigación.

- On the south, Paseo de la Reforma.

- On the east, Avenida General Mariano Escobedo and Colonia Anzures.

- On the west, Blvd. Manuel Ávila Camacho (Anillo Periférico) and the colonias of Lomas de Chapultepec, Reforma Social and Residencia Militar.

Here are some neighbourhoods to avoid

- Doctores

- Tepito

- Iztapalapa

Many moving to Mexico may never make the trek to Mexico City. But honestly, you should carve out a week once you get established and go and visit the sites there.

Here, in no particular order, are the best things to do in Mexico City. Many are free; some have an entrance fee.

1. MUSEO NACIONAL DE ANTROPOLOGIA

Located within the famous Chapultepec Forest, the Museo Nacional de Antropología (National Museum of Anthropology) "holds artifacts from Mexico's pre-Columbian era, dating from about 100 B.C. to A.D. 1521. The facility houses artifacts, including the famous Aztec Calendar Stone, Piedra del Sol, the famed 16th-century statue of Xochipilli, the Aztec god of art, games, beauty, dance and dance maize (among others). The museum looks at how tradition, culture and life were formed in all regions of Mexico.

The museum is so extensive that many travellers claim you

can spend a whole day exploring the many collections and exhibits and recommend giving yourself plenty of time to explore. As one of Mexico's largest and most visited museums, the grounds are also home to a gift shop, a cafeteria, a locker room and the National Library of Anthropology and History.

2. BASILICA DE SANTA MARIA DE GUADALUPE

The Basílica de Santa María de Guadalupe (Basilica of Our Lady of Guadalupe) is an important religious site in Mexico City. The first shrine built to honour the Virgin Mary of Guadalupe was erected in 1531 on Tepeyac hill, but the first basilica dedicated to the Virgin Mary was not built until 1695. However, nearly 300 years' worth of construction and environmental damage threatened the integrity of the basilica, so a new basilica was built on the same plaza in the 1970s.

Today, the complex has many features, including the basilica, the ancient church, a gift shop filled with religious items, a museum and a library. Visitors extolled the basilica, saying it is a must-see whether you are Catholic or not. Though Mass is held frequently, reviewers noted that the layout of the buildings helps visitors avoid interrupting worship.

In addition, past travellers said various tours were available from Mexico City (some of which included Teotihuacan) and said it was a great way to have a fully-informed experience. The basilica is often featured as a stop on hop-on, hop-off bus tours.

The basilica is open daily, though the hours at each site are within complex variables.

Admission to the museum is 10 pesos (about 50 cents), while the rest of the complex is free (though you may wish to make a cash donation).

3. PALACIO DE BELLAS ARTES

The Palacio de Bellas Artes (Palace of Fine Arts) is considered the cultural centre of Mexico City and is a must-visit. The palace's exterior showcases art nouveau and art deco-style architecture, while the inside features marble floors and vaulted glass windows.

In addition to its architectural grandeur, the building hosts cultural events in the national theatre, including music, dance, theatre, opera and literary performances.

The museum at the palace also holds several famous murals, including the work of the renowned Mexican muralist Rufino Tamayo.

On the top floor, you'll find the National Museum of Architecture, showcasing renowned Mexican architects' work and lives and multiple art museums and galleries.

Many say that the palace is sure to be one of the most beautiful sights you'll see in Mexico City and add that if you get the chance, watch a performance in the world-class theatre.

The palace is open daily from 10 am to 7 pm, while the museum is open from Tuesday through Sunday from 10 am to 6 pm (the last entrance is at 5:30 pm). Admission to the museum is 70 pesos (about $3.70), but you can save money by visiting on Sundays when admission is free.

Rates for performances vary by discipline."

4. TEMPLO MAYOR

"Before Spanish colonization, Templo Mayor served as the religious centre for the Aztec people. When Spanish conquistadors arrived in the late 14th century, the temple was among many destroyed and built over. It wasn't until 1978 that the temple dedicated to the Aztec gods Huitzilopochtli and Tláloc (gods of war and water) was unearthed in the heart of Mexico City. Today, the area remains an active archeological site and the adjoining museum houses more than 7,000 artifacts from the site.

Recent visitors said it's fascinating to see the ancient ruins tucked away in the city's centre. Many said it's worth spending time in the museum," but the site and scale can't match the massive Museo Nacional de Antropología. Still, the whole complex has been deemed a UNESCO World Heritage site and is one of Mexico City's most popular attractions.

The Templo Mayor and its museum are located one block northwest of the Zócalo metro station. The museum and ruins are open Tuesday to Sunday (closed Mondays) from 9 am to 5 pm. Admission costs 75 pesos (about $4) for adults and is free for children and senior citizens. Do not visit on a Sunday when admission is free for Mexican residents. if you're hoping to avoid crowds,

5. TEOTIHUACAN

One of many UNESCO World Heritage sites in the Mexico City region, Teotihuacán (teh-oh-tee-wa-can) contains some of the largest pre-Columbian pyramids in all of Mexico. The site has many famous constructions, including the Palace of the Plumed Butterfly, which showcases various columns of winged creatures, and the fantastic Pyramid of the Sun, which sits at the heart of the small city. The nearby museum, Museo de la Sitio, also holds many artifacts from the period.

While many travellers are amazed by the daunting monuments, here are a few tips to make your trip easier: The souvenirs are pricey, but some haggling in Spanish will help you score a better deal.

Bring a bottle of water (or 2), wear sensible shoes and apply sunscreen, as the site provides very little shade. Also, if you're able, climb the Pyramids of the Sun and the Moon for a bird's-eye view of the massive complex. Another good idea is to book a guide and transportation ahead of time to fully enjoy the experience.

Teotihuacán is about 31 miles (50 km) northeast of Mexico City. You can access the site via public transportation from Autobus del Norte bus station (located just off the yellow line metro station by the same name).

To avoid crowds, get there early and avoid going on Sundays if possible, as residents of Mexico receive free admission that day. Entry fees are modest (about $4).

6. ZOCALO
(PLAZA DE LA CONSTITUCIÓN)

Officially known as Plaza de la Constitución, El Zócalo is the main public square and one of the most recognizable places in Mexico City. It contains a giant Mexican flag at its centre and has been the centrepiece of public gatherings since the days of the Aztecs.

The site also hosts annual, widely attended religious events during Holy Week and for Corpus Christi. Several historic buildings also border the square, including the city's national cathedral, the National Palace and federal buildings.

You could spend a couple of hours looking around the Zócalo, and some travellers suggest you start your visit at sunset.

CHAPTER 10: QUICK SUMMARY

- Mexico's capital is Mexico City, the largest city and the most populous city in North America.

- In 2022 Mexico City's population was estimated to be 22,085,140, which makes it the second-largest metropolitan area in the Western Hemisphere (behind Sao Paulo, Brazil), the eleventh-largest agglomeration, and the largest Spanish-speaking city in the world. It is estimated that as many as 700,000 Americans live in Mexico City, the largest population of Americans living outside of the United States.

- Greater Mexico City is formed by Mexico City, 60 municipalities from the State of Mexico and one from the state of Hidalgo. Greater Mexico City is the largest metropolitan area in Mexico and the area with the highest population density.

- Mexico City is a cosmopolitan city with a thriving nightlife and an endless array of things to do, places to see, and foods to experience.

- The most recognizable icon of Mexico City is the golden Angel of Independence on the wide, elegant avenue Paseo de la Reforma, modelled by order of the Emperor Maximilian of Mexico after the Champs-Élysées in Paris.

- Mexico is home to 35 UNESCO (United Nations Educational, Scientific and Cultural Organization) World Heritage Sites.

For those of you who want a slower-paced life near the beach, or in the mountains, in Chapter 11, we will look at the best places to live as an expat or retire to.

BEST CITIES FOR EXPAT LIVING

LAS MEJORES CIUDADES PARA VIVIR EXPATRIADOS

It is better to live rich than to die rich.

SAMUEL JOHNSON

As we are learning, Mexico is a big country with many geographical differences. We have the mountains that are cool in temperature and pleasant for those that don't love the heat but want the sun, then there is living inland, where it is less cool, more heat with tons to do, and then we have the beautiful beaches with the warm sand and sun virtually every day.

In the last chapter, we looked at Mexico City and what she had to offer. Now, we're going to look at other cities within Mexico to assess if they are right for you, whether you are still working, have a family, or it's time to retire, and you're looking for the perfect place to settle down.

First, let's look at some ideal cities if you want to move to Mexico. These are cities with expats and retirees.

ACAPULCO

In the 1940s, 50s and '60s, Acapulco was a cosmopolitan celebrity hotspot with its breathtaking bay, jagged cliffs, and turquoise water. Today, Acapulco remains a popular area for expats to take up residency.

Acapulco is one of Mexico's oldest beach resorts. The people of Acapulco are warm, friendly, and engaging. You can jump on one of the local buses that constantly drive along La Costera, the coastal road from the Icacos naval base on the east side to Caleta.

The bus costs 8 pesos (.40 cents US), and you can flag them down and get off wherever you want along the route. Each bus is painted in bright and vibrant colours and blasts different kinds of music.

Acapulco has unique street art everywhere, and shopping is a high priority with vibrant Mercado Municipal outdoor food markets everywhere.

Acapulco is a coastal city that existed before the Europeans invaded the American continent. There is the Acapulco with the lavish hotels, beaches and tourists, and the Acapulco of old, wherein the open-air marketplace, one can still hear indigenous people speaking Nahuatl, the language of the Aztecs. Acapulco was so crowded at one time that the Mexican government created Cancun, which now attracts the most casual tourists. The stratagem worked, and Acapulco has recovered its quiet loveliness.

"Because Acapulco isn't some whitewashed, scrubbed-cheek tourist theme park where nature is kept at bay and corporate dullness rules. It's lusty and visceral and noisy, with its Hollywood pastels and bending palm trees and a huge heart and generous soul. it has taken everything the earth can throw at it and still emerges, if not always smiling, then at least unscathed.

But it needs us to have faith, to go back and revel in its ways. there's no point denying Acapulco has problems, but it's equally ridiculous to write it off, too. It's one hell of a town. so, man up. and take the plunge. a great and grateful Acapulco awaits."

Here are a few of my favourite things to do and see if you're considering Acapulco as your new home.

LA QUEBRADA

Here, you can watch the cliff divers jumping from a height of 130 ft (40 m) and safely landing in the water below. The show starts around 1 pm, and you will be in awe when you see how skilled the divers are.

TAXCO

If you're up for a nice drive, visit the city of Taxco. It's a small and romantic city located between Acapulco and Mexico City. The streets are cobblestone, where you'll find quaint cafes to enjoy your favourite cup of coffee.

PALMA SOLA ARCHAEOLOGICAL SITE

What's nice about this site is that very few people visit here, so it's quieter, and you can take your time. It is located deep within the forest, 4 miles (6 km) northeast of Acapulco's old town within El Veladero National Park. This site dates back to 200 BC to 600 AD and houses petroglyphs done by the Yopes, who were indigenous people of the region, which today, is known as Guerrero in southern Mexico. I would suggest taking a guided tour and learning about the petroglyphs in detail.

Food writer Tom Parker Bowles put it best in an article he wrote for Esquire magazine:

BAJA CALIFORNIA PENINSULA

Baja California Peninsula in Northwestern Mexico. It separates the Pacific Ocean from the Gulf of California. The peninsula extends 775 miles (1247 km) from Mexicali, Baja California, in the north to Cabo San Lucas, Baja California Sur, in the south. It is half the distance from Maine to Miami – and 110 miles (177 km) across at the widest part near the US border.

The Baja Peninsula is a great place to live well on less money. Whether you are a retiree or a digital nomad, we've found in our research that Baja has a lower cost of living, great medical care, low crime, and fantastic real estate.

Expats love Baja, and the growing English-speaking population means that learning Spanish is not as important as if you were living in Mexico City. However, I would encourage all expats to learn Spanish; it will improve your life in ways you can't imagine right now.

Over the years, realtors and tourism promoters have dubbed the northern part of the peninsula, especially the 68 mile (109 km) stretch of Pacific coastline just south of San Diego, the Baja Gold Coast.

Many expats from the west coast of the USA, and some from the Rocky Mountains, gravitate to the Baja peninsula. Those seeking a cooler climate, rugged cliffs, and good waves for surfing usually chose the Pacific Coast side of the peninsula – often the area from Rosarito to Ensenada. Sun worshippers and beach lovers prefer life on the Sea of Cortez or the southern part of the peninsula.

The air is fresh from unpolluted northwesterly winds sweeping across the Pacific Ocean. The climate is much like coastal San Diego – mostly sunny, not too cold, and not too hot. The humidity is usually comfortable; the only significant rainfall is about 2 inches (5 cm) a month from late November to early March. Sometimes, fog and ocean mist blanket the shoreline until late morning and the evening.

This area of the northern Baja peninsula also has rugged cliffs and sweeping ocean vistas, like the Big Sur area of California, and enough sand and surf and riding trails to please almost everybody from beachcombers to surfers and horse lovers.

Many expats live in the northwestern Pacific Coast corner of the peninsula because San Diego is only an hour away. For expats who don't want to cut ties with the USA, the ability to drive to and from the USA in a single day is a big plus compared with other places in Mexico. Many expats drive to San Diego frequently for doctor visits, banking, shopping, or other errands and return home for dinner.

The San Ysidro border crossing between San Diego and Tijuana is the busiest in the world, with almost 17 million cars annually and about 46,000 daily coming and going.

If you're anything like me, you want to see everything your new location offers. Don't be one of those expats who come to a new city or country and never get involved in what's happening. Even if your Spanish is a little rusty or non-existent, or you don't have a car, there are ways to figure out how to get around. You can rent a car, see if a new neighbour would like to show you, or hire an Uber for the day. You can see a ton in Mexico for about $35 USD.

Here are a few popular places to visit along the Baja Coast.

Cave Paintings

The Baja peninsula has some impressive cave paintings dating back 6,000 years. Cueva del Raton is one of the most accessible sites, a little more than halfway down the peninsula between Guerrero Negro and San Ignacio. The easiest way to visit the site without getting lost is to hire a tour guide in Guerrero Negro or San Ignacio for a 1-day excursion.

Quinceanera

If you ever get an invitation to a quinceanera in Mexico, don't miss it. It's the special Spanish ceremony celebrating the transition from a girl to a young woman.

Baja's Wine Country

Most people outside Mexico don't know that some of the finest wines in North America come from the Valle de Guadalupe.

Baja 1000 Off-Road Race

Each year, Ensenada hosts the Baja 1000 off-road race and the 125-nautical mile International Yacht Race that starts at Newport Beach, California.

Sierra de San Pedro Martir National Park

The park is a mountain range that runs north-south along the middle part of northwestern Baja California and is known for its pine trees and granite rock formations. Its name is Spanish for "mountains of Saint Peter the Martyr." Picacho del Diablo (Devil's Peak) is the park's highest peak in Baja, California, with its summit reaching 10,157 ft (3,096 m).

PUERTO VALLARTA

Puerto Vallarta, or PV as the locals call it, is where the Sierra Madre mountains meet the Pacific Ocean and is no doubt one of the most beautiful cities in the world. Once a tiny fishing village, Puerto Vallarta has become a sophisticated tourist destination and is perhaps the most gay-friendly city in Latin America.

Situated on the Bay of Banderas, Mexico's largest bay, PV, with its cobblestone streets and old Mexico charm, is perfect for a large and growing expat community.

PV is positioned at the same latitude as the Hawaiian Islands, giving it a similar climate with dry winters and rainy summers. The average daily high temperature is 86°F (30°C), and the average daily low temperature is 70°F (21°C).

It is a 3-hour flight from Los Angeles, a 4.5-hour flight from New York, and just under 5 hours from Toronto.

You'll need to hire a boat to get to a few beaches like Quimixto, Las Animas, or Yelapa. If you make it to Yelapa, be sure to look for the women on the beach selling slices of homemade tropical pie. Many consider the trip to Yelapa beach worth it just for the pie, with banana cream being a favourite. But come early as the pies sell out quickly, and when they're gone, business is done for the day.

Food, did you say Tacos? You can find a taco stand on every street corner, and they are always busy. Another favourite is grilled marlin or red snapper.

If you haven't tried Ceviche, then this is the place for you. We have Ceviche everywhere in Panama, and I'm a huge fan. Being on the coast in Mexico, you'll be able to find it everywhere.

For you walkers, explore the Malecon or boardwalk as we call it. If you love the smell of the ocean and getting out each morning or as the sun sets, make your way here. It stretches for miles along the oceanfront and is filled with art, statues, shops, restaurants and street food vendors.

If you are a diver, you will love living in Puerto Vallarta. The Pacific waters are mostly calm and clear, making for ideal scuba diving conditions. Whether you're already certified or considering taking lessons, you'll find a dive shop to suit your needs.

Some of the best dive spots around Puerto Vallarta include Las Caletas, Los Arcos and the famous Marietas Islands. Divers in Puerto Vallarta often encounter many types of different fish, octopus, schools of dolphins, turtles, giant manta rays, and the occasional humpback whale or whale shark. When diving offshore, you can explore cave systems and shipwrecks.

Puerto Vallarta's old town, with cobbled streets and white stucco buildings, is a huge draw for tourists and history buffs.

The Church of Our Lady of Guadalupe is the central feature of the town's skyline.

It is dedicated to the patron saint of Mexico and the destination of thousands of Catholic pilgrims during the 12-day Festival of Our Lady of Guadalupe each December.

RETIRING IN PUERTO VALLARTA

Puerto Vallarta has become a popular retirement destination for US and Canadian retirees. This has created several neighbourhoods within the Puerto Vallarta region that cater primarily to real estate tourism; the Hotel Zone, which stretches from downtown Vallarta to the airport and Marina Vallarta (near the airport), and Amapas and Conchas Chinas, which are built into the mountain slightly south and behind Puerto Vallarta, and overlook the city and bay.

Most recently, in the downtown area, especially in Emiliano Zapata (also known as the Romantic Zone), a somewhat controversial trend has commenced where traditional homes are being demolished to construct condominium buildings.

This region in recent years has been popular for real estate tourism, with nearly 25% of all real estate sales for the region taking place here in 2019. The controversial construction of condominium towers has also been taking place along the coastline heading south in Conchas Chinas and along the South Shore.

The Vallarta tourism real estate market comprises full-time retirees and second-home owners, primarily from the United States. On average, about 40% of buyers are American, with nationals consisting of 30% and Canadians and other foreign buyers making up the remaining 20%.

Mexicans favour destinations such as Puerto Vallarta, Los Cabos and Cancun not just for the sun and beach but also as real estate investment to hedge their pesos as real estate in these regions is priced in USD rather than in pesos like the rest of the country.

Puerto Vallarta can be classified as a medium-ranged real estate market with a market consisting primarily of condominiums with an average price of around $320,000 USD in 2019. Higher-end real estate can be found primarily in Conchas Chinas. However, Punta Mita, at the northern point of Banderas Bay in the neighbouring state of Nayarit, has become increasingly more popular with wealthier buyers over the past 10 years.

To the East of each zone are many residential areas with a short walk (10-30 minutes, depending on how far into the residential area you want to live) to the beaches along the coast. Add to the other beaches mentioned are Bucerias, Sayulita, Conchas Chinas & Mismaloya, with several between each of these.

Summers are hot, but you can run errands in the mornings and hibernate at the movies for 32 pesos/$1.50 USD and come out to play in the evenings during the summer. You will find that many people don't require a/c between November-May.

If you ask most expats and retirees why they have chosen Puerto Vallarta to live in, it's because of the people. They are warm and inviting; if you can't remember that simple Spanish word, they don't fret. They laugh and help you the best they can.

One thing to be mindful of is the poverty of the locals. Many areas of the city are still poorly served by roads and sewers. With 45,000 regular dwellings, 10% do not have a potable water supply (they have to carry their water from a public tap), 8% do not have connections to a sewer system or septic system, and 4% do not have electricity.

Here are a few of my favourite places in Puerto Vallarta.

VALLARTA BOTANICAL GARDENS

Vallarta Botanical Gardens is impressive as you explore its different sections: the Cactus Garden, with species of various forms and sizes; the Tropical Fruit Orchard, with a fantastic collection of oaks, wild palms and agave plants; and the Conservatory of Orchids and Native Plants, with almost 300 species native to Mexico - out of 1000 found in the country.

When you finish visiting the greenhouses and gardens, you can walk deeper into the forest, cross the hanging bridge and admire the magnificent trees that inhabit the area.

CUALE RIVER ISLAND

The Cuale Cultural Centre offers painting, sculpture, dance, drama, and music workshops, as well as free access to the Cuale Archaeological Museum, exhibiting the archaeological findings in the area and general information on Mesoamerican history and art.

LOS ARCOS MARINE PARK

Los Arcos Marine Park is in front of Mismaloya beach and is a natural paradise where you can scuba dive and snorkel. Discover the abundant marine life in its depths due to its light ocean currents that allow great visibility even at more than 1500 feet deep (480 m).

Los Arcos is also an ideal place to practice stand-up paddling and kayaking and explore the caves formed around the huge granite rocks that emerge in the middle of the ocean.

This protected area is a natural habitat for many marine birds, such as blue-footed boobies, parrots and pelicans. At the bottom of the sea, its reefs are home to multicoloured fish, including clownfish, puffer fish, stingrays and octopuses.

SAN MIGUEL DE ALLENDE

Nestled in Mexico's northern central highlands sits charming and cultured San Miguel de Allende. Long a favourite hangout of artists and romantics, San Miguel offers a step back in time to cobblestone streets, colourful Colonial architecture, and breathtaking views.

San Miguel de Allende is located in the far eastern part of Guanajuato, Mexico.

It is part of the Bajio region, is 170 miles (274 km) from Mexico City, and is only a 10-hour drive from the US border. A historic town and World Heritage site since 2008, it has fresh springs, which was its appeal in 1542. It's the town where the nation of Mexico was declared to be free and separate from Spain. This was done by a wealthy local clique who had no authority to do so, but it worked all the same because people were sufficiently open to the idea of change and were ready to fight for it. It has architectural controls that make it nearly impossible to remodel any exteriors in the historic centre. If you took away the cars, much of it would look like 1750.

San Miguel has a population of 174,615, with estimates of expats ranging from 20,000 to 25,000, with at least half of these from the United States and the remaining from Canada and Europe. They are attracted by the mild climate, cultural opportunities, and low crime.

Despite being less than 5% of the total municipal population, foreign residents have a considerable cultural and economic impact on the city. Most foreign residents are retirees from the United States, Canada, and Europe who have come for the mild climate, cultural opportunities, and low crime.

The large expat community has established several institutions here, most notably the Biblioteca Pública in the former convent of Santa Ana, which has the second-largest English-language book collection in Mexico and serves as a community center for foreigners. There is also a chapter of the Lion's Club (est. 1987). A post of the American Legion and the Veterans of Foreign Wars and Mexico's only Audubon Society chapter is located there.

Since there are a ton of expats, this is one of the safest places in Mexico. The cost of living is low, the temperature is fantastic, and there is a ton of culture and arts. You can rent a 2-bedroom apartment on a long-term lease for around $600 USD per month on the city's outskirts. Something downtown will be closer to $1000 USD per month.

If you want to purchase your home and want something pretty nice, expect to pay around $300,000 USD in a great neighbourhood in town. You can always go a little further out to find some great bargains.

You can buy fresh fruits, vegetables, eggs, cheese and meats daily from the indoor food markets at a very reasonable price.

Here are some great things to see and do in San Miguel de Allende,

ARTS, MUSIC AND LITERATURE

San Miguel was the largest recipient of funding for the arts in the Spanish colonial period. The city was full of wealthy art patrons from the start of the 1500s. Affluent Spanish families like the Condes de la Canal paid for the sumptuous Chapel of Loreto and employed artists in all aspects, including baroque music compositions.

A fragment of that musical past is used in the Holy Week music accompanying the celebration of mass around Easter. Religious and secular music continues to be a town focal point, with the English composer and pianist Michael Hoppe performing frequently.

The town hosts an important free film festival annually, the GIFF (Guanajuato International Film Festival). The event caters to the writing community, bringing authors, editors and literary agents together. The 2009 event attracted names such as Erica Jong, Todd Gitlen and Josephine Humphreys. Writers have lived here since the mid-20th century.

SANCTUARY OF JESÚS NAZARENO DE ATOTONILCO

Situated just 8 miles (13 km) away is the Sanctuary of Jesús Nazareno de Atotonilco. UNESCO calls Atotonilco's interior church decoration a masterpiece of 18th-century Mexican baroque art, particularly for its murals. Walker Simon of Reuters writes, "Others have compared the frescoes' scope, quality and biblical sweep to the Vatican's Sistine Chapel."

FESTIVALS

Many festivals here are purely Mexican, combining social activity with religious expression. There are pilgrimages, all-night vigils, ringing church bells, processions and fireworks throughout the year.

The year's most significant celebration is that of the town's patron saint, the Archangel Michael. The angel's feast day is 29 September, but festivities take place for an entire week. Activities include private parties, sporting events, cultural events, indigenous dance and more. The week is popularly called the Fiestas de San Miguel de Allende. The finale is a procession of the actual image of St. Michael that is usually high on the main altar of La Paroquia. He is taken on a flower-covered dais to "visit" the leading churches in the historic district.

Fireworks are a part of all festivities. Elaborate structures that spin and light in sequence, called "castillos"—castles—are installed in the esplanade at the Jardín and sometimes at other churches in town.

Holy Week begins with an exhibition of altars dedicated to the Virgin of Sorrows and ends with the Procession of Silence. Before the Procession of Silence, there is a reenactment of the judgment of Jesus by Pontius Pilate on one side of the San Miguel Parish. Then the procession begins, representing the Passion's fourteen scenes before his crucifixion.

Many townspeople participate in the event, with children dressed as angels and adults in period clothing carrying statues of Jesus. The procession winds its way along the main streets of the historic centre completely in silence.

The annual Festival de Música de Cámara, or Chamber Music Festival, occurs each year in August in the city's historic center. One of the purposes of the event is to bring this type of music to streets and other public venues as well as traditional concert halls such as the event's home, the Angela Peralta Theater.

Other events include the Jornada de Cultura Cubana in March, the Festival de Tìteres in April, the Festival de Convivencia y Hermandad Universal in May, the Desfile de Locos in June, the Festival Expressiones Cortos in July, the Feria Nacional de Lana y Latón and the festival de Jazz y Blues in November and the Festival de San Miguel de Allende in December.

The most-important political celebration is the reenactment of the "Grito de Dolores" as the original occurred in the nearby town of Dolores Hidalgo, marking the beginning of the Mexican War of Independence.

As the birthplace of Ignacio Allende, the town was a focal point of the 2010s Bicentennial celebrations, with reenactments of events such as the arrival of the message from Querétaro from Josefa Ortiz. Bicentennial celebrations also included events such as the Ballet Mazatl.

Festivities were concentrated in and around the Jardin Principal, the Ignacio Allende House and the Centro Cultural.

SMART is a multi-media cultural festival held annually in May that combines exhibits by Mexican artists with various culinary and social events at local hotels, including the festival founder Hotel Matilda, Dos Casas Hotel and L'Otel.

MERIDA

One of the most popular places in Mexico is Mérida. It is the largest city on the Yucatan Peninsula and is about 22 miles (35 km) off the coast of the Gulf of Mexico. To the east is the state of Quintana Roo, to the west is the state of Campeche, to the north is the Gulf of Mexico, and far to the south is the state of Chiapas.

Along with Merida, the Yucatan Peninsula is also the home of Cancun and the island of Cozumel, two of Mexico's most frequently visited tourist meccas.

Merida is home to over a million people and has a large expat population and a significant indigenous Mayan population.

The city is also located in the Chicxulub Crater. It has a very flat topography and is only 30 ft (9 metres) above sea level.

The land outside of Mérida is covered with smaller scrub trees and former henequen fields. Almost no surface water exists, but several cenotes (underground springs and rivers) are found across the state.

Merida has a charming city centre, colourful old mansions, and a flat, easy-to-walk landscape. A short 22-mile (35 km) drive takes you to beautiful beaches on the Gulf of Mexico.

Folks considering a move to Merida should be advised that while she has much to offer, the summers are HOT. May temperatures (Merida's hottest month) boast an average high of 100°F (37°C).

Merida's culture is a distinctive blend of traditions inherited from the ancient Maya civilization dating back to 2600 BC and customs brought by Spanish conquistadors, who began colonizing the territory in the 16th century. Many historians believe that Mérida is the oldest continually occupied city in the Americas.

CULTURE

Mérida has been nicknamed "The White City" (La Ciudad Blanca), though this moniker's exact origin is unclear. Some explanations include the typical colour of its old buildings painted and decorated with "cal" or the fact that the residents keep the city clean. Mérida was named after the Spanish town of the same name, originally (in Latin) Augústa Emérita.

Mérida served as the American Capital of Culture between 2000 and 2017.

As the state and regional capital, Mérida is a cultural center featuring multiple museums, art galleries, restaurants, movie theatres, and shops. Mérida retains an abundance of colonial buildings and is a cultural center with music and dancing playing an important part in day-to-day life. At the same time, it is a modern city with a range of shopping malls, auto dealerships, hotels, restaurants, and leisure facilities. The famous avenue Paseo de Montejo is lined with original sculptures. Each year, the MACAY Museum in Mérida mounts a new sculpture installation featuring works from Mexico and another chosen country. Each exhibit remains for ten months of the year.

YUCATÁN'S MAYA MUSEUM

Mérida and the state of Yucatán have traditionally been isolated from the rest of the country by geography, creating a unique culture. The conquistadors found the Mayan civilization to be incredibly resilient, and their attempts to eradicate Mayan tradition, religion, and culture thankfully failed.

The surviving remnants of the Mayan culture can be seen daily in speech, dress, and written and oral histories.

It is especially apparent in holidays like Hanal Pixan, a Mayan/ Catholic Day of the Dead celebration. It falls on October 31, November 1, and November 2 (one day for children, one day for adults, and one day for all souls) and is commemorated by elaborate altars dedicated to dead relatives.

It is a compromise between the two religions, with crucifixes mingled with skull decorations and food sacrifices/offerings. Múkbil pollo is the Mayan tamale pie offered to the dead on All Saints' Day, traditionally accompanied by a cup of hot chocolate.

Many Yucatecans enjoy eating this on and around the Day of the Dead, and while complicated to make, they can be purchased and even shipped via air. (Muk-bil means "to put in the ground" or to cook in a pib, an underground oven).

For English speakers, Mérida has the Mérida English Library, a lending library with an extensive collection of English books, videos and children's books.

The library is also the site for expat meetings, children's storytelling hours, and other cultural events.

Mérida is also home to the Yucatán Symphony Orchestra, which plays regular seasons at the José Peón Contreras Theatre on Calle 60 and features classical music, jazz, and opera.

SAFETY

You can't beat Mérida in terms of safety in Mexico. There are a ton of expats here, so if your Spanish is still at the beginner level, you will feel reasonably comfortable. As cities go, Mérida feels like any other US city, so you will feel at home here.

FOOD

Yucatán food has its unique style and is very different from what most people consider "Mexican" food. It includes influences from the local Mayan cuisine, and the Caribbean, Mexican, European and Middle Eastern foods. Tropical fruits, such as coconut, pineapple, plum, tamarind and mamey, are often used in Yucatán cuisine.

There are many regional dishes. Some of them are

Poc Chuc, a Mayan/Yucateco version of boiled/grilled pork

Salbutes and Panuchos. Salbutes are soft, cooked tortillas with lettuce, tomato, turkey and avocado on top. Panuchos feature fried tortillas filled with black beans and topped with turkey or chicken, lettuce, avocado and pickled onions. Habanero chiles accompany solid or puréed dishes and fresh limes and corn tortillas.

Queso Relleno is a gourmet dish featuring ground pork inside a carved Edam cheese ball served with tomato sauce.

Pavo en Relleno Negro (also known locally as Chilmole) is a turkey meat stew cooked with a black paste made from roasted chiles, a local version of the mole de guajalote found throughout Mexico. The meat soaked in the black soup is also served in tacos, sandwiches, panuchos, or salbutes.

Sopa de Lima is a lime soup with a chicken broth base, often accompanied by shredded chicken or turkey and a crispy tortilla.

Papadzules. Egg "tacos" bathed with pumpkin seed sauce and tomatoes.

Cochinita pibil is a marinated pork dish, by far the most renowned from Yucatán, that is made with achiote. Achiote is a reddish spice with a distinctive flavour and peppery smell.

Bul keken (Mayan for "beans and pork") is a traditional black bean and pork soup. The soup is served at home on Mondays in most Yucatán towns. The soup is usually served with chopped onions, radishes, chiles, and tortillas. This dish is also commonly referred to as frijol con puerco.

Brazo de reina (Spanish for "The Queen's Arm") is a traditional tamale dish. A long, flat tamal is topped with ground pumpkin seeds and rolled up like a roll cake. The long roll is then cut into slices. The slices are topped with tomato sauce and a pumpkin seed garnish.

Tamales colados is a traditional dish with pork/chicken, banana leaf, fresh corn masa and achiote paste seasoned with roasted tomato sauce. Hot sauce in Mérida is usually made from the indigenous chiles in the area, including, Chile Xcatik, Chile Seco de Yucatán, and Chile Habanero.

DON'T MISS:

PRE-HISPANIC CITY OF CHICHEN-ITZA

Chichen-Itza, which sits about 75 miles (120 km) from Merida on the Yucatan peninsula, was built by the Mayan civilization and is one of the world's seven wonders. Chichen-Itza was one of the most important city-states in pre-Hispanic America and is one of Mexico's most visited archaeological sites today.

This sacred site was one of the greatest Mayan centres of the Yucatán peninsula. Throughout its nearly 1,000-year history, different peoples have left their mark on the city.

The Maya and Toltec vision of the world and the universe is revealed in their stone monuments and artistic works. The fusion of Mayan construction techniques with new elements from central Mexico makes Chichen-Itza one of the most important examples of the Mayan-Toltec civilization in Yucatán. Several buildings have survived, such as the Warriors' Temple, El Castillo and the circular observatory known as El Caracol.

You may have seen familiar images of the ancient ruins at Chichen-Itza, the incredible murals on the buildings of the central university city campus of the Universidad Nacional Autonoma de Mexico in Mexico City, or the intricate cathedral in San Miguel de Allende, Uxmal, another UNESCO-listed Maya ruin located an hour and fifteen minutes south of Merida, is celebrated for its precise construction and ornate stone carvings.

The towering Pyramid of the Magician is in remarkably good condition, as are the surrounding structures, which can be enjoyed with fewer crowds than in Chichén-Itzá.

When a deadly asteroid slammed into the seafloor off the coast of the Yucatán Peninsula 66 million years ago, wiping out the dinosaurs, it also created more than 6,000 freshwater sinkholes and caves called cenotes.

For centuries, the crystal-clear groundwater pools were used as sacred wells by the Maya, where they performed offerings and spiritual rituals to communicate with the gods. Local shamans still perform these rituals today.

PRE-HISPANIC TOWN OF UXMAL

The Mayan town of Uxmal, in Yucatán, was founded c. AD 700 and had some 25,000 inhabitants. The layout of the buildings, which date from between 700 and 1000, reveals a knowledge of astronomy.

The Pyramid of the Soothsayer, as the Spaniards called it, the Pyramid of the Soothsayer dominates the ceremonial centre, which has well-designed buildings decorated with a profusion of symbolic motifs and sculptures depicting Chaac, the god of rain.

The ceremonial sites of Uxmal, Kabah, Labna and Sayil are considered the high points of Mayan art and architecture.

CANCÚN

Cancún is a city in southeast Mexico on the northeast coast of the Yucatán Peninsula in the Mexican state of Quintana Roo. It is a significant tourist destination in Mexico and the seat of the municipality of Benito Juárez.

The city is on the Caribbean Sea and is one of Mexico's east-ernmost points.Cancún is just north of Mexico's Caribbean coast resort area known as the Riviera Maya.

Apart from the island tourist zone (part of the world's second-longest coral reef), the Mexican residential section of the city, the downtown part of which is known as "El Centro." follows a master plan that consists of "supermanzanas" (superblocks), giant trapezoids with a central, open, non-residential area cut in by u-shaped residential streets.

Cancún's mainland or downtown area has diverged from the original plan, with development scattered around the city.

The remaining undeveloped beach and lagoon front areas outside the hotel zone are now under varying stages of development, in Punta Sam and Puerto Juarez to the north, continuing along Bonampak and south toward the airport along Boulevard Donaldo Colosio. One development abutting the hotel zone is Puerto Cancún; Malecon Cancún is another large development.

Cancún has a tropical climate, wet and dry climate, with little temperature difference between months. The city is hot year-round and moderated by onshore trade winds, with an annual mean temperature of 80°F (27°C).

Unlike inland areas of the Yucatán Peninsula, sea breezes restrict high temperatures from reaching 97 °F (36 °C) on most afternoons.

Annual rainfall is around 52 in (1,340 millimetres), falling on 115 days per year.

The rainy season runs from May through late October, when hot temperatures, high humidity, and quick but intense summer thunderstorms are common.

The dry season usually begins in December and runs through April, when more temperate conditions occur as the northeast trade winds bring northerly breezes, sunshine, and relative humidity is lowest.

MAYA ARCHEOLOGICAL SITES

There are some small Mayan vestiges of the pre-Columbian Maya civilization in Cancún. El Rey (Las Ruinas del Rey) is located in the Hotel Zone.

El Meco, a more substantial site, is found on the mainland just outside the city limits on the road north to Punta Sam.

Close by in the Riviera Maya and the Grand Costa Maya, there are sites such as Cobá and Muyil (Riviera), the small Polé (now Xcaret), and Kohunlich, Kinichná, Dzibanché, Oxtankah, Tulum, and Chacchoben, in the south of the state.

EXPAT COMMUNITY

Cancun and nearby Playa del Carmen are very expat-friendly communities. With the big tourist economy, many Mexican locals speak some English, and the cities are easy for English speakers to navigate. Plus, a busy international airport means you can return to the USA in as little as two hours.

BEST AREA TO LIVE

You can choose to live in the city instead of the famous Hotel Zone as you might want a more authentic cultural experience by living right in the city among your Mexican neighbours.

Cancun is a big, small city with most of the conveniences you are accustomed to in the US or Canada. You can live in an area called SM18. Most shopping areas are no more than 5 minutes away by car or taxi. Cancun also has a fantastic public transportation system. You can walk to Walmart, Sam's Club, Costco, City Club and the beautiful, modern, amazing Plaza Las Americas. The local "Triple-A" baseball park and soccer stadium are nearby. Plaza Las Americas has a wonderful VIP movie theatre featuring leather recliners, each with a personal table and lamp. The price of admission is approx. $6 USD.

Cancun is known for its fantastic scuba diving, and you can dive all year long in the crystal clear waters off of Cancun, Cozumel, Puerto Moreles, and Isla Mujeres. The fishing, boating and snorkelling are also fantastic here. You can take art lessons and learn how to paint. In addition, you can slowly eat your way through the hundreds of restaurants in the area.

COZUMEL

Cozumel is a 34-mile-long by 11-mile-wide (54 km by 17 km) island off Mexico's Riviera Maya. Cozumel is quite unlike its neighbour. It's largely undeveloped, with expanses of jungle and untouched shoreline that are a rarity on the mainland. The city of San Miguel has a laid-back vibe and stunning stretches of untouched nature can be found along the eastern and southern shores.

Just off Cozumel's southwestern coast lies the world's second-longest coral reef system (only Australia's Great Barrier Reef beats it). The Mesoamerican Reef System spans about 175 miles (281 km) from the Gulf of Mexico to the coast of Honduras. The exceptionally clear waters put Cozumel high on many divers' bucket lists.

It's common for divers to see vast coral heads, vivid sponges, tropical fish, and tunnels and caves housing species found only here, such as the Cozumel splendid toadfish. The Arrecifes de Cozumel National Park, a popular diving area, is home to several endangered creatures, including the loggerhead sea turtle, the queen conch, and black coral. The seafloor is also incredibly varied here, with ledges and cliffs creating dramatic underwater vistas.

Cozumel has low crime rates that should alleviate any fears of living here, with violent crime almost non-existent. The nice thing about Cozumel is that they use the US dollar and speak English in most places.

Home and apartment rentals are available on a "leased" basis from six months to two years. Or, if you want something more permanent, you can buy a condo in one of the developments that line the beach on the north and south sides of San Miguel.

Although $850 USD per month is the average rent, two-bedroom places are available for as little as $600 USD per month. Utilities average $120 – $250 USD per month, depending on your need for technology. Property taxes are very low by US standards. Figure $750 USD/year or less, even for a very large home.

Food prices are similar to what you'd find in a grocery store in a smaller US city. Restaurant prices range from delicious lunches in small Mom and Pop places as low as $7 USD to high-end pricing with entrees in the $12 to $25 USD range.

High-speed internet is readily available. Cable TV now features a sizable number of English-language channels. You can even stream on Netflix, Hulu, YouTube and the like.

There are several small English lending libraries. There are now enough Big Box stores to satisfy "first world country" tastes–three enormous groceries, Sam's Club, and two large Coppel department stores. A ferry ride across the channel takes you to a Home Depot, Walmart, and Costco.

Good medical care is available from several locations on the island, including the Clinica San Miguel and the CMC. For maintenance care and general practice — from cuts and broken bones to stabilization after a heart attack — Cozumel gets high marks.

Doctors and nurses are never in a hurry. They are very compassionate and caring. And then have all the modern medications and techniques.

Prices are lower than in the US, and many US and Canadian insurance companies will now cover care here.

Most locals make the short air trips to either Cancun (20 minutes by plane) or Merida (60 minutes by plane) for complicated or specialized surgery. World-class doctors and facilities are available to effectively treat anything you can name and at relative bargain prices. Merida, the capital city of Yucatan, has become a mecca for worldwide medical tourism. Many of the doctors at places like Star Medica trained at prestigious institutions in the US. It also bears mentioning that most prescription drugs are available in Cozumel's farmacias, and the majority do not require a prescription!

Dental work is very inexpensive in Cozumel. Several excellent dentists charge half or less than what you would pay outside the country for something like a crown or a root canal.

The people of Cozumel, mostly Mexicans and Mayans, are charming, sweet people. If you live here, you will interact with them daily in the stores, restaurants and everywhere.

Due to Cozumel being an island, if you want to go to the mainland, you'll need to take the ferry. That being said, you could come to Cozumel and never leave. It has everything you could ever want or need.

OAXACA

Oaxaca, Mexico, is best known for such archaeological wonders as the Zapotecan city of Monte Alban and its Pacific Coast beaches. Oaxaca has intensely colourful weaving and handicrafts available. In these isolated mountain valleys, 16 indigenous ethnicities; the largest being the Zapotec; groups, draw on a wealth of native plants, including chepiche, pitiona, and hoja santa, to create one of the world's great idiosyncratic cuisines.

Everywhere you turn, in the markets, outside the cathedrals, surrounding the zocalos – the anti-modern appeal of Oaxacan crafts is a powerful testament to the artistic isolation of the surrounding villages.

Oaxaca is so colourful. The architecture, clothing, textiles, festivals and food are all bursting with colour, and the weather is unbeatable. Most days are sunny and 20 degrees, with maybe a little rain at sunset.

Over the past 25 years, the expat community has grown by more than 1,000%.

One of the most appealing aspects of living in Oaxaca is the cost of living. An American expat can expect to pay around $350 USD for a 2-bedroom apartment just 10 minutes from Centro Oaxaca, including utilities and internet.

Food will run you around $150 USD monthly, allowing you to spend $500 USD per month.

If you want to go out for dinner, to the movies, have a drink with friends and go shopping, then expect to spend an additional $400 USD. That brings your total to $900 USD per month. Okay, how else can I spend money?

You'll want to travel outside Oaxaca for a few weekend adventures or for some great escape when friends visit. I would add an additional $400 USD.

The cons of living in Oaxaca

- There are no beaches. Getting to the beach is about a 6-hour drive. Native Mexicans say that Oaxaca is the 'real' Mexico.

- The internet is not like in the bigger cities. Some days are good, others not so much, so if you make your living online, then maybe this little oasis isn't for you.

- Along with the internet is electricity. The electricity is government-managed, and there is no option to have it work effectively. A generator is always helpful in these cases.

- The city is always celebrating something, which makes the streets extremely noisy. They love to party and have nightly fireworks and fiestas all the time, day and night, so if quiet is what you're looking for, Oaxaca is not the place for you.

- If you've been to the beaches in Mexico, you're well accustomed to the street vendors trying to sell you something; well here, it is no different. It happens every day, all day.

- Healthcare is not great in Oaxaca. You will need to be in a larger city if you have any health issues.

- Nothing is marked when you enter a store. They price it according to your looks. So if you look like a Gringo, expect to pay higher prices, especially if you can't speak Spanish. You will likely get a much better deal if you can converse with the locals in Spanish.

There are some incredible places around Oaxaca that you can visit if you choose to live here. Less than 2 hours away is the petrified waterfall, Hierve el Agua, Teotitlan del Valle, and El Tule, the widest tree in the world. To the south, about a half-hour drive, are the woodcarvers of Arrazola, who create the famous painted animals called alebrijes or the potters of San Bartolo Coyotepec, who create beauties of black clay.

CAMPECHE

Another extremely safe area in Mexico is Campeche. Officially called the Free and Sovereign State of Campeche, it is in Mexico's southeast region on the Yucatan Peninsula's west side, has a coastline to the west with the Gulf of Mexico, and is home to about 1 million people.

The city was built in 1517 and is an excellent retirement destination for several reasons. The most important being the low cost of living, affordable real estate, high degree of safety and colourful colonial heritage.

Home to a large number of Mexico's indigenous people, Campeche is, for the most part, still "off the tourist radar," and therefore, more "Mexican" than the many other areas that have made the economic trade-offs necessary to attract the tourist industry.

It's a UNESCO World Heritage City with a beautiful, well-preserved Spanish colonial centre. And it lies on the Gulf of Mexico, where sea breezes cool Campeche's warm weather.

Campeche is very affordable if you are on a budget. You could survive quite nicely on 1000 USD per month, including food, rent and health care. Many expats pick Campeche because it is quiet, has a good quality of life, and has lots to do.

Campeche has two full-service hospitals, Hospital Dr. Manuel Campos and Sanitorio Clinica Campeche, a Red Cross facility (Cruz Roja) and several clinics.

Grupo San Miguel, Centro Médico Carmen and Central Quirúrgica Del Carmen. But, you may have to go to Merida for specialty medical services or surgeries.

FOOD

Camarones al Orégano — shrimp dish seasoned with oregano

Camarones al Coco — shrimp dish seasoned with coconut

Pejelagarto — alligator-head fish (Lepidoseus viridis), a freshwater fish with a long snout typically cooked on a grill, seasoned with lime juice, chilli, etc.

Frijoles Negros con Carne de Cerdo — black beans with pork

Sweets

Postre de Chicozapote — a dessert made from the chicozapote fruit from the native chicle tree, from which chewing gum originally was made; simply a wonderful fruit to taste

Alcoholic Drinks

Balche — a mildly alcoholic drink served ice cold, made from fermented pineapple rind.

MAZATLÁN

Here, the beaches are uncrowded, allowing you to walk for miles and miles. Located halfway along Mexico's Pacific coast, life here is affordable all the way around. Food is inexpensive, and so is the rent.

One of the nice things about living or retiring in Mazatlán is that it is close to 700 miles (1126 km) south of the Arizona border, which would be about a 14-hour drive down Highway 15D. You could easily move everything down here and start your new life without too many hassles.

The city was founded in 1531 by an army of Spaniards and indigenous people. By the mid-19th century, many immigrants had arrived from Germany. Over time, Mazatlán developed into a commercial seaport, importing equipment for the nearby gold and silver mines.

As of this writing, roughly 466,000 people are living in Mazatlán. A car ferry crosses the Gulf of California from Mazatlán to La Paz, Baja California Sur.

FOOD

The main dishes in Mazatlán are heavily influenced by seafood. Food specialties include ceviches, zarandeado fish, and aguachile. Other standard and prominent foods are smoked marlin and tuna, chilorio, bearded tamales (made with shrimp), Governor tacos, fish crackers and Sinaloa-style grill-roasted chicken.

The local cuisine offers a variety of fresh drinks such as horchata, barley, coconut, coconut horchata, Tejuino, wines and a range of beers, of which the best known is the local beer called Pacífico, which has its factory in the harbour. Another well-known drink in the region is a vanilla-flavoured beverage called "tonicol."

Typical sweets include coconut candies, jamoncillos, and other candies made with coconut marshmallows from the region.

MAZATLÁN CARNIVAL

Mazatlán Carnival is held in late February/early March. It is one of the most important carnivals in Mexico as the first parade on Sunday brings together more than 600,000 people for over three hours in the coastal area of the city on the "Avenida del Mar." A novelty that allows tourists to come from all over the world to witness this festival is called "Burning of humour." This tradition says to burn a character (Monigote) representing someone who people think has done a misdeed, which usually means politicians, presidents, or as in 2013, "influenza" was burned.

This is followed by the famous "Naval Combat," depicting the battle against French vessels seeking to land at the port.

CONCLUSION

Whether you are looking for authentic markets and charming shops or big box stores like Sam's Club and Walmart, these cities have it all.

You will be able to get most of the things that you are accustomed to buying at home in any of these cities.

For those things that are on your 'must-have' list but just can't be found in Mexico, Amazon has arrived on the scene and seems to work pretty well for the most part, at least in the larger cities. (https://www.amazon.com.mx). From my understanding, you can just use your Mexican address for Amazon, and they will deliver to your door.

CHAPTER 11: QUICK SUMMARY

- There are some fantastic cities either on the beach or in the mountains. Here are a few of the most expat-friendly cities and some exciting things to do when you live there.

- Acapulco is one of Mexico's oldest beach resorts where you can watch the cliff divers jumping from a height of 130 ft (40 m) and safely landing in the water below. The show starts around 1 pm, and you will be in awe when you see how skilled the divers are

- Baja California Peninsula is in Northwestern Mexico and separates the Pacific Ocean from the Gulf of California with a lower cost of living, great medical care, low crime, and fantastic real estate

- Puerto Vallarta, or PV as the locals call it is one of the most beautiful cities in the world

- San Miguel de Allende is located in the far eastern part of Guanajuato, Mexico. The population is 174,615 and estimates of 20,000 - 25,000 expats, half being American and the rest from Canada and Europe

- Mérida is also located in the Chicxulub Crater, about 22 miles (35 km) off the coast of the Gulf of Mexico and has a charming city centre, colourful old mansions, and a flat, easy-to-walk landscape

- Chichen-Itza, sits about 75 miles (120 km) from Merida on the Yucatan peninsula and is one of the most important city-states in pre-Hispanic America and is one of Mexico's most visited sites today.

- Cancún is a city in southeast Mexico on the northeast coast of the Yucatán Peninsula in the Mexican state of Quintana Roo.It is hot year round and has a very friendly expat community

- Playa del Carmen is a very expat-friendly community

- Cozumel is a 34-mile-long by 11-mile-wide (54 km by 17 km) island off of Mexico's Riviera Maya land is largely undeveloped, with expanses of jungle and untouched shoreline that are a rarity on the mainland

- Campeche is another extremely safe area in Mexico, built in 1517 and is an excellent retirement destination

- Mazatlán, is where the beaches are uncrowded, allowing you to walk for miles and miles

Chapter 12 is all about your furry friends; your pets. How to bring them to Mexico, whether you drive or fly, and what has to happen before they enter the country.

CHAPTER 12

PETS

MASCOTAS

Handle every stressful situation like a dog. If you can't eat it or play with it, just pee on it and walk away.

UNKNOWN

In Mexico, dogs and cats are not typically spayed/neutered for reasons intertwined with both culture and religion. Pets in some families are considered disposable and are treated poorly by any standard, and by others, valued members of the family, and family is cherished in Mexico.

CAN I BRING MY PET WITH ME?

Two dogs or cats may be brought in per person, with their accessories, appropriate import certificates and other documentation. Beyond this limit, there is a fee. You are only allowed to have enough food to feed the animals on the day of arrival. Your pet's leash, collar, and harness are permitted to accompany him/her.

Information on importing pets from the U.S. to Mexico can be found on the APHIS/USDA https://www.gob.mx/senasica/documentos/informate-y-consulta-los-requisitos-194242?state=published website or Mexico's government website https://www.aphis.usda.gov/aphis/pet-travel/by-country/pettravel-mexico, but bear in mind that rules change regularly so it is always a good idea to check Facebook pages or websites specific to the area you will be visiting to verify current policy before you travel.

If you can find one, a vet well accustomed to preparing animals for travel to Mexico is your best bet. Well-meaning veterinarians unfamiliar with the current rules and regulations can cost you anxiety, time, and money if you arrive only to find that you have not completed the required preparation or do not have the proper documentation for your pet.

As of December 16, 2019, a health certificate from a USDA-certified vet is no longer required to enter Mexico with your dog or cat. Rules for pets entering Mexico from the U.S. or Canada in effect as of this writing; https://www.gob.mx/cms/uploads/attachment/file/565030/If_you_are_traveling_with_your_pet2.pdf

Once you arrive at the airport (with your pet in a clean carrier containing no disposable bedding such as a newspaper or any edible products like treats or chews), you will be directed to the Mexican Animal and Plant Health Inspection Office (OISA) to see the official personnel working with SENASICA.

They will verify the following:

- That the animals do not present signs of infectious disease

- That the animals are free of ectoparasites

- That the animals do not present fresh wounds or wounds in process of healing

If your pet is small enough to fly in-cabin on an airplane, each airline will have its own rules, procedures, and forms to fill out, so be sure and check the airline's website.

If your pet will be flying cargo, it is important to note that many airlines will not fly a pet in cargo if temperatures are likely to be above a certain limit at any travel point. You do not want to risk your dog or cat being stranded in a warehouse unattended after being deplaned due to high temperatures, so check with the airline to see their specific policies.

Several companies offer international pet relocation services, and they will be up to date on what is required for your pet. If you can afford it and want someone to take care of the process of relocating your pet for you, some options are

- https://www.petrelocation.com

- https://www.happytailstravel.com

- https://www.airanimal.com

- https://www.petmovers.com

The same rules apply when driving across the border into Mexico with pets, so be prepared with the same documentation and information as you would have if you were flying in.

Once in Mexico, many expats become involved in volunteer work with animal rescue organizations that rehome Mexican street dogs and cats. So, if you meet and fall in love with a shelter pet or even befriend a street dog or cat that you can't stand to leave behind, it is quite possible to bring your new furry friend home when you leave Mexico.

Most tourist and expat communities have organizations to help you get the proper immunizations and documentation to get your fur buddy imported to the US or Canada. Veterinary care is abundant and excellent in most tourist and larger cities and for significantly less money than you are used to spending on vet care at home.

If you are bringing a pet into Mexico, be prepared for the

possibility that you may not be able to find the same pet food in Mexico that your fur baby eats at home.

Many vet clinics will carry a good selection of premium pet foods, but Mexican grocery stores will not have the variety or quality of pet foods to which you may be accustomed.

If you find that a change to a different brand becomes necessary, try to choose a product with the same primary ingredients as what you currently use. For example, if your dog eats food with chicken and rice as the main ingredients, you should be able to find a substitute with the same ingredients, at least.

USING A CUSTOMS BROKER

You don't need to hire a customs broker if your pet is travelling with you, even if they are in the hold as excess baggage. A customs broker clears goods that pass through customs and is responsible for making the customs declaration for pets for import or export. Therefore, it will only be necessary to hire them when the animal travels alone or is sent as Live Cargo.

AIRFARE FOR PET – HOW TO TRAVEL IN PEACE WITH YOUR PET

Buying a pet air ticket is among the main questions for those who want to travel with their dogs and cats in the aircraft cabin.

Flying with your pets involves advance preparation and a lot of bureaucracy.

Therefore, you need to be aware of airline rules regarding the transport of dogs and cats before planning trips like this. This is because there is no specific legislation for pets about this issue. Thus, each company determines which breed it will transport, the size and weight allowed, and the amount of the pet's airfare, among others.

Unlike what happens when travelling with children, it is not necessary to buy a pet air ticket. In other words, you don't need to buy a specific ticket. However, you need to inform the airline about your pet's transport when you purchase your ticket.

Also, if you want to travel in peace with your dog or cat, you will need to have a reservation and travel authorization. Both are mandatory and must be presented at the time of check-in at the airport.

The reservation is essential due to the limit of animals that each company can carry per segment.

DOCUMENTS REQUIRED TO BUY PET AIRLINE TICKETS

When requesting a pet air ticket, reservation and authorization, it is unnecessary to present any documents. However, some are mandatory for your pet to travel with you, including a medical certificate, proof of vaccination and CVI, for international travel.

WHICH BREEDS ARE PROHIBITED FROM TRAVELLING BY AIR

Although airlines allow the transport of animals, some breeds are prohibited, including

- American Bulldog

- Griffon of Brussels

- Boston Terrier

- Pitbull

- Boxer

- Pekingese

At the time of this writing, no breed of dog or cat is banned from entering Mexico.

WHERE IS THE BEST PLACE FOR YOUR DOG OR CAT TO BE WHEN TRAVELLING TO MEXICO?

Animals can travel in the plane cabin, together with their guardian. However, your carrying case should go under the seat in front of you. They can also go in the aircraft hold.

To travel in the cabin, the animal's weight and its carrying case cannot exceed the stipulated maximum weight, which varies by airline. In cargo, the total weight can be up to 45 kg.

There is a limit of three animals inside the plane cabin, one per passenger.

The number of pets in the aircraft hold varies depending on the model of the aircraft and the chosen airline.

SHIPPING KENNEL FOR YOUR PET

To bring dogs and cats to Mexico, it is necessary to pay attention to the rules related to the kennel.

Each airline has specific requirements for kennel size, weight and detail. However, in general, they need to be strong, well-ventilated, and the ideal size for the animal. In addition, they must have locks that make it impossible for the dog or cat to leave.

See below the main requirements of international airlines: (they are done in metric as this is airline policy)

KLM: The pet carrier must be a maximum of 46cm x 28cm x 24cm, and the weight must be a maximum of 8 kg.

United: The pet carrier must be a maximum of 52" x 32" x 34", and the total weight must not exceed 8kg.

Air Canada: The pet carrier must be a maximum of 23cm x 40cm x 55cm, and the total weight must not exceed 22 lbs, including the carrier.

There are exceptions with all of the above airlines. Please check for updated information and the difference when flying on one aircraft instead of another.

You don't want to arrive at the airport to transport your dog to find out that the carrier you have is too big for the aircraft she will be flying on.

ADAPTING YOUR PET TO THEIR KENNEL IS VERY IMPORTANT

It is common for pets to be uncomfortable with their first experience in their travel case. I would suggest a few trial runs to see how they manage the stress.

If they can go in alone and stay there for a few hours, you will be happier knowing they are not stressed on the flight.

KENNEL FOR DOGS AND CATS TRAVELLING BY PLANE

Your dog or cat kennel is highly complex when travelling by plane, mainly because employees don't always know the correct information for boarding. Follow these basic rules so that you don't have any unwanted surprises at check-in:

- Your dog or cat should be able to stand upright – without touching their head to the ceiling

- Be able to walk around the body

- Cannot get any part of their body out of the box – no paws, no muzzle, no tail

- They should be able to lie down comfortably inside their kennel.

For boarding in the cabin, animals cannot exceed the maximum weight allowed, and the kennel material can be malleable (fabric) or rigid (plastic). Specific marks for this type of transport are not required. Generally, the average size of a kennel for animals travelling in the cabin is 25 cm high, 40 cm long and 30 cm wide. Maximum weight 7 to 8 kilos.

For trips in the hold or the cargo compartment, only rigid plastic, wood or metal boxes that comply with the standards of the IATA (International Air Transport Association), the body that regulates air transport, whether for humans or animals, are accepted. In other words, not every brand and model sold on the market can be used in this situation.

Be careful with the weight and size allowed by airlines, even if your dog is in cargo. The kennel, plus the dog, cannot exceed 45 kilos.

Animals that exceed this limit must be transported as live cargo, requiring a customs broker for their release and a carrier that performs this service, so this is not ideal.

Another important item is that the kennel must be clean. It cannot, under any circumstances, be dirty or smell bad at boarding. Also, don't forget to bring toys for your pet in your suitcase. Some airlines prohibit some items from going into the kennel, so pack them in your carry-on just in case.

IT'S BEST TO ARRIVE AT THE AIRPORT EARLY

As for any flight, I would check in with your pet/s at least 3 hours in advance at the airport. It is recommended that you arrive 4 hours in advance and carry out all the necessary procedures calmly without anxiety to your pet.

This is also a great opportunity for you to prepare your pet before boarding and take them for a walk outside the airport so that they can do the necessities before entering the airport's departure area. Even if your pet does everything before boarding, I suggest covering the kennel with a hygienic mat to avoid accidents.

PET RELOCATION SERVICES

If you look for pet relocation on the Internet, millions of companies will pop up offering relocation services to places worldwide.

Each provider offers different services. They usually offer to handle the paperwork (but you might need to go to the vet yourself) and then picking up the pets. Some companies also handle all processes, including flight reservations, crates, veterinary services, to pet delivery.

Some companies will have representatives at major airports at the destination or work with a local company, but some leave you alone. Check and get written confirmation about this issue.

CHAPTER 12: QUICK SUMMARY

- You may bring up to 2 dogs or cats, per person, with their accessories, appropriate import certificates and other documentation

- To bring dogs and cats to Mexico, it is necessary to pay attention to the rules related to the kennel for each airline

- Animals can travel in the cabin of the plane, together with their guardian

- In general, the average size of a kennel for animals travelling in the cabin is 25 cm high, 40 cm long and 30 cm wide. Maximum weight 7 to 8 kilos.

- How to travel peacefully with the animal? - PETFriendly Turismo. https://www.petfriendlyturismo.com. br/en/2020/12/29/airfare-for-pet-how-to-travel-peacefully-with-the-animal/

- Airplane travel with a dog and cat: 3 common mistakes. https://petfriendlyturismo.com.br/en/blog/2020/06/22/ airplane-travel-with-a-dog-and-cat-3-common-mistakes/

- https://www.klm.us/information/pets

- https://www.united.com/ual/en/us/fly/travel/animals/ crates.html

- https://www.aircanada.com/ca/en/aco/home/plan/ special-assistance/pets.html

Chapter 13 is all about learning Spanish and how important it is to get into a good routine so that when you arrive in Mexico, you can converse with the locals and not feel intimidated.

LANGUAGE

IDIOMA

One language sets you in a corridor for life. Two languages open every door along the way.

FRANK SMITH

While Mexico has no government-declared official language, Spanish is spoken by almost 92% of the people, along with indigenous languages in some areas.

English is widely spoken in tourist areas and larger cities, but you will find daily life and interactions with potential friends, co-workers, merchants, and neighbours much easier if you try to learn at least a little Spanish. Many programs are available online, some free and some not, that will provide low-stress Spanish language learning.

Group Spanish classes and one-on-one tutors will be easy to find in cities and tourist areas. Facebook groups for expats in your area can provide this and plenty of other information that will be helpful. My experience has been that it is a must to learn the language of the people you will be working and interacting with daily. You must put forth the effort and learn the best you can. I'm not saying it's going to be easy, it won't be, but it will be worth it.

HOURS NEEDED TO LEARN A SECOND LANGUAGE

There have been studies that going from absolute beginner to fluent (meaning you can speak the language and have everyday conversations in the street) take roughly the following hours based on the target language (this is assuming you are

214

coming from a native English level):

Level One Languages – 575 – 600 hours of study (easiest for native English speakers to pick up):

- Spanish

- French

- Italian

- Portuguese

- Romanian

- Dutch

- Swedish

- Afrikaans

Level Two Languages – 750 hours:

- German

Level Three Languages – 900 hours:

- Malaysian

- Indonesian

- Swahili

Level Four Languages – 1100 hours:

- Vietnamese

- Russian

- Turkish

- Hindi

- Polish

- Tagalog

- Persian

Level Five Languages – 2200 hours:

- Chinese

- Japanese

- Korean

- Arabic

So keep all that in mind when planning your routine for learning a second language.

During my late teens and early 20's, I travelled through Central America, and no one spoke English. If I wanted to enjoy my time there, I had to learn Spanish. I stayed with a family that only spoke Spanish, I went to school to learn the language, and after three months, I could speak the language fairly well.

Twenty years go by and Spanish is still lurking in my brain, but I am no longer fluent because I have not used it very often.

I decided to move my family to Panama, a predominantly Spanish-speaking country. I would say 85% speak Spanish, and maybe 15% can also speak English. So I needed to learn to speak, write and read the language.

Here's how I did it in about one year

One of my favourite teachers while learning Spanish has been Olly Richards programs https://StoryLearningCourses.com. Here are my thoughts about Olly Richard's Course Review, and I've attached My Insane Language Routine.

I want you to understand that I live this life every single day. No matter where I am in the world -whether vacationing in Costa Rica for 3 weeks or living in Brazil for several months, I've found that if I let any of this lapse for very long, I lose my habit quickly. Living in Brazil, the national language is Portuguese, and if I wanted to learn a 3rd language, I would follow the exact routine and be fluent using this study guide.

Active Study — Spanish Uncovered By Olly Richards

I use a story-based system called Spanish Uncovered by Olly Richards for most of my active study time. It follows an entertaining story, chapter by chapter. The course is broken down into bite-size pieces. I am constantly learning new vocabulary skills while reading the story. The pace is designed to take you at the perfect speed, and each chapter builds on the previous chapter.

Sometimes I switch things up from Spanish Uncovered and use the Olly Richards Grammar Hero course. I find this course is a little more advanced, so when I feel I need a push to learn new words, I do a few weeks of this course in the morning. It also follows story-based learning that Olly Richards is famous for, but it's more hyper-focused on Grammar.

Dead Time – Conversations By Olly Richards

Deadtime is the term Olly Richards describes when you must do something else unavoidable, like driving your car, waiting for the bus or sitting on the train. I work from a home office, so these times do not apply to me, but I enjoy going for a walk in the park once a day.

For many people, these periods would be spent listening to music or staring into space. I recommend using this time to listen to an audio program in your chosen language. I have tried many different things like Spanish Audiobooks, podcasts, and even the news in Spanish. But what I found works best is an Olly Richards course called Conversations. This is a brilliant system where they have recorded short conversations between two native speakers on various topics. Some of the advantages are:

- You have context (you know what the conversation is going to be about before you start listening)

- The conversations are short and easy to understand

- The people speaking are native speakers and have clear accents

- They talk the way people speak on the street, so you get an ear for the sounds.

During my walk, I aim for 30 minutes on Olly Richards Conversations audio program daily.

ITALKI

iTalki is a marketplace matching students and teachers in hundreds of languages. Classes start at around $5.00 an hour and go up from there. They have tutors who will practice and have conversations with you, or you can have lectures with high-end teachers who have teaching degrees.

Currently, I have a bunch of different teachers I use on iTalki. I use this on the weekends and cycle through my classes with them based on their availability. For Spanish, I find you can get an excellent teacher for about $8.00 an hour. For $5 of FREE credit on iTalki after signing up for your first lesson, go to https://expatmoneyshow.com/italki

PRIVATE TUTORING

Twice a week, we had a Private Tutor from Chile come to our house. We used this time to work specifically on conjugating verbs and learning grammar that is not covered in my Grammar Hero course. A private tutor that comes to your house is an excellent way to learn a language but is probably the most expensive method.

DOWNTIME

Downtime is the time at the end of the day when maybe your brain is a little mush from work, and you don't have the energy for active studying.

I suggest that instead of forcing yourself to focus on studying, you would typically do something in your chosen language. For example, if you enjoy watching movies, find a film in the language you are studying.

The key is not to watch the movie with English subtitles because your brain will automatically switch to English and not translate what you hear. Your best bet is to put the subtitles in the language you are studying to have a higher chance of understanding what is happening. So, for example, at night, I might look for a movie on Netflix from Mexico and watch it in Spanish with Spanish subtitles on. Sometimes it can be challenging to gather all the nuances of what is happening, but this helps with immersion.

One other point I would like to bring up with immersion is this: even though I live in a Spanish-speaking country, most of my time is spent working in English. I think it is possible to accomplish full immersion in any language while still in your home country. Don't wait until you move abroad to start studying the language. Start today.

BONUS: USEFUL BOOKS FOR LEARNING SPANISH

Below are a couple of books I have found helpful while learning Spanish.

- 501 Verbs in Spanish – Barrons

- Short Stories in Spanish for Beginners – Olly Richards

- Short Stories in Spanish for Intermediate Learners – Olly Richards

MY DAY TO DAY ROUTINE

This is what a typical day looks like for me:

- 8:00 am – Wake up, bathroom, a large glass of purified water with ACV and a double espresso on the side

- 8:30 am – Active Spanish study time, either Spanish Uncovered or Grammar Hero

- 9:30 am – Exercise

- 10:00 am – Work

- 12:30 pm – First meal (I am currently following intermittent fasting – which is not as tough as you might think lol)

- 1:00 pm – Work

- 4:00 pm – Dead Time – walk in the park, listen to the Conversations program by Olly Richards

- 4:30 pm – Work

- 6:30 pm – Second meal, family time

- 8:30 pm – Downtime – Spanish movies or TV

- 10:00 pm – Work – answer final emails for the day

- 10:30 pm – Electronics off, read one of my Spanish books or review the new words I learned

- 11:30 pm – Lights out, bedtime

PUTTING IT ALL TOGETHER

Back in 2020, I did 452 hours of Spanish studying (including my Netflix binge-watching), and yes, I track this stuff and write it all down; it's the only real way to know if doing it properly.

Let's add up all the hours I plan on doing in the coming year:

- 260 hours of focused study time using the course I told you about (1 hour every day, Monday to Friday)

- 260 hours of private tutoring (1 hour every day, Monday to Friday)

- 100 hours of Netflix in Spanish

TOTAL: 620 hours of study time.

It kind of sounds like a lot, but please keep in mind that a good portion of it is also entertainment time, and as my language progresses, it will be more and more natural and doesn't require much effort.

In 620 hours, you could go from complete beginner to advance in Spanish, even if you have no history of learning a second language.

READING AND COMPREHENSION

I picked up reading in Spanish, this was not an easy task for me, but the reward was great. Reading in Spanish exposed me to tons of new words that I otherwise would not have had a chance to encounter (continuing with reading will also assist in my problem with vocabulary).

 It was slow going at first, but it was worth the effort. I used my friend Olly Richard's books on Kindle and worked through them with my language tutor; I worked on these books:

- Short Stories in Spanish for Beginners

- Short Stories in Spanish for Intermediate Learners

- 101 Conversations in Mexican Spanish: Short Natural Dialogues to Learn the Slang, Soul, & Style of Mexican Spanish

- 101 Conversations in Social Media Spanish: Conversations, Comments, & Private Messages to Learn Authentic Social Media Spanish

- 101 Conversations in Intermediate Spanish: Short Natural Dialogues to Boost Your Confidence & Improve Your Spoken Spanish

Olly does books teaching all the popular languages, and you can pick them up on Amazon for cheap; they are an affordable way to get some good reading practice.

FINAL THOUGHTS ABOUT LEARNING SPANISH

Using different language learning methods is fun and will keep your motivation going. I think it's funny that now when I go out with my mates on the weekend, I have to order all the food and translate everything from Spanish for them even though some of them have been here in Panama ten times as long as I have been. Don't let yourself fall into the expat trap where you only converse with people from your own country while abroad; using quality programs will have you learning a new language in no time.

The last thing I will mention before wishing you success in your language-learning journey and we move on to our next chapter, is this. If you have any false belief pattern that says you can't learn a new language because you are too old, don't have the talent, do not have enough time, have no motivation, etc., it's all rubbish. You can do this. Follow what I have laid out, invest in yourself, and believe you can do this; because you can.

CHAPTER 13: QUICK SUMMARY

Learning a new language is essential when you move to a new country, especially one that doesn't speak English. Here are some tips and tricks to help with the learning process.

- Level One Languages – 575 – 600 hours of study (easiest for native English speakers to pick up)

- Level Two Languages – 750 hours

- Level Three Languages – 900 hours

- Level Four Languages – 1100 hours

- Level Five Languages – 2200 hours

- Using different language learning methods is fun and will keep your motivation going Using your dead time like driving your car, waiting for the bus or sitting on the train to learn Spanish

- Online programs like iTalki and private tutoring can be beneficial

- Make studying Spanish a daily habit.

Chapter 14 is all about the food in Mexico. The different fruits and vegetables that can be found in specific areas of the country.

CULINARY AND FOOD

CULINARIA Y COMIDA

People who love to eat are always the best people.

JULIA CHILD

Mexico offers you a combination of local cuisine and vast networks of American/international food chains. Especially in cities of any size, most anything you could desire food-wise is available, including plenty of regular American fare. But, as they say, when in Rome, do as the Romans do. Don't be afraid to try some of the local dishes. There's a misconception that all Mexican food is really spicy–but although there are a lot of spices used in Mexican cuisine, not all of them are hot. Mexican food is varied and offers flavour profiles that you won't find in other countries.

Some popular local dishes include

Chilaquiles — A breakfast dish made with fried corn tortillas and topped with green or red salsa. It's also served with scrambled or fried eggs, a topping of cheese, and pulled chicken.

Pozole–Historians believe the Pozole is one of the cultural remnants of prehistoric Mexican civilizations. The modern version of the soup is made with chicken, pork, and beef, stewed overnight, and served with lettuce, radish, onion, lime, and chilli toppings.

Enchiladas — First known to be eaten by the ancient Mayans, enchiladas are corn or flour tortillas filled with any of the following: meat, cheese, seafood, beans, and vegetables. While Enchiladas are commonly found in Mexican restaurants in the U.S., they are not routinely on menus in Mexico!

Tamales — These were also developed by the Mayans, Aztec and Inca tribes that once inhabited Mexico. These are pockets of corn dough stuffed with sweet or savoury fillings, steamed while wrapped in banana leaves or corn husks.

Tacos — The versatile taco is perhaps the most famous and best-loved of all Mexican foods. Tacos can be found anywhere and everywhere from the most elegant dining establishment to the lowliest street stand. Typically a corn tortilla filled with beef (beef, pork or chicken) and topped with cilantro, lettuce, tomato, cheese or avocado, tacos are one of the many reasons you will never starve in Mexico!

Mole sauce — Mole is a traditional sauce made with onion, nuts, chilli peppers and chocolate, among other ingredients. This unusual-sounding combination offers a surprising and pleasing flavour experience.

If you're not a fan of the local food, then you'll most likely quickly find food chains like Burger King, Baskin Robbins, Chuck E. Cheese and other American restaurants. Sustaining yourself in Mexico shouldn't be a struggle for anyone.

If you are concerned about obtaining the groceries to which you are accustomed in Mexico, fear not. Most medium to large-sized cities and cities with a large expat and tourist population will often have international grocery stores that should have almost anything you want or need.

It is also common in these places to find organic grocery stores with many hard-to-find ingredients. Cities with Costco, Sam's Club and Walmart will have a great variety of international products to cater to the expat community.

TAJIN SEASONING

Here is something you must purchase, it's called Tajin. This classic Mexican seasoning is put on watermelon and cantaloupe to mangos, cucumbers, and vegetables. It is a spicy chilli mixture typically put on fruit or around the rim of a drink. I have also seen it used to spice meat, as well as an avocado or street corn.

While I was in Colombia last year, they served Tajin with shredded mango. It was delicious, and here in Panama, one of my favourite restaurants has its signature drink called 'Diablo Rojo', and the glass is rimmed with these amazing flavours.

FRUITS

If you're from Canada or the USA, you have likely had most of the fruits and vegetables grown in Mexico. Most are imported for our pleasure. Some of these would be

Avocado

Avocado is Mexico's national fruit; of all the places I've eaten avocado in the world, I ate the best ones in Mexico. Avocados are also used to make the famous guacamole.

Among the main benefits of adding avocado consumption to a diet are, a decrease in cholesterol levels, control in blood pressure, anti-inflammatory properties, control in blood sugar levels, helps prevent birth defects, decreases the risk of strokes, protects against cancer, helps eliminate bad breath and cleanses the intestine, increases nutrient absorption, skincare and anti-ageing. In addition, avocado has a high content of fatty acids, helps speed up metabolism, controls blood fat levels and helps you feel satiated.

There are many varieties of avocados, but I would say the most popular and most tasty is the Hass variety. Hass avocados make up 95% of all the avocados eaten in the USA.

Mango

The mango is native to South Asia, but the mangoes grown in Mexico are delicious and shouldn't be missed. The Ataulfo mangoes are in season from March to September and are primarily grown in Jalisco, Michoacan, Sinaloa, Veracruz, and Chiapas. It's a sweet variety that is well-paired with some chilli served on a stick.

Guanabana

Known as soursop in English, the guanabana fruit will most likely be a familiar flavour and name to those who have visited Mexico. It is a popular ice cream flavour and tastes similar to that of a tart, strawberry-banana hybrid. You'll also find juices made of guanabana. Strangely spiky on the outside, the fruit itself is quite large and has a white interior dotted with black seeds. It's very beneficial for your health, too.

Maracuyá

Maracuyá is a passion fruit grown in Mexico and commonly used for juices or as a mixer for mezcal. Some Mexicans eat them raw with chilli and lime. It's related to the Granadilla, which is sweeter than Maracuya.

Pitaya

Pitaya is one of the most characteristic Mexican fruits and is commonly known as Dragon fruit in other parts of the world. It's a cacti fruit endemic to Central America, although it's also grown extensively in Southeast Asia.

Jocote

Jocote fruits are native to Central America and have been used in medicine and food for thousands of years by the indigenous people. The Jocote fruit is rich in Vitamins C, A, and B, as well as various minerals. It has a sweet taste, somewhat similar to a plum, and its pulp is yellow when it's ripe.

VEGETABLES

With its fantastic weather, Mexico grows some of the essential vegetables around the globe. Here are a few of my favourites to cook with and eat raw:

Poblano Pepper

Poblano is a fresh hot pepper that is dark green, and when fully ripe, the colours become dark red or brown. The flavours are mild, and the Scoville Heat Unit ranges from 1,000 to 2,000. Poblano peppers are usually roasted and peeled, then canned or frozen.

They can also be stuffed to make chiles rellenos. The most famous dish prepared with these peppers is chiles en nogada, which is especially popular on Mexican Independence Day as it incorporates green, white, and red ingredients. The dried version of these mild peppers is known as Ancho pepper.

Tomatillo

Tomatillos are fruits of a plant called Physalis ixocarpa. They resemble green tomatoes with a papery husk and are extensively used in Mexican cuisine to produce salsa verde and guacamole. The flavours are slightly less sweet and more acidic than regular tomatoes, with hints of lemon, herbs, and apples.

On the inside, the texture is less watery and denser. Tomatillos develop flavour when boiled and can be used raw to keep the flavours bright and acidic. Although technically a fruit or a berry, the tomatillo is mainly used as a versatile vegetable.

Chipotle

Chipotle is a variety of hot pepper that is a smoked and dried ripe jalapeño. This hot pepper is derived from the Nahuatl word chilpoctli, which means smoked chile. Traditionally, chipotle is made in a sealed smokehouse.

Since there are numerous types of jalapeños, not all chipotle peppers are alike. They are characterized by a medium heat level ranging from 5,000 to 10,000 on the Scoville scale. The most popular variety is called chipotle morita, characterized by its deep red colour.

Calabaza

Calabaza is a round, pumpkin-like squash with variable sizes. It is primarily cultivated in the Caribbean and throughout Central and South America. Calabaza is characterized by its firm, bright orange flesh with a sweet flavour similar to that of butternut squash.

The seeds are also edible when toasted, known as pepitas. The squash is often used in cakes, stews, and candies, while the flowers, or flor de calabaza, are commonly used in quesadillas, empanadas, and pupusas as an ingredient.

DRINKS

There's an array of popular Mexican drinks to choose from. They range from family-friendly breakfast champurrado bowls to hard-hitting Cerveza margarita highballs. Other traditional local drinks include jarritos, aguas frescas, horchata, tejate, Mexican ponche, margarita, palome, and tequila.

Aguas Frescas

If you've ever been to a busy street market in Mexico, you might have noticed one or two food carts selling bright-coloured fruit juice in large plastic containers. These are agua fresca. The term agua fresca roughly translates to fresh water and is a very popular refreshment in Mexico. It's affordable, accessible, easy to make, and, most importantly, delicious. The natives love this Mexican street food so much it is often sold by the litre.

Agua fresca is about as simple as a drink can get. It consists of nothing but fresh fruit juices mixed with water—sometimes, vendors will also sprinkle in some sugar to make their drinks a bit sweeter. Popular flavours include papaya, lime, watermelon, cinnamon oats, tamarind, and hibiscus. Natives claim that agua fresca has been around even before the colonization of modern-day Mexico.

Historical records suggest that the ancient Aztecs' diets primarily consisted of the wild fruits growing around Tenochtitlán—now Mexico City—so it's not unlikely for them to create refreshments using wild fruits.

Jarritos

Jarritos is the leading Mexican soft drink brand in the American market today. What popularized them is their diverse set of flavours. They come in guava, mandarin, tamarind, strawberry, and pineapple—all of which are non-conventional carbonated drink flavours.

Champurrado

Champurrado is a corn flour-based chocolate drink locals often have for breakfast or lunch. Think of champurrado as your favourite hot chocolate drink, but far richer and denser thanks to the extra cornflour or, as the locals call it, masa.

Atole

Atole is another popular corn flour-based drink in Mexico. You'll see large pots of atole served right beside champurrado as the locals would usually have either of the two for breakfast.

The only difference between champurrado and atole is that the latter does not have cocoa. Other than that, they're essentially the same warm, rich, thick breakfast drink. Also, champurrado is a type of atole. What makes atole so amazing is that the popular Mexican drink already existed long before the Spanish conquistador Hernan Cortez colonized the Aztec empire to create modern-day Mexico City in 1521.

CHAPTER 14: QUICK SUMMARY

- Mexico offers you a combination of local cuisine and vast networks of American/international food chains. Especially in cities of any size, most anything you could desire food-wise is available, including plenty of regular American fare.

- If you're from Canada or the USA, you have likely had most of the fruits and vegetables grown in Mexico. Most are imported for our pleasure. Some common fruits would be avocado and mango, and some not so common would be guanabana, maracuyá, pitaya and jocote

- Common vegetables are poblano peppers, tomatillos, chipotle peppers and calabaza

- Drinks are aguas frescas, jarritos, champurrado and atole

Chapter 14 is all about the food in Mexico. The different fruits and vegetables that can be found in specific areas of the country.

CHAPTER 15

COST OF LIVING

COSTA DE LA VIDA

Life is too important to be taken seriously.

OSCAR WILDE

CURRENT COST OF LIVING INDEX BY CITY

One of the most essential factors in deciding where you want to live and work is the cost of living.

How much you have to spend factors into how much you need to make, what type of lifestyle you can afford, and where you'll need to live.

This is especially true if you live on a fixed income or if you are a retiree. In Latin America, prices can change pretty quickly.

The cost of living in Mexico is 55.57% lower than in the US, according to Numbeo.com, and rent is, on average, 73.24% lower than in the US.

The average monthly cost for a family of four in Mexico City is $1,732.31 USD, not including rent. The average monthly cost for a single person in Mexico City is $475.63 USD, not including rent.

Compare this to average monthly costs for a family of four in New York at $4,807.63 USD and $1,304.32 USD for a single person, not including rent or $3,874.81 USD for four in Miami, or $1,071.56 USD for a single person in Miami, not including rent.

The cost of living index in Mexico City is 63.65% lower than in New York, and rent in Mexico City is, on average, 82.21% lower than in New York.

Let's look at some general comparisons between different cities in Mexico and other parts of the world

CITY	CONSUMER PRICES	RENT	GROCERIES
Monterrey vs. Toronto	50.50% lower	76.59% lower	47.91% lower
Queretaro vs. Tel Aviv	63.24% lower	78.19% lower	59.30% lower
Guadalajara vs. London	60.77% lower	82.63% lower	49.00% lower
Merida vs. Sydney	59.52% lower	85.84% lower	55.48% lower
Tijuana vs. Chiang Mai	59.52% lower	85.84% lower	55.48% lower

COST OF LIVING 2022 -BASED ON 139 COUNTRIES SUBMITTED

These indices are historical and they are published by Numbeo.com. This is a snapshot of the current indices as of the day of writing.

RANK	COUNTRY	COST OF LIVING INDEX	RENT INDEX	RESTAURANT PRICE INDEX	LOCAL PURCHASING POWER INDEX
1	Bermuda	146.04	98.58	159.17	81.07
2	Switzerland	123.35	53.54	122.09	118.44
18	New Zealand	75.66	36.06	76.35	87.99
25	Canada	70.22	34.33	67.86	87.98
26	USA	70.13	42.07	70.07	106.34
27	UK	69.65	31.84	76.79	88.78
38	UAE	58.33	43.28	61.53	92.17
46	Spain	53.88	21.25	53.96	70.04
51	Panama	51.43	21.75	43.38	33.09
64	Portugal	47.94	20.73	40.26	46.80
67	Costa Rica	47.01	14.70	41.69	39.88
75	Thailand	43.21	14.69	22.59	31.56
100	Mexico	35.35	12.55	32.67	38.62
112	Brazil	33.24	8.27	25.24	27.85

ABOUT COST OF LIVING INDICES FROM NUMBEO

These indices are relative to New York City (NYC). This means that for New York City, each index should be 100%. If another city has, for example, a rent index of 120, it means that on average, in that city, rents are 20% more expensive than in New York City. If a city has a rent index of 70, that means, on average, rent in that city is 30% less expensive than in New York City.

Cost of Living Index (Excl. Rent) is a relative indicator of consumer goods prices, including groceries, restaurants, transportation and utilities.

The Cost of Living Index does not include accommodation expenses such as rent or mortgage. If a city has a Cost of Living Index of 120, it means Numbeo has estimated it is 20% more expensive than New York (excluding rent).

Rent Index estimates the prices of renting apartments in the city compared to New York City. If the Rent index is 80, Numbeo has estimated that the rent price in that city is, on average, 20% less than the price in New York.

Restaurants Index compares prices of meals and drinks in restaurants and bars compared to NYC.

Local Purchasing Power shows relative purchasing power in buying goods and services in a given city for the average net salary in that city. If domestic purchasing power is 40, the inhabitants of that city with an average salary can afford to buy, on average, 60% fewer goods and services than New York

City residents with an average salary.

QUALITY OF LIFE INDEX 2022
BASED ON 87 COUNTRIES *higher is better*

Rank	Country	Qualityof Life Index *	Safety Index*	Health care Index*	Traffic Time /lower is better
1	Switzerland	195.27	78.32	74.85	28.50
9	New Zealand	176.81	56.70	73.32	30.78
15	USA	170.72	51.84	69.06	32.85
16	Japan	169.48	77.88	80.49	40.65
18	Spain	168.48	66.13	78.37	29.24
20	Portugal	162.63	69.42	71.97	29.85
22	UK	161.74	53.53	74.83	34.40
23	Canada	160.38	57.05	71.31	33.61
24	UAE	160.38	84.68	68.73	36.19
30	Singapore	151.59	72.36	71.07	41.22
47	Mexico	124.90	46.32	72.83	39.29
50	Costa Rica	122.07	46.14	62.75	60.19
57	Panama	114.32	56.08	61.15	37.12
65	Brazil	107.04	32.99	57.84	41.28
72	Thailand	100.97	60.69	77.65	39.62

ABOUT QUALITY OF LIFE INDICES FROM NUMBEO

Quality of Life Index (higher is better) is an estimation of overall quality of life by using an empirical formula which takes into account: purchasing power index (higher is better), pollution index (lower is better), house price to income ratio (lower is better), cost of living index (lower is better), safety index (higher is better), health care index (higher is better), traffic commute time index (lower is better) and climate index (higher is better).

Generally speaking, whether you are from the U.S., Canada, Europe or almost anywhere else on the globe, the cost of living in Mexico will be significantly lower than what you are accustomed to. Many people are delighted to find a better quality of life than they had at home in Mexico for much less money.

If you are exchanging US dollars to spend in Mexico, your money will go a long way as the dollar is, and has been, very strong against the peso. Of course, exchange rates fluctuate by the minute, but the bottom line is that your US dollars will go a long way in Mexico. It is advisable to get the XE.com app on your phone to convert prices on the spot without having to calculate in your head.

Rent is, of course, a significant variable. Modern apartments, condos, and homes will be readily available in most larger cities and tourist areas. These will command a higher price than smaller, more basic, local-style accommodations. Tastes and lifestyle choices vary widely from individual to individual, and rent prices will reflect that. While it might be possible to find a small apartment in a local, working-class, less touristic area for $300 USD per month, one might find that a nice condo in an appealing area with lots of amenities could run as much as $ 2,000 USD per month or more. Beware of guides and articles that promise outrageously low rents in Mexico. While this is certainly possible, it may not be possible for you, depending on your standard of living.

COST OF LIVING IN ACAPULCO

- Family of four estimated monthly cost is $1,691 USD without rent.

- A single person's estimated monthly costs are $464 USD without rent.

- Acapulco is 65.89% less expensive than New York (without rent).

- Rent in Acapulco is, on average, 80.91% lower than in New York.

COST OF LIVING IN MEXICO CITY

- Family of four estimated monthly costs are $1,849 USD without rent.

- A single person's estimated monthly costs are $507 USD without rent.

- Mexico City is 62.01% less expensive than New York without rent.

- On average, rent in Mexico City is 80.44% lower than in New York.

COST OF LIVING	ACAPULCO	MEXICO CITY
Milk (regular, 1 gallon)	$ 4.49	$ 4.11
Loaf of Fresh White Bread (1 lb)	$1.46	$ 1.50
Rice (white), (1 lb)	$ .60	$ .61
Eggs (regular/12)	$ 1.61	$ 1.60
Local Cheese (1 lb)	$ 2.73	$ 2.62
Chicken Fillets (1 lb)	$ 2.22	$ 2.30
Beef Round (1 lb) (or Equivalent Back Leg Red Meat)	$ 3.09	$ 3.48
Bananas (1 lb)	$ .50	$ .48
Bottle of mid-range wine	$11.00	$ 9.70
Domestic beer (.5 litre bottle)	$ .85	$ 1.14
Imported beer (12 oz small bottle)	$ 1.75	$ 2.40
Cigarettes – 20 pack Marlboro	$ 2.67	$ 3.10
UTILITIES (MONTHLY)		
Basic (Electricity, Heating, Cooling, Water, Garbage)	$ 31.04	$ 43.44
1 min. of Prepaid Mobile Tariff Local (No Discounts or Plans)	$ .12	$ .09
Internet (60 Mbps or More, Unlimited Data, Cable/ADSL	$ 24.69	$ 26.70
SPORTS AND LEISURE		
Fitness Club, Monthly Fee for 1 Adult	$ 27.00	$ 43.00
Cinema, International Release, 1 Seat	$ 3.40	$ 3.88

RESTAURANTS	ACAPULCO	MEXICO CITY
Meal, Inexpensive Restaurant	$ 3.76	$ 7.27
Meal for 2 People, Mid-range Restaurant, Three-course	$ 38.00	$ 34.00
McMeal at McDonalds (or Equivalent Combo Meal)	$ 4.61	$ 5.82
Domestic Beer (1 pint draught)	$ 1.46	$ 1.94
Imported Beer (12 oz small bottle)	$ 3.00	$ 3.39
Cappuccino (regular)	$ 2.40	$ 2.29
Coke/Pepsi (12 oz small bottle)	$ 1.02	$ .85
Water (12 oz small bottle)	$ 1.00	$ 65
TRANSPORTATION		
One-way Ticket (Local Transport)	$ 0.49	$ .29
Monthly Pass (Regular Price)	$ 15.00	$ 12.55
Taxi – within 10 min drive	$ 2.43	$ 3.00
Gasoline (1 litre)	$ .86	$ .95
CHILDCARE		
Preschool (or Kindergarten), Full Day, Private, Monthly for 1 Child	$ 135.00	$ 300.00
International Primary School, Yearly for 1 Child	$ 4,873.00	$ 6,400.00
BUY APARTMENT PRICE		
Price per Square Feet to Buy Apartment in City Centre	$ 175.00	$ 216.00
Price per Square Feet to Buy Apartment Outside of Centre	$ 119.00	$ 126.50

RENT PER MONTH (FURNISHED)	ACAPULCO	MEXICO CITY
Apartment (1 bedroom) in City Centre	$ 592.62	$ 637.36
Apartment (1 bedroom) Outside of Centre	$ 339.97	$ 436.46
Apartment (3 bedrooms) in City Centre	$ 1,075.94	$ 1,296.89
Apartment (3 bedrooms) Outside of Centre	$ 879.61	$ 789.64

Let's compare two cities in Mexico. You'll see that there is very little difference here. **Canada is 1.9 times more expensive than Mexico and the United States is 2.3 times more expensive.** We plugged in the cost of living in an average Canadian and American city to see how Mexico would fare. The table on page 245 is converted from Pesos and Canadian funds to USD. I find it easier to compare.

	MEXICO	CANADA	USA
Basic meal with drink at inexpensive restaurant	$3.76	$13.78	$14.25
Fast food combo meal (McDonalds, or similar)	$4.61	$8.68	$7.75
Bottle of Coca-Cola (0.33 litre)	$1.02	$1.83	$1.90
Cappuccino in mid-range area	$2.40	$3.44	$4.18
Bread	$1.46	$2.36	$2.71
Local cheese (500 grams)	$2.73	$5.37	$5.56
Milk (1 liter)	$2.10	$2.08	$0.85

Monthly public transit pass	$15.00	$68.16	$63.05
Internet Connection	$24.69	$67.33	$67.11
1-Bedroom apartment in downtown area	$592.62	$997.16	$1225.46
Utilities for 2 (including electric, gas & water)	$31.04	$108.01	$128.68
International Middle school for 1 child, two semesters	$4873.00	$10449.85	$15195.09

MEXICAN SUPERMARKETS

When talking about grocery shopping in Mexico, it is not uncommon for locals to mention traditional markets or "tianguis" as their chosen destinations for shopping for fresh ingredients. However, despite the cultural importance of markets and specialty food stores, supermarkets and convenience stores have also become a relevant part of the shopping experience for many families.

The supermarket landscape in Mexico is shaped by four major companies: Walmart de México, Organización Soriana, Grupo Comercial Chedraui, and Grupo La Comer. Accounting for the various needs and shopping habits of the population, these corporations are present in different formats, with discounts, premiums, and regular supermarkets available for consumers. Overall, Mexican shoppers tend to prefer regular and discount formats.

According to January 2022 data, Walmart and Bodega Aurrerá – Walmart de México's classic and low-cost brands – were the most popular Mexican supermarket chains on Twitter. In terms of sales, it is also Walmart that leads the market.

The American company is followed by its Mexican competitor Organización Soriana, whose most common format, "Soriana Hiper," is one of its regular brands. Another nice thing about the grocery stores in Mexico is that they have food stalls.

They sell everything from tacos de Cabeza (the roasted head of an animal taco) to barbecued (barbacoa) tacos. Grilled onions are also common additions and different types of salsas. Each stand typically offers one red and one green sauce. Also, they usually offer a large bowl of halved Mexican limes for a squeeze into your taco.

DIFFERENCES AND SIMILARITIES BETWEEN MEXICO GROCERY STORES AND US GROCERY STORES

Various dairy items in Mexico are processed quite differently than in the United States. Eggs are not power washed, nor are they chemically treated. They do not need refrigeration.

Almost all Mexican cheeses are from goat's milk. Therefore, their texture and colours are different. Mexico even sells non-homogenized milk, which needs no refrigeration.

Meat products like chicken, beef and pork are not as bright red because of the lack of sodium nitrates used in these meat products. Typically, fish is seen openly displayed on ice and sliced. And since Mexico is so close to the sea in various regions, seafood plays a big part in Mexican diets. For them, it is plentiful and inexpensive.

MEXICAN STORES – NO FREEZERS, BUT MEAT COUNTERS!

Frozen foods are not common in Mexican grocery stores, unlike the endless freezer aisles in Canadian stores. Canadians are used to seeing prepackaged meat in the meat section which is different in Mexican grocery stores.

The meat counter displays fresh pieces of meat for people to pick and choose which type of cut they want to buy. You will find many cuts of meat, including thinly sliced meats and sausages like chorizo. Depending on the grocery store, you can choose your bread and have it weighed or you can ask to have a specific weight of bread to be packaged.

CHAPTER 15: QUICK SUMMARY

- One of the most essential factors in deciding where you want to live and work is the cost of living. How much you have to spend factors into how much you need to make, what type of lifestyle you can afford, and where you'll need to live.

- The cost of living in Mexico is on average 55.57% lower than in the US, according to Numbeo.com. Rent is, on average, 73.24% lower than in the US.

- The average monthly cost for a family of four in Mexico City is $1,732.31 USD, not including rent. The average monthly cost for a single person in Mexico City is $475.63 USD, not including rent.

- Family of four estimated monthly costs are $1,849 USD without rent. A single person's estimated monthly costs are $507 without rent. Mexico City is 62.01% less expensive than New York without rent.

- Rent in Mexico City is, on average, 80.44% lower than in New York.

- Grocery stores in Mexico have food stalls, and they sell everything from tacos de Cabeza (the roasted head of an animal taco) to barbecued (barbacoa) tacos.

- Meat products like chicken, beef and pork are not as bright red because of the lack of sodium nitrates used in these meat products. Typically, fish is seen openly displayed on ice and sliced.

Chapter 16 discusses Mexico's healthcare system, including private and public hospitals, insurance, vaccines, assisted living facilities, death and medical tourism.

HEALTH CARE

CUIDADO DE LA SALUD

The art of medicine consists of amusing the patient while nature cures the disease.

VOLTAIRE

LIVING HEALTHY IN MEXICO

Mexico's mild climate makes it easy to get outside and exercise almost daily. In addition, the abundance of fresh fruits and vegetables is a wonderful substitute for processed foods. It's essential to make healthy choices.

When it comes to health care, we all want the best coverage we can afford, and needless to say, the options can be staggering, whether it be from the different benefits offered or the costs involved.

HOSPITALS

Hospitals in México range from small-town clinics to third-level government hospitals with prestigious research departments and cutting-edge technology. The same can be said for private hospitals.

The best hospitals in Mexico are in Guadalajara, Mexico City, and Monterrey, meaning if you need very specialized treatment, you might want to go there. You can obtain a complete list of hospitals from your own insurance carrier or the https://mx.usembassy.gov/. Here are a few hospitals in Mexico for foreigners and Expats.

Star Médica Hospital
Calle Paseo de la Victoria 4370,
Partido Iglesias, 32618 Juárez, Chih.
+52 614 432 6600

Christus Muguerza Hospital
Carretera Nacional 6501 Col. La Estanzuela,
Monterrey N.L. 64988
+52 81 8399 3400

Angeles Group Hospital
Av. Paseo de los Héroes #10999,
Zona Río, 22010 Tijuana, B.C.
+52 664 635 1800
1 800 678 8966 (from US)

Hospital Shriners para Niños
Ave del Iman No. 257, Coyoacan
+52 55 5424 7850

Hospital Trinidad
Calle Manzanillo No. 94, Cuauhtémoc
+52 55 1085 2760

Hospital General de México
Cuauhtémoc
+52 55 2789 2000

Amerimed in Cancun
Av. Tulum Sur 260 Supermanzana

7 Manzana 4 77500
Cancún, Quintana Roo México

Amerimed in Puerto Vallarta

Blvd. Francisco Medina Ascencio #3970,
Marina Vallarta, Puerto Vallarta
Phone: (322) 226-2080

AFFILIATIONS WITH US PROVIDERS

Many US providers have established affiliations with some of Mexico's leading hospitals. Baylor University Medical Center and the Methodist Hospital of Houston have affiliations with the American British Cowdray Medical Center (ABC) Hospital in Mexico City.

The CIMA Hospital in Monterrey has affiliations with the Mayo Clinic and Children's Hospital Boston. As the demand for medical tourism grows, other US academic institutions and medical institutions are expected to establish footprints in Mexico.

Private Care: If emergency surgery is required, you can assume they will follow up with excellent care. Private hospitals do not accept insurance policies from north of the border and require a patient to pay upon release. They facilitate paperwork for patient reimbursement. More and more, private hospitals are accepting insurance policies for payment, but ask at the time of admission or before.

Hospitals expect a family member or friend to stay in the

room with you, and a couch or cot is provided.

Many Mexican physicians do postgraduate training in Europe, the US or Canada and are fluent in English. Nursing staff tend to be less fluent in English. A little bit of Spanish works wonders when facing this problem.

PRICE COMPARISON

Overall, healthcare costs in Mexico are less expensive than in the US, based on friends' accounts and interviews with clients in both countries.

On average, the cost of medical and dental procedures in Mexico is inexpensive compared to the US.

- Outpatient laser surgery on both eyes by a top-notch private physician is less than $1,300 USD, including all preoperative diagnosis and post-op care over 10 days.

- A 4-day stay in the Intensive Care Unit of a world-class private hospital in Mexico averages about $2,500 per day USD, including lab tests, doctors, and medicines. Compare that with the average USA cost of about $16,000 per day for the same ICU care, NOT including lab tests, doctors, and medicine.

- A Cesarean delivery during a 3-day stay in a top-notch private hospital in Mexico costs about $2,500 USD for EVERYTHING - doctors, nurses, lab tests, medicine - and includes a private suite (with a separate visit area where visitors can eat at a table with four chairs or sleep overnight while the new mama is resting in the other room). How much would that cost in the USA?

- A 1-hour office visit with a private physician in a medical office complex at an excellent private hospital costs between $60-$85 USD to diagnose and prescribe treatment for bacterial bronchial pneumonia. During the appointment, the doctor will examine the patient, walk the patient to the onsite facilities for lab tests and X-rays, and wait for the X-rays to discuss with the patient. The lab tests cost about $200 USD, and X-rays cost between $80-$100 USD. That means the total cost for an hour with a private physician including tests and X-rays is between $340-$385 USD, paid with cash or credit card unless you have insurance coverage. Prescription generic medicine for 10-14 days might add another $85 USD to the bill.

- A hip replacement may cost only $15,000 USD in private hospitals, compared to about $100,000 in the USA.

- Major back surgery may cost less than $20,000 USD, compared with more than $100,000 in the USA.

DENTISTS

Dental care is also significantly less expensive in Mexico, and even smaller towns and cities will often have many dental clinics and providers from which to choose. Expat groups in the area you are interested in can be a great source of recommendations and reviews of different doctors, dentists, and clinics.

You may wonder if it is safe to have dental work done in

Mexico. I can assure you it's safe as your own dentist. Tens of thousands of Americans have received high-quality dental work in Mexico. I suggest border towns like Tijuana or Puerto Vallarta, or Merida.

Then there is the dentist. Where have they been trained? Do they speak English? When you talk with a dentist, don't be afraid to ask tough questions.

You are putting yourself at risk by not thoroughly going over everything with them. And don't feel bad if you don't get a good feeling from them. Leave and find a new dentist.

Here are some average prices of dental work in Mexico. Prices vary, same as in the US or Canada and are quoted in USD.

- Dental Crown $250 - $600 USD per tooth

- Full set of dentures $600 USD

- Teeth cleaning $28 USD

- Porcelain Veneers $450 USD per tooth

- Whitening $150- $312 USD

- Composite Fillings $38 -$150 USD

- Root Canal $250 USD

- Non-complicated extractions $70 USD

- Metal Braces $400- $3,500 USD

- Damon Braces $805 – $3,500 USD

- Invisalign Braces $2,518 – $5,104 USD

- Ceramic Braces $350 – $3,800 USD

YOU MIGHT NOT EVEN REALIZE

Did you know that dental filling costs are based on how many surfaces are being treated and the filling material? So even if you are quoted a lower price, ensure that it reflects the same procedure. If you're not making an "apples-to-apples" comparison, you can't assume the lower price is the best or most accurate.

One of the questions we get asked is why it is so much less expensive in Mexico than in the US or Canada. Right off the bat, the main reason is that US dentists leave school with over $200,000 of debt. That can take a lot of time to recoup, and the only way to recoup is to charge large sums of money for their work. And once the debt is repaid, they are not likely to reverse their pricing; they might even increase their prices.

In Mexico, the schools are considerably cheaper, and the Mexican government subsidizes dental schools, so Dentists don't open their first practice in debt. And even if they do, it's nowhere near $200,000 USD, so they charge less, and everyone is happy.

The other significant difference between Canada, US and Mexico is that the dental assistant does much of the work, and the dentist just does the heavy lifting. In Mexico, the dentist does everything.

INSURANCE

IMSS COVERAGE - MEXICAN SOCIAL SECURITY INSTITUTE

Many individuals obtain IMSS coverage, a great affordable medical option in Mexico. However, some applicants have been informed to lie on the application about pre-existing conditions. This is a serious no-no. Doctors are not fools. If something happens to you, they could discover the problem where you will require IMSS.

We have had clients who have explained their pre-existing conditions to the IMSS doctors and have not been refused coverage. There were some limiting conditions, but overall coverage was not affected. This will apply to any insurance plan you decide to purchase.

While reading all the fine print in your applications for medical coverage, make sure you also pay close attention to the payment schedule your insurance plan has.

When speaking with an insurance company representative, they will tell you that certain procedures are covered but sometimes fail to mention how much they will pay for a procedure. Insurance companies take an average of what these fees are from many different sources.

This can be an issue when you think you are fully covered, and you choose a high-end hospital and have the procedure completed only to find out that the insurance company will only pay X amount of dollars for the said procedure when, in fact, the hospital charges three times that amount. This can leave you with a substantial bill.

We must also be careful from the hospital end. Ensure you get details from the hospital, including all extra costs involved with your stay. For example, if you're going in for an angioplasty, find out what ALL the costs are, not just the procedure costs, but the support costs too.

I know someone who was quoted 50,000 pesos for an angioplasty, which was acceptable, but the final bill came to 130,000 pesos. All the additions included the room, nursing staff, surgeon, etc.

When a medical facility charges these types of fees, they will want a guarantee of payment if you can't pay upon leaving. Please be careful what you sign with these facilities, especially if you have a relative looking after you or you are the relative looking after someone else.

In some instances, you may be asked to sign as a witness (Testigo) on one of these bills, but you may end up signing a statement that reads "El Aval", which means you assume responsibility for the cost if the patient defaults.

If you sign such a document, it doesn't matter what false pretenses someone might have had you sign it under; you ARE responsible. And this rule applies to anything you sign, whether it be a deed, lease, or contract of any type.

You must keep vigilant about these matters. It is always better to be informed and protected beforehand because it will always cost more and be more of a problem afterwards.

INSURANCE POLICY

When reviewing your insurance policy, please read the fine print. Even though it may be a full-service medical plan, some things may not be covered.

Also, make sure you meet all the requirements set out by the insurance company. Otherwise, you may be dropped when you need the actual coverage. Here is the company that our family uses for worldwide coverage: https://expatmoneyshow.com/insurance

PRIVATE INSURANCE FOR HEALTHCARE IN MEXICO

Foreigners can buy private insurance from many international firms to cover medical treatment in Mexico and other countries. Premiums vary widely from less than $1,000 USD a year for catastrophic insurance to more than $12,000 USD a year for expanded coverage. Enrollees may have to pay annual premiums in advance. After patients meet the requirements for deductibles, these insurance plans usually pay all remaining costs. Most of these plans require a physical and may require a letter from a personal physician attesting to no pre-existing conditions.

A few private hospitals and doctors in major cities in Mexico accept insurance coverage with pre-approval from companies such as Aetna, BlueCross/BlueShield, and Cigna. In such cases, the hospitals bill the insurer directly. Almost all larger hospitals in Mexico have offices to explain coverage to patients before hospital admission. Some large private hospitals have special offices with English-speaking staff to explain coverage and assist patients in submitting forms for reimbursement from insurance companies.

Your Medicare or other US insurance plan will not cover you while you are in Mexico. This will likely be true for any other insurance plan from any other country. So you will need to make other arrangements for health insurance coverage in Mexico. Visit this page for relevant Medicare regulations, which aren't easy to understand and change every year. https://www.ecfr.gov/current/title-42/chapter-IV/subchapter-B/part-406.

SELF-INSURING (PAYING OUT OF POCKET)

You may think that paying out of pocket is a good idea, considering the costs seem pretty cheap. But what if something major happens and you need emergency surgery that costs you $5,000 USD? It's not worth it. And you could probably handle $5,000, but what if it was $100,000? Where would you come up with that sort of cash?

As of 2020, if you live in Mexico legally, you will have INSABI for catastrophic events. While primary care can save your life, you may wish to consider private insurance as an option if you can afford it. Many expats return home because of medical issues, don't let that be you.

Several companies cater specifically to expats for health insurance if you are moving to Mexico permanently, including but not limited to:

- https://healthcaremx.com

- https://guardianinsurancemx.com/

There is a Mexican universal health care plan (Seguro Popular) which you may qualify for if you are a Permanent Resident. Still, most expats opt for other private insurance if they wish to be insured. If you have a pre-existing condition, you will want to investigate your options in the area where you intend to live.

Bring any medications you currently take with you. If you have left the medication you need at home, there will be a 'Farmacia' or pharmacy on just about every corner in every city. They often have an impressive selection of pharmaceuticals.

Many medications that require a prescription in the US or Canada do not require a prescription in Mexico. Farmacia clerks can usually look up drugs, and you may be able to have your prescription refilled without a doctor's prescription. Should that not be the case, seeing a doctor to renew a prescription will not be expensive.

If you are mobility impaired, some areas will be more difficult for you than others. Hilly or mountainous areas like Puerto Vallarta, San Miguel de Allende or Guanajuato will be quite challenging for those in wheelchairs or unable to climb many stairs and navigate steep streets.

Cobblestone streets and broken or nonexistent sidewalks are not uncommon, even in other areas that are not so rough to negotiate. You will want to consider the general geography of the area if mobility is an issue. If you have any pre-existing health issues or concerns, visit your doctor before planning your move to Mexico.

Excellent health care is available in many places, but you may want to make sure that a specialist is available in the area you are interested in before making further plans. Bring copies of your medical records with you. Getting them once you've arrived in Mexico may be difficult.

TRICARE, CHAMPS, ETC.

US veterans living in Mexico can receive health care insurance coverage under 3 US programs:

- **TRICARE** is a health care program serving active duty service members, National Guard and Reserve members, retirees, families and survivors worldwide.

- **CHAMPUS** is a federally-funded health program.

- **Foreign Medical Program (FMP)** is for disabled veterans.

A few Mexican doctors and hospitals may agree to handle billing for these programs. However, most will expect payment from the patient, who has to seek reimbursement from the insurance program.

VACCINES

No special additional vaccines or immunizations are required to enter Mexico. If you are particularly cautious and are not opposed to immunizations, a tetanus booster might not be a bad idea, but otherwise, no special precautions should be necessary. Of course, recommendations are based on the worldview of the one making the recommendation.

Some recommend hepatitis A, B, and typhoid vaccines before travelling to Mexico.

MOSQUITOES

In some jungle or coastal areas with a hearty mosquito population, mosquito-borne illnesses like Dengue Fever may be at risk. Other diseases carried by mosquitoes and spread through their bites include the Zika virus, West Nile virus, Chikungunya virus, and malaria.

Dengue Fever is not entirely uncommon in some areas of Mexico; some years seem worse than others. These diseases can also be contracted in other places, in pretty much any area where mosquitoes are an issue, and they can be severe or even fatal.

Mosquitos in tropical jungle and coastal areas can be utterly relentless and challenging to combat. Recommendations for what 'really works' to repel mosquitos abound, and it seems that everyone has their favourite natural answer that 'really works.' These include but are not limited to lime juice, tequila, essential oil-based repellents, Mexican vanilla, and many others. The reality is this: if you are travelling to a tropical, coastal, or jungle area of Mexico, you will need a mosquito repellent with a high percentage of DEET. And you will need to bring it with you as you may not be able to find an effective mosquito repellent with DEET once in Mexico. DEET is a strong chemical that some people feel uncomfortable putting on their skin, which is understandable.

Special care will need to be taken when applying as it will literally eat nail polish off your nails if you get it on them. Despite that, if you are in a mosquito-prone area, any possible adversity to using DEET should probably be secondary to the dangers of being attacked by a swarm of hungry mosquitos. And this can be a very regular occurrence in some places. Of course, mosquitos are not a problem in many places, such as highland areas.

ASSISTED-LIVING FACILITIES

As more and more expats are retiring to Mexico, there is a growing demand for assisted-living facilities.

Assisted Living and nursing homes in Mexico run roughly half—or less—than what you would pay north of the border and also include three home-cooked meals a day, laundry, and cleaning service with doctors' home visits regularly. Many facilities offer 24/7 nursing care.

Some of these homes have the option for you to live in your own home or apartment and be taken care of whenever the need arises. Others are long-term care facilities where trained staff care for all your needs.

DEATH

There are many laws, regulations, and bureaucratic rules if a foreigner becomes ill and dies in Mexico, just as in other countries. Planning is critical and should include registering with the foreign Consulate. At a minimum, just in case, foreigners should arrange for a personal physician in Mexico and a mortuary.

Procedures in Mexico differ depending on whether the death occurs in a hospital, at home, in a public place, or in an accident. Even with planning, many foreign deaths in Mexico involve lengthy police interviews, removing the body from a government morgue, and embalming. Authorities often override personal and religious preferences regarding autopsy, embalming, and cremation.

To alleviate some problems, foreigners should have a Notario prepare a Certificate of Ratification, which can cut through much of the Mexican bureaucracy surrounding death. The document must be in Spanish, certified and legally filed by a Notary. An immigration professional can arrange all of this.

If a personal physician can certify the cause of death at home or in a hospital, this document may bypass the coroner and an autopsy. Even with the Certificate of Ratification, next-of-kin must provide specific documents to prove a relationship to settle a foreigner's estate; a birth certificate, driver's license, passport, and any documents with name changes such as marriage certificates and divorce decrees.

If the Certificate of Ratification specifies a mortuary, this may bypass the government morgue. The mortuary can obtain the necessary permits to send the body to another country for burial, facilitate cremation, and transport the ashes. Be prepared to pay cash to everyone involved.

All of this is more critical if the nextof kin cannot travel to

Mexico immediately after the death. If you are considering cremation costs, including the pick up of the body and delivery of the urn, the average cost is about $500 USD. That, of course, is after you have done the paperwork. Some funeral homes, especially those in large expat communities, offer programs where you can prepay for funeral services. They will expect payment in advance, and your representative should be prepared to cover these costs if you have not done so already. Your executor should contact the local embassy in Mexico for precise instructions on dealing with the death of a loved one in Mexico.

Americans – for the death in Mexico, the Special Consular Services (SCS) unit of the US Citizen Services section at the US embassy can assist family and friends in the event of the death of a US citizen in Mexico. Contact the US embassy for further information.

Canadians – The death of a Canadian in Mexico requires a family representative to go to the Canadian Embassy. This person must have their Canadian passport and birth certificate. Power of attorney is required if you are not immediate family and is recommended under any circumstances. They must also have the deceased person's passport and the original or a certified copy of the death certificate.

Mexican Wills – If you own property or have any Mexican holdings, including a bank account, I highly recommend having a Mexican will. Creating a will in Mexico is considerably different than doing one in Canada or the US. In September, wills are drawn up at half-price nationwide. They call it "National Will Month."

Your will can take considerable time to create and draft several appointments. An official translator will be involved unless you are fluent in Spanish, as well as three personal witnesses you bring with you. It's considerably different than in Canada, where if you write it on a piece of paper and sign it, it's legal.

MEDICAL TOURISM

Medical tourism is growing in popularity, and procedures performed by highly skilled professionals can cost from 1/4 to 1/2 of what they do in other first-world countries. Cosmetic surgery, operations to correct obesity, hip and knee replacements and Lasik eye surgery are only a few of the procedures opted for in Mexico. Of course, cosmetic surgery prices and all other procedures vary per factor involved.

While visiting Colombia in 2021, I filmed a full video on Medical Tourism. You can watch it on YouTube for free by following this link https://ExpatMoneyShow.com/medical-tourism. Medical tourism is something that I have believed in for decades and am a huge proponent, Here is a story from Mark G from our Private Facebook Group on April 5, 2021:

I am on my way to Mexico for dental work.

I will have the mercury amalgam fillings removed I got as a child, plus the removal of a root canal, then a complete tooth replacement with a couple of zirconia implants. The cost for these implants in the U.S. is $5,000 – $8,000 per implant.

In Mexico, they are $1,950/tooth. For changing the removal of the mercury fillings, the charge is $60/tooth, and the fillings are $30. So $90/tooth. The entire trip should cost less than $5,000. If I only need one implant, it's under $3,000. You can't get this *kind of surgery in the U.S. for this amount of money.*

Another story, a friend of mine just had a car accident and his face got all banged up. If he had gone to Mexico and had full implants, not zirconia, he could have gotten the top and bottom done for well under $10k. He paid $40k in the U.S.

Here is a list of leading hospitals and dental clinics in México that I found quite reputable. I have listed the ones that are near the border of the US and México, in case you are still living in the US and want to do Medical Tourism to México.

- http://avilasdentalgroup.com/ Rosarito, Mexico

- https://hospitalcer.com/cerhospital Los Algondones, Mexico

- http://www.ramlanzdental.com/ Mexicali, Mexico

- http://www.visionmendez.com/ Tijuana, Mexico

- https://www.oasisofhope.com/ Tijuana, Mexico

- https://dentaris.com.mx/ Cancun, Mexico

- https://www.hospitalguadalajara.com/ Tijuana, Mexico

- http://www.clinicasanjuan.com.mx/ Tijuana, Mexico

WHAT NEEDS TO BE PAID BEFORE LEAVING THE HOSPITAL

In general, patients in México have to pay the total costs for the hospital and doctors before leaving the hospital.

Therefore, foreigners without private insurance need to analyze the costs and benefits of paying cash in Mexico vs. returning to their home countries. Government-subsidized programs such as Medicare in the USA might cover almost all costs, and hospitals back home might agree to bill patients later.

AIR AMBULANCE

This company, Air Ambulance, https://www.airambulance1.com/location/tijuana-me is located in Tijuana. They are available 24/7 for international and domestic flights.

They provide these services:

- Domestic and International Air Ambulance Transport

- Long Distance Medical Escort

- Organ Transport

- VIP Medical Transportation

- Commercial Stretcher

- Neonatal / NICU patients

- Bariatric patients transport

CHAPTER 16: QUICK SUMMARY

- When it comes to health care, we all want the best coverage we can afford, and needless to say, the options can be staggering, whether it be from the different benefits offered or the costs involved.

- The very best hospitals in Mexico are in Guadalajara, Mexico City, and Monterrey, which means if you need very specialized treatment, you might want to go there. You can obtain a complete list of hospitals from your own insurance carrier or https://mx.usembassy.gov/

- On average, the cost of medical and dental procedures in Mexico is inexpensive compared to the US

- Insurance providers in Mexico cover all healthcare in the country, and people can choose between private or public healthcare providers

- Foreigners can buy private insurance from many international firms to cover medical treatment in Mexico

- No special additional vaccines or immunizations are required to enter Mexico

- Medical tourism is growing in popularity, and procedures performed by highly skilled professionals can cost from 1/4 to 1/2 of what they do in other first-world countries

In chapter 17, we discuss education in Mexico. Public and private schools and what you can expect from alternative education and, most importantly, online schools like https://expatschool.io/

EDUCATION

EDUCACIÓN

The more that you read, the more things you will know, the more that you learn, the more places you'll go.

DR. SEUSS

PUBLIC AND PRIVATE, UNIVERSITIES, HOMESCHOOLING

Many educational options exist for expats and foreign nationals with school-aged children living in Mexico. Public education has had its share of issues in Mexico due to corruption and lack of funding. Some expats choose to send their children to a Mexican public school for half the day and homeschool in the afternoons. This helps assimilation.

Most internationals go the private school route. In any of the larger cities, there will likely be at least a couple of schools.

Mexico City is home to a whopping 23 international schools (https://www.international-schools-database.com/in/mexico-city), including a private French school with two campuses, a German school with a curriculum approved by the German government, and a Japanese school with a curriculum according to the Japanese Ministry of Education.

International schools can also be found in Guadalajara, Queretaro, Monterrey, Nuevo Leon, Puebla, Puerto Vallarta, Torreon, Tijuana, and Tampico, among others. Even mid-sized Puerto Vallarta has both British and American schools, so if tuition costs are not an issue, private education is widely available.

Even smaller cities, in areas favoured by expats, will often offer a surprising variety of school options. Cabo San Lucas, Cancun, Playa del Carmen, Tulum, and the islands of Isla Mujeres and Cozumel all have private or international school options for expat children.

Understand that in Mexico, as it is almost everywhere else, private education can be an expensive undertaking. Yearly tuition for some schools, especially international schools, can easily compare with college tuition, with costs being slightly lower for lower grades and increasing with progressing grades.

Nevertheless, if private education for your children is your preference, do not be deterred. There are many private and international school options in Mexico's cities, and some internet research will reveal that some are far less expensive than others.

To enroll your child, you must pay a yearly inscription fee which averages $350 – $400 USD. This covers registration costs. The books, school supplies, and uniforms are additional.

Determine the city or area where you need to locate a school, search online for the schools available in that area, and either go to the school's website or call them to discuss tuition and fees. This is much easier once you know where you will be living. Commute time will be a factor in some cities such as Mexico City. You don't want to find a great school only to discover that a home in the perfect neighbourhood would involve an impossible commute to get the kids to school every day.

EXPAT INTERNATIONAL SCHOOL OF FREEDOM & ENTREPRENEURSHIP

This school is possibly one of the most innovative and intelligent learning methods I have ever seen. I helped to create this school with my business partner Michael Strong who has been in the education field for over 30 years.

Expat International School is a virtual school for students ages 8-19. They educate your child through interactive peer learning that leads to high-level academic skills development. They are warm, purpose-driven, and effective. They specialize in working with international families to tackle challenges.

The Novice Program is for students 8-11 years old. It is based on Montessori principles adapted to a virtual environment, including rich online and offline learning activities and adapted for international families. We've carefully created a set of experiences that combine personalized learning, Socratic dialogue, and offline learning experiences that develop your child's heart and mind within a warm community, ensuring both personal well-being and academic success.

The Middle School Program is for students 11 – 14 and addresses the essential needs of children in this highly sensitive transitional phase of development. Students integrate Socratic dialogue texts with conversations and one-on-one coaching on personal growth.

Our STEM program allows for radical personalization and group problem-solving experiences that engage curiosity while developing thinking skills needed for superior SAT performance in high school. Our Wednesday program combines art, music, and tech experiences to complement our academic core.

The High School Program is for students 14 – 19 years old and provides one of the most personalized programs anywhere. It combines ongoing Socratic and personal growth conversations and one-on-one coaching with increasingly sophisticated personal projects and entrepreneurial ventures based on the student's interests.

Streamlined graduation requirements mean that students can take courses that are both interesting and relevant to their post-high school plans rather than being forced into a one-size-fits-all-school program. We provide the best of community and individual choice.

To check out our online programs, visit the website at

https://expatschool.io/

UNIVERSITY

There are many to choose from for those wishing to attend a university in Mexico. A quick search on https://www.topuniversities.com/universities/level/undergrad/country/mexico reveals 83 universities in Mexico City and other cities, and this is probably not an exhaustive list.

Most university classes are taught in Spanish, so fluency in Spanish would be necessary. While some schools offer

Spanish courses for international students during the semester, students need to have some Spanish proficiency before being admitted.

ALTERNATIVE EDUCATION

Homeschooling is an option for those dubious of Mexican public education and not willing or able to pay for private education. The array of online educational opportunities and curriculums is nothing short of staggering.

Finding local Spanish language tutors can also be pretty easy via social media. Private or group Spanish language tutoring is usually inexpensive and readily available in almost any city.

This can be a great way to ensure that your children's experience in a country that is not their own is positive by allowing them to make local friends while fully experiencing the culture more easily.

HOMESCHOOLING - WHAT IT IS

Homeschooling is the education of school-aged children at home or in various places other than school. Usually conducted by a parent, tutor, or an online teacher, many homeschool families use less formal, more personalized and individualized methods of learning that are not always found in schools.

The actual practice of homeschooling can look very different. The spectrum ranges from highly structured forms based on traditional school lessons to more open, free forms such as unschooling, which is a lesson – and curriculum-free implementation of homeschooling.

Some families who initially attended a school go through a deschool phase to break away from school habits and prepare for homeschooling.

While "homeschooling" is the term commonly used in North America, "home education" is mainly used in Europe and many Commonwealth countries. Homeschooling shouldn't be confused with distance education. Distance education generally refers to the arrangement where the student is educated by and conforms to the requirements of an online school rather than being educated independently and unrestrictedly by their parents or by themselves.

Homeschooling is legal in Mexico.

WHAT IS WORLD SCHOOLING

Worldschooling is the deliberate inclusion of travel and learning from the world around you to educate children, using the world as your classroom!

Worldschooling is a state of mind – it's seeing education more inclusively. Understanding that learning happens everywhere and throughout the day. It's opening your children up to the world beyond their immediate four walls and teaching them through experiences by doing, being, touching, smelling, and feeling.

WHAT DOES WORLD SCHOOLING LOOK LIKE?

For some, this means selling everything and travelling the world full-time; trading in a mortgage, car payments, electricity bills, and a stationary life for airfares, accommodation, experiences, and adventures.

For others, it is travelling 3-6 months of the year while children are enrolled in a traditional school setting. For some, it's just travelling at every possible opportunity but valuing the educational benefits their children receive from travel.

Whether you choose to be a full-time, part-time or casual world schooling family, Worldschooling is unique to the individuals. What it looks like in one family can be completely different from what it looks like in another.

Worldschooling is about creating an incredible lifestyle perfectly tailored to your family's needs, your children's learning styles, and your interests.

Many of our clients world-school their children and are part of ExpatSchool.io. These two concepts work together to create highly educated and functional children.

MONTESSORI

The method was originally developed by Italian educator Maria Montessori in the mid-twentieth century.

Popularly known for the rooms decorated with furniture and objects within reach of the little ones, the Montessori teaching methodology is supported by six educational pillars: self-education, knowledge of science, cosmic education, the prepared environment, the prepared adult and the balanced child.

The method seeks to create a learning scenario that promotes the development of autonomy through this set of elements, to form independent, creative, confident citizens and protagonists of change actions.

The bottom line is that a move to Mexico does not mean the death of your children's education. Quite the contrary, quality educational opportunities are abundant and relatively easy to find, especially in mid-sized and larger cities.

If you and your children view this new, unfamiliar educational experience as an adventure, that's exactly what it will be. Mexico has a rich heritage and a fascinating history, and your kids will get to learn about it while being there. How exciting is that!

CHAPTER 17: QUICK SUMMARY

- Many educational options exist for expats and foreign nationals with school-aged children living in Mexico.

- There are many to choose from for those wishing to attend a university in Mexico. Here are but a few choices; https://www.topuniversities.com/universities/level/undergrad/country/mexico

- Alternative education for parents who are not in favour of the Mexican education system, homeschooling is an option, or online schools like Expat International School, a virtual school for students ages 8-19

- To check out our online programs, visit the website at https://expatschool.io/

Chapter 18 is about the Immigration process from your home country to Mexico. We discuss what citizenship is and is not and how you can acquire citizenship here in Mexico.

We then delve into the different types of visas that you will require to enter Mexico, both to live temporarily and for long-term residency.

IMMIGRATION

IMMIGRACIÓN

Immigration policy should be generous; it should be fair; it should be flexible. With such a policy we can turn to the world, and to our own past, with clean hands and a clear conscience.

JOHN F. KENNEDY

LET'S FIRST TALK ABOUT WHAT IS CITIZENSHIP?

A citizen is someone able to exercise his/her political rights by voting, being a candidate, etc., and also comprehending full civil rights and social rights.

CITIZENSHIP AND NATIONALITY

Nationality and Citizenship are two of the most misunderstood terms in the world. For ordinary people, citizenship works as a substitute for nationality and vice versa. But both are distinct concepts with different meanings.

Nationality denotes where an individual has been born or holds citizenship with a state. Nationality is obtained through inheritance from his/her parents,

Citizenship is a legal status in a political institution such as a city or a state. The relationship between a citizen and the institution that confers this status is formal.

NATIONALITY	CITIZENSHIP
Nationality denotes where an individual has been born or holds citizenship with a state. Nationality is obtained through inheritance from his/her parents	Citizenship is a legal status in a political institution such as a city or a state. The relationship between a citizen and the institution that confers this status is formal,
Ethnic or Racial	Legal or Juristic
The place or country where the individual has taken birth	The individual is designated as a citizen by the government of the country
Birth and Inheritance (subject to the rules prevalent in the country)	Birth, Inheritance, Marriage, Naturalization,
Nationality cannot be changed	Citizenship can be changed
An example of nationality is Brazilian to a person with Brazilian roots born in the United Kingdom	An example of citizenship is a Panamanian being con- ferred US Citizenship upon clearing a citizenship test

MEXICAN PASSPORT

You must follow a specific process to apply for and acquire Mexican Citizenship, also known as 'naturalization.' As a minimum, you must have applied for and been granted per- manent resident status; however, some exceptions apply to this rule, depending on a variety of factors, for example, marriage to a Mexican national, which may enable natural- ization with a shorter qualification period.

To have a Mexican passport, you have to be a Mexican citizen. You are allowed to have dual citizenship as well.

The advantage of having a passport from Mexico is that there are some countries that you can visit that Americans or Canadians are not allowed to visit. There are countries where you can do business that Americans are not allowed to do business with.

THE ADVANTAGES OF A MEXICAN PASSPORT

As of January 2023, Mexico's passport ranks as the 25th most powerful passport in the world.

The strength of a passport depends on how many countries it lets you access without a visa and gets you a visa on arrival.

Mexican nationals can enter 160 countries worldwide visa-free or visa on arrival. This is an extremely powerful passport, with only 67 countries requiring a visa.

Few passports in the world could offer you as much mobility as a Mexican passport. With the authorization to travel to almost the entire world without a visa, you can create more opportunities to invest in a business and real estate across the globe.

Getting a passport from Mexico can open quite a few gates for you.

HOW TO GET CITIZENSHIP IN MEXICO

Mexican nationality is based on both the principle of jus soli (right of soil) and the principle of jus sanguinis (right of blood). The Mexican constitution also distinguishes between nationals of Mexico and citizens of Mexico.

The legal means to acquire a nationality and formal membership in a nation differ from the relationship of rights and obligations between a national and the nation, known as citizenship.

ACQUISITION OF NATIONALITY

According to the 30th article of the Constitution of Mexico, there are two ways in which a person can acquire Mexican nationality: by birth or by naturalization.

NATIONALITY BY BIRTH

The Mexican Constitution states that Mexican nationals by birth are: (see the section on Birth Tourism for more information)

- People born in Mexican territory regardless of their parent's nationality.

- People born abroad to a Mexican citizen.

- People born abroad to a naturalized Mexican citizen.

- People born on Mexican ships or aircraft for military or merchant use.

NATIONALITY BY NATURALIZATION

Mexicans by naturalization are

- those who obtain from the Secretariat of Foreign Affairs a letter of naturalization and

- an individual married to a Mexican national residing in Mexico who fulfills the requirements outlined in the Mexican nationality law: to have lived with the spouse for two years immediately before the date of the application.

The Nationality Law also establishes that a foreigner that wishes to naturalize must do the following:

- present the application to the Secretariat of Foreign Affairs;

- formulate the renunciation of the person's country of origin and take the oath of sole nationality to Mexico. Once this has been given;

- prove knowledge of Spanish and Mexican history; integration to the national culture; and

- prove residence in Mexico for five years immediately before the submission of the application, or

- two years of residency if

- a direct descendant of a Mexican by birth; or

- is the mother or father of a Mexican by birth, or

- is a national of a Latin American or Iberian country; or

- to the judgment of the Secretariat, she or he has performed or created outstanding works in a cultural, social, scientific, technical, artistic, sports or business area that benefit the nation, in which case, the foreigner is not required to have resided in the country for the number of years prescribed in the law; or

- one year of residency if adopted by a Mexican national. Minors who are second-generation descendants or have been under the tutelage of a Mexican national.

MEXICAN CITIZENSHIP

Mexican law differentiates between nationality and citizenship as in most other countries in the Americas.

Nationality is the attribute of the person in international law that describes their relationship to the State.

In contrast, citizenship is given to those nationals (those who hold Mexican nationality) with certain rights and responsibilities before the State.

The 34th article of the Mexican constitution establishes that Mexican citizens are those Mexican [nationals] who are 18 years of age or older and have an "honest way of living." Mexican citizens have these rights:

- vote in all elections

- be elected in all elections

- gather or associate freely to participate in the political affairs of the nation

- enlist in the Mexican Army or the Mexican National Guard to defend the Republic and its institutions

- exercise the right of petition

Mexican law also distinguishes between naturalized citizens and natural-born citizens in many ways.

The Mexican constitution prohibits naturalized citizens from serving in a wide array of positions, primarily governmental. Naturalized Mexicans cannot occupy any of the following posts:

- The Mexican military during peacetime

- Policeman

- Captain, pilot, or crew member on any Mexican-flagged vessel or aircraft

- President of Mexico

- Member of the Congress of Mexico

- Member of the Supreme Court of Mexico

- Governor of a Mexican state

- Mayor or member of the legislature of Mexico City

LOSS OF NATIONALITY AND LOSS OF CITIZENSHIP

The 37th article of the constitution establishes that Mexicans by birth (natural born Mexicans) can never be deprived of their nationality, as defined in the Nationality law, in the acquisition of another nationality. However, naturalized Mexicans may lose their nationality by doing the following:

- voluntarily acquiring another nationality, presenting themselves as foreigners or accepting nobility titles that imply a submission to a foreign state;

- Even though Mexican nationals by birth can never involuntarily lose their nationality, Mexican citizenship, and thus its prerogatives, may be lost if a person does the following:

    - accepts nobility titles from foreign countries;

    - serves in a foreign government without the authorization of the Congress of the Union;

    - accepts or uses foreign distinctions, titles or functions, without the authorization of the Congress of the Union, except for those that are literary, scientific or humanitarian in nature;

    - helps a foreign citizen or government against Mexico in any diplomatic claim or before an International Tribunal.

Mexican nationals can give up their nationality to acquire another nationality.

MULTIPLE NATIONALITY

The nationality law acknowledges that a Mexican may possess another nationality. However, if that is the case, such an individual must always enter and leave the country as a Mexican (by presenting a Mexican proof of citizenship).

The law also established that regardless of possession of another nationality, an individual will always be considered a Mexican national and cannot claim protection from a foreign country in some instances:

- participating in the capital of an entity or a company if they are constituted according to the Mexican law; if

- giving credits to such entities, and if

- possessing property in Mexican territory.

All Mexican nationals by birth who possess another nationality cannot be elected for, or work in, public office.

Only in those cases where the law establishes that they must not acquire another nationality.

If in such a case, she or he can request a Certificate of Nationality from the government, renouncing the other nationality.

BIRTH TOURISM (NATIONALITY BY BIRTH)

Birth Tourism is giving birth in a country that grants citizenship based on jus soli and provides benefits to all children born there. This will give your child a better quality of life and entitles them to a second passport immediately from birth.

In many cases, parents of such children also enjoy a faster naturalization timeline.

When determining a child's citizenship at birth, countries usually apply one of two rights: jus soli (right of soil) or jus sanguinis (right of blood). Jus soli grants citizenship merely based on being born "on the soil" of the country in question. Jus sanguinis determines the child's citizenship based on the parents' nationality.

The process of "jus soli" is generally available to anyone who has a child within the territory of a country with birthright citizenship, even if they are a temporary resident or an illegal alien.

The only people whose children do not qualify for instant citizenship are diplomats.

These countries offer "absolute jus soli," meaning that the biggest hurdle you'll face in some countries is registering your bundle of joy with the local authorities to secure your passport.

Here is a list of the best countries in which to give birth:

Argentina	Jamaica
Belize	Mexico
Bolivia	Nicaragua
Brazil	Pakistan
Canada	Panama
Chile	Paraguay
Costa Rica	Peru
Dominica	Portuga
Ecuador	St. Kitts & Nevis
El Salvador	St. Lucia
Fiji	St. Vincent and the Grenadines
Grenada	Trinidad and Tobago
Guatemala	Tuvalu
Guyana	United States
Honduras	Uruguay
	Venezuela

BENEFITS OF LIVING IN A COUNTRY THAT OFFERS BIRTHRIGHT CITIZENSHIP

One of the most significant benefits of living in a country that upholds birthright citizenship is that it grants citizenship to anyone born in that country with no other requirements.

This can give the child valuable legal rights, such as protecting them from unwarranted extradition or enabling them to benefit from social programs that would otherwise be available.

Benefits such as this are why expectant parents are sometimes compelled to move to a country that offers birthright citizenship. Depending upon their current situation, they can sometimes secure a better life for their children simply by giving birth in a different country — provided it has birthright citizenship.

My wife and I decided to give birth to our second child in Brazil for the reasons I mentioned above. At birth, he is an automatic Brazilian citizen. Because I am Canadian, he will also qualify to receive his Canadian citizenship (with a little work from our side). Then, we are residents of Panama. He will therefore be allowed to receive his permanent residency in Panama.

I think that is amazing. He has three countries that he can live and work in potentially for the rest of his life.

One of the other benefits for us as a family is that we got to spend six months in Brazil. Seeing the country, living life as a Brazilian, the food, nature, and way of life.

If we had not chosen this path for our son, we would never have been able to spend six months in a country that we loved, as we had travelled there many times over the years. And now, we will continue to visit Brazil, spend more and more time there and instill in our children the love of travel.

Here is a story of giving birth in Mexico, by Ryan & Sabrina

My name is Ryan, from the US, and I had been in a relationship with my girlfriend, Sabina, from Kazakhstan for a bit over a year. We are the couple you envision watching the tv show "90 Day Fiance". We first found out that we were expecting our first child early in 2020, right as the pandemic was just starting to be news.

We had researched a few countries such as Panama, Costa Rica, and Brazil, but we settled on going to Chile to give birth, after researching the country in depth. I was already a permanent resident of Mexico so we thought it would be nice to give our child citizenship in South America, providing them with one of the best passports in the world and easy access to almost all of South America.

As countries quickly began to shut down, I knew that our options would soon be limited. As Sabina's Kazakhstani passport did not offer visa-free travel to any of the countries that were still open, we zeroed in on Mexico, as it was virtually the only country open to both of us. We did not want our child born in the US and I was unable to enter Kazakhstan due to them shutting their borders as well.

Fortunately, Mexico was ready for us. My father had been living in Cancun for many years and welcomed us with open arms. We had experience with a good hospital in Cancun and I had been in touch with various doctors. Although the doctor I decided on trying out first did not speak English, she turned out to be absolutely amazing.

Sabina was very worried at first but I assured her that I could handle the Spanish and that she seemed to be an excellent doctor affiliated with an excellent hospital. We put a lot of trust in her and it paid off.

We went to several appointments before she set a deadline for the baby to be born. Nothing happened as we waited and waited. We survived a very strong hurricane. On the night of Hurricane Delta, we were praying that she did not go into labor as there was no way we would be able to make it to the hospital. Thank goodness, she did not. The next day looked like the apocalypse had struck.

The day of the deadline finally came with no birth. My parents drove us to the hospital where we had everything already set up and our doctor was ready for us. They tried to induce labor, but nothing happened. Finally, the doctor decided to perform a C-section that evening. We were obviously extremely nervous but everything ended up perfect, with a strong and healthy baby girl being born. We ended up staying at the hospital for 3 nights. The room was very nice. It was almost like a hotel room with a view, a private bathroom, and a futon for me to sleep on. The hospital staff and doctors could not have been better. Although only one doctor spoke English, everything was great. The staff were very welcoming and helpful. We are forever thankful to them and our doctor.

Getting documents for our baby was so simple. It was way easier than we imagined it would be. We were able to pick up the birth certificate after making an appointment with the civil registry a few days before. Due to the pandemic, we were basically the only people there. The process was pretty simple, though there was a small hiccup with Sabina's place of birth on her birth certificate since it was from the Soviet Union and did not match exactly her passport. The situation was remedied quickly though and we walked out with our baby's birth certificate in under an hour.

Getting a Mexican passport was also quite easy. We made an appointment online and made our way to the passport office in downtown Cancun on the specific day. While this was a bit more intense than getting the birth certificate, we did it all on our own. We walked out with our child's passport in under 2 hours.

The hard part was getting an appointment for the US passport at the consulate in Merida. They had no appointments of course, and after pulling some strings I was able to get us an appointment. We missed it due to another hurricane that hit the Yucatan peninsula. I was able to secure another appointment.

Although we ended up getting an emergency passport the same day of the appointment, it was pretty crazy due to a low-level staffer who did not like how I filled out the form stating that I did not list every time I left the US since I was 14 (really?!).

I demanded to speak to the actual consular officer and that situation was also remedied after she clearly noticed that my child qualified for US citizenship based on my citizenship and we told our story of how we met. Though its a pretty crazy story, she claimed it was not the craziest that she had heard! We were told to return later that afternoon to pick up the passport, which we did, before driving back to Cancun.

We then traveled to the Kazakh embassy in Mexico City so that our baby could receive a visa to go home with mom to Kazakstan (visa-free travel for US and Mexico passports was suspended due to the pandemic, and Kazakhstan does not allow dual citizenship, even if a parent is a Kazakh citizen). We roamed around Mexico City for a few days and eventually got the visa. We then traveled back to the US and the two of them departed for Kazakhstan a few days later. The first part of our Mexican adventure had come to an end.

Following up almost 2 years later; On a subsequent trip to Mexico, Sabina was granted permanent residency and received her card in less than a week. The baby is healthy and doing fine, and we are exploring destinations for our next birth tourism adventure.

— Ryan and Sabina

California, USA and Nur Sultan, Kazakhstan

IMMIGRATION VISAS

WHAT IS A VISA?

A visa is an official document allowing the bearer to enter a foreign country legally.

The visa is usually stamped or glued into the bearer's passport. There are several different types of visas, each of which affords the bearer different rights in the host country. Citizens of the United States, Canada, Great Britain, and most European nations may visit Mexico for a maximum of 180 consecutive days. No visa is necessary.

WHAT IS A TRANSIT VISA?

Travellers may sometimes require transit visas to pass through a country that is not their destination. Transit visas are typically necessary if you have a layover in a country of more than a few hours.

WHY DO I NEED A VISA TO TRAVEL?

Visas are necessary if you'd like to travel to a country that does not have a visa policy in place with your home country.

Many countries have visa policies and agreements that allow their citizens to travel freely without needing a visa. For example, Canadians and Americans do not need visas to travel to each other's countries, only valid travel documents. However, Canadians need visas to travel to Russia, for example, since no visa agreement exists between the two nations.

WHEN DO I NEED A VISA?

It depends on where you'd like to go. If your home country has a visa agreement with the country you intend to travel to, you likely will not need to apply for a visa beforehand.

However, if your home country does not have a visa agreement with your intended destination, you must apply for a visa before travelling.

WHAT IS A VISA POLICY?

A country's visa policy is a rule that states who may or may not enter the country. The policy may allow passport holders of one country to enter visa-free but not passport holders of another country.

Most visa policies are bilateral, meaning that two countries will allow visa-free travel to each other's citizens, but this is not always the case. For example, Canadian passport holders may travel to Grenada visa-free, but Grenadians must apply for a visa to travel to Canada.

There are no hard and fast rules for countries when determining visa policies. However, some typical considerations include diplomatic relations with the other country, the history of illegal immigration from the country, cost and tourism factors, and more.

WHAT IS AN EVISA?

An eVisa, or electronic visa, is a digital visa stored in a database rather than stamped or glued into the bearer's passport. The eVisa is linked to the individual's passport number.

Applications for eVisas are typically made over the Internet, and the applicant will receive a paper document to present while travelling.

WHAT DOES A VISA LOOK LIKE?

Traditional visas can either be stamped or glued into your passport. If your visa is glued into your passport, it is usually a small document that includes your name, passport number, place of birth, travel reason, and expiration date.

Stamped visas typically have less information on them. They

usually only have the destination and date from which the visa is valid and official instructions stating how many days the visa is valid.

WHAT IS A TRAVEL/TOURIST VISA?

Travel visas allow the bearer to enter a foreign country for touristic and leisure purposes only and stay for a predetermined amount of time. These visas do not entitle the holder to work or engage in business activities in the host country.

ARRIVAL IN MEXICO

If you are arriving by plane, you must carry a current passport valid for at least six months from your arrival in Mexico. If your passport is expired, the airline will not allow you entry onto the plane.

If you arrive by land at the US/Mexico border, you can use a passport or, if you are a US citizen, a Passport Card. The information you will find in this book on Immigration is updated as of January 1, 2022.

VISAS & TOURIST CARDS

There are several visa options for those visiting Mexico for an extended period or planning to make Mexico their permanent home.

There are numerous visas granted by the Mexican government that will allow you entrance into the country.

VISITOR PERMIT

A visitor permit is something like a tourist visa that allows you to stay in the country for 6 months. The fee for this visa is $25 USD and is usually included in the price of your airline ticket, which you can see under taxes and fees.

IF YOUR ARE APPLYING FOR FM2 OR FM3 THIS FMM IS REQUIRE CONTACT JORGE GONZALEZ BY EMAIL AT JORGE@SANDIEGOLEISURE.COM

If you arrive by road and leave within seven days of your arrival date, there is no fee for the permit. If you arrive by ship, you will have to pay for this permit separately.

You must be a passport holder of one of the many countries which don't require a visa to enter Mexico. For this purpose, The USA, Canada, and many other countries are allowed entry. You must present at arrivals:

- Passport or valid ID and travel that is valid under international law

- FMM properly filled out

- The immigration authority may request the foreign person to verify the reason for his/her trip using one of the following documents:

- Hotel reservation, return tickets (itinerary), tour tickets (itinerary).

- Letter mandated in the Spanish language from the parent company, subsidiary or foreign subsidiary indicating that the foreign person is employed by the parent company and that they (he/she) will pay for the services provided in the national territory.

- Copy of the contract for the transfer of technology, patents and trademarks, the sale of machinery and equipment, technical training of personnel, or any other related to the production process of a company established in Mexico or linking the foreign party to the Mexican party, or constancy of appointment by the shareholders' meeting of companies legally established in Mexico.

- Letter of the organization or public or private institution inviting the foreign person to participate in any unpaid activity in national territory, stating the object of the visit and the estimated time of stay. If the organization or institution suffers the travel and stay costs of the foreign person in the national territory, a responsive letter must be attached.

- Letter of invitation or acceptance of any institution belonging to the National Education System to carry out courses, studies, research or training projects for a maximum of one hundred and eighty days.

- If you arrive by land, you must get a visitor's permit at the port of entry.

- If you fly to Mexico, flight attendants on international flights hands out the visitor permit forms before the flight lands. They are also available at Mexican airports, near the immigration desks.

- If you are visiting a Mexican port as part of a cruise, you'll need to get a visitor's permit at your first Mexican port of call.

Keep Your Visitors Permit (FMM) Safe

Once completed, the immigration officer at the port of entry will stamp both halves of the form and hand you the smaller half, stamped with the date you entered the country. It's essential to keep this document safe, as you will need to surrender it when you leave Mexico. If you depart Mexico on a flight, your airline will insist you surrender your stamped half of the Visitors Permit to them before they allow you to board.

Suppose you lose your Visitors Permit while you are in Mexico; In that case, you will need to visit one of the local immigration offices in towns and cities across the country or at the airport. You will have to apply for a replacement before you can leave.

This will cost $40 USD, which you do at the bank and a fair amount of paperwork. You will then return to the immigration office to receive your replacement Visa. So, be very careful with this form. I would suggest that you keep it inside your passport so that you have it handy when leaving the country.

If you have a Visitor's Permit and are leaving the country by land, you should voluntarily surrender your form to an immigration official before departure. Failure to do so might cause delays the next time you try to enter Mexico.

The Visitor's Permit is valid for 180 days from the date you enter Mexico.

Each time you enter Mexico, you will be allowed another 180 days from that date.

You cannot renew or extend a Visitor's Permit. The only way is to leave, come back through a port of entry and fill out the Visitors Permit again. That does not mean that the Immigration officials will allow you entry back into Mexico; however, it is usually safe to do.

If you get turned away, ask when you will be allowed back in the country and explain your situation to the official. Having a good use of Spanish will be highly beneficial at this point.

You cannot work in Mexico while living on a visitor permit. But if you need to do so (maybe you're just getting a feel for what Mexican life would be like, and you have to work while you're at it), you can purchase a "permission to work" visa for only 175 USD.

The only stipulation is that you cannot be paid in Mexico for your services. If you're working remotely from a company back home, they'll just continue to pay you via your home bank account.

OVER-STAY ON YOUR VISITORS PERMIT

If you have overstayed on your visitor's visa, you will be required to see an immigration officer and pay the fine before leaving the country. The amount of the fine depends on how long you have overstayed. It is calculated daily; however, the penalty will never exceed MX 8,000 pesos.

If you are flying out of a Mexican airport, I suggest you visit the Immigration Office a few days before your flight with your expired Visa in hand and explain the situation. Complete the required forms, pay the bank's fine and get an exit permit because if you attempt to do this at the airport, you will likely miss your flight.

RESIDENCY IN MEXICO

Applying for legal residency is the start of a new adventure in Mexico. Following, you will find several different visas for which you can apply. I am going to talk about short and long-term visas.

If you are going for an exploratory visit, you will require a tourist visa.

If you are going to live in Mexico and will not be leaving the country within 180 days, please begin the process of a temporary visa in your home country and go from there.

In 2012, Mexico enacted a sweeping immigration reform law that consolidated its immigration rules and qualification criteria for would-be residents and job seekers. More broadly, it brought Mexico's immigration rules closer to international protocols.

Since 2013, all temporary and permanent resident visas must be pre-approved by the consulate closest to your home. So you must begin the process outside of Mexico.

IMMIGRATION LAWYERS

Depending on your level of Spanish, you can apply for a Mexican visa directly in person at any Immigration Office, or you can hire a lawyer to do the paperwork and administration for you. Honestly, doing immigration work on your own can be extremely difficult and time-consuming.

Making an error can cost you much more than you might have to pay your lawyer. I never do immigration work alone.

I always hire a professional who does this type of work day in and day out. They know the system, and often they know someone that can expedite your paperwork.

A good immigration lawyer will understand the process completely and be up-to-date on any changes that have occurred during the last year.

Hiring a lawyer and a notary will help you avoid several trips to the immigration department and also help with fingerprinting and which documents you must have with you.

VISA PROCESSES

As you are now aware, you can't just show up in Mexico and stay forever. There are proper methods and routes you'll need to follow to get your Mexico visa.

The duration of your stay will determine which visa you'll need. Visitor Visas or FMM Visas, which is a short-term permit to enter the country, allow you to stay up to 180 days, but this visa cannot be extended or renewed. You must leave the country when it expires.

The fee is $25 USD, and if you fly into Mexico, it is included in the price of your flight. If you enter by road or ship, you must pay separately. Because the FMM is valid for six months, many retirees who want to live in Mexico part-time, like snowbirds, never get any other visa. However, if you want to stay longer, you have two other options.

TEMPORARY RESIDENT VISA

If you want to live in Mexico for more than six months but not longer than four years, the temporary resident visa is what you want. This visa is issued one year at a time, and unlike the FMM, you can renew this visa for another 1-3 years. It also allows unlimited entries into Mexico (and exits from Mexico), so you don't need to worry about your visa permissions if you plan to travel. A temporary visa can also permit you to work if you hope to get a job there. But you must apply for a lucrative temporary visa versus a non-lucrative one. It's a simple classification difference when applying.

Main Requirements For Getting A Temporary Visa

One of the critical requirement factors for any type of visa is proving to the Mexican government you have sufficient funds or investments to sustain yourself while living in Mexico. That can be done by showing a consistent monthly income. For example, the minimum monthly income for a single applicant is $1400+ USD. However, that number can change depending on which consulate you apply from and which calculation they use. For that reason, it's best to contact your nearest consulate for details about Mexico residency requirements.

Suppose you are applying as a couple or family. In that case, your spouse or dependent will add a minimum of $520 USD to your proof of monthly income. Or you can provide your last 12 months' bank statements with an average balance of at least $24,000+ USD. Again, contact your consulate for the exact number.

Another way to achieve a temporary residency visa is if you own a property in Mexico with a minimum value of $207,000 USD.

Temporary Resident Benefits

- You can open a bank account

- Import household goods without paying duty

- You'll have unlimited exit/entry

- You can retain a permanent residency after four years

- You can temporarily bring your US car into Mexico

- You can buy a Mexican car

What Can't Temporary Residents Do?

- You can't vote

- You can't extend the visa after four years. After that, you must either convert your visa to a permanent visa or leave Mexico

- You can't buy beachfront land unless you put it in a trust

How to Apply For a Temporary Residence Visa

Step 1: The process must be started from a Mexican consulate in your home country.

Step 2: Once you've proven you meet the requirements, the consulate will process and pre-approve your application. They will add a visa sticker to your passport.

Step 3: When you arrive in Mexico, you'll need to find the local immigration office within 30 days. When you meet with them, they'll give you a temporary resident permit, and a plastic card.

PERMANENT RESIDENCE VISAS

If you want to live for more than four years or permanently in Mexico, your best bet is to apply for a permanent residence visa.

Who is Eligible for the Mexican Permanent Resident Card?

Not everyone is eligible for a permanent residence visa in Mexico. There are rules and requirements you must meet. Typically, there are five ways to qualify:

- You can have family ties in Mexico. For example, you could be of Mexican descent but born in another country.

- You can be married to a Mexican

- Have political asylum or residency on humanitarian grounds

- Have lived four years in Mexico as a temporary resident

- Apply for a Mexico retirement visa through economic solvency.

There are two ways to go about it.

- You can apply immediately for a Mexico permanent resident visa

- You can first apply to become a temporary resident. After four years, you can apply for and transfer your visa from temporary to permanent status.

- The benefit of going this route is the income requirements to retire in Mexico are significantly less than if you were to apply for permanent residency straight away.

Requirements For The Mexican Permanent Resident Card

Just as with the temporary visa, you need to prove economic

solvency. But to apply directly for a permanent visa, you'll need substantially more money.

The minimum monthly monetary requirement for a single person is $2600+ USD. Expect to add at least $520 USD for a spouse or dependent. Or you can show savings of $43,000+ USD over the last year. Because the Mexico retirement visa requirements can change, contact your nearest consulate for exact monetary requirements.

Mexican Permanent Resident Visa Processing Time

Like everything bureaucratic, patience is a virtue when applying for your Mexican permanent residency.

Some places are notoriously slow, while others offer same-day service. So, it all depends. But expect to wait two weeks. which is still mighty fast.

CHANGING A TEMPORARY RESIDENCE CARD INTO A PERMANENT RESIDENCE CARD

After having a temporary visa for four consecutive years, you can apply to exchange it for a permanent residency visa. You can apply for this swap within Mexico.

You usually don't need to show any more documents or prove economic solvency.

There will be some admin fees and Mexico permanent resident visa application forms but it's pretty straightforward.

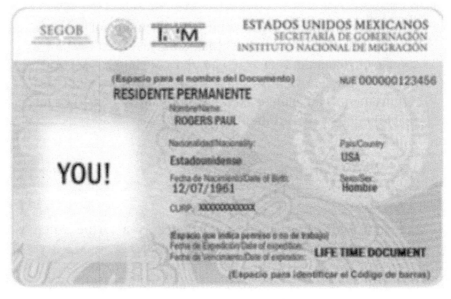

Benefits of the Mexico Permanent Resident Card

- You can open a bank account

- No need to apply yearly. This is a permanent visa

- You can work or be employed without applying for consent

- You'll have unlimited exit/entry

- Temporarily bring your US car into Mexico

- You can buy a Mexican car

What Can't Permanent Residents Do?

- You still can't vote

- You can't import a foreign-plated car

- You can't buy beachfront land unless you put it in a Trust

What is the Duration of a Mexico Permanent Resident Card?

Once you get your permanent visa card, you are set for life.

How to Apply for the Mexican Permanent Resident Card

Step 1: For the most part, permanent resident visas can't be issued from within Mexico. So, you must find your nearest Mexican consulate in your home country and apply from there.

You'll have to fill out paperwork and pay a fee of around $36 USD.

Step 2: They will pre-approve you and place a visa sticker on your passport.

Step 3: When you arrive in Mexico, go to immigration and swap your sticker for a permanent residence permit card. You have 30 days to make the swap.

Step 4: You're a permanent resident.

SPOUSAL VISA

People ask me if it is easy for my spouse to get a visa too. Yes, it can be done inside Mexico. I would highly recommend using your lawyer for this process, as it is quite a tricky endeavour. This also applies to your children.

ADDITIONAL CONSULATE REQUIREMENTS

- One up-to-date passport-sized photo measuring 39 x 31 mm

- $40 USD cash

- Mexican consulate visa application form to be printed, completed and taken with you. On question 21, for a temporary resident pre-approval, check 'more than 180 days and less than four years and for a permanent resident, check 'definitive'. Complete questions 1-25.

- Passport

- Financials 12 months of individual printouts for savings/investments and/or six months of individual bank printouts showing income and/or proof of homeownership in Mexico. Take as much proof of financials as possible. You can never have too much.

- Appointment confirmation form

NOTE: When entering Mexico with your pre-approved visa from the consulate, they will give you a white card. It must be marked 'canje' on the lower left side by immigration (not 'tourist').

Your pre-approved visa holograph contained in your passport is also to be stamped at the same time. When coming by air, you will receive a white card from the airline, and again it must be marked 'canje' by immigration services. You will be sent back to the border if this is not done.

CURRENT VISA FEES - AS OF JANUARY 2023 IN USD

Please note that with the possible fluctuation of the peso, these prices may vary.

Temporary resident:

* 1 year $270

* 2 years $404

* 3 years $512

* 4 years $607

Permanent resident:

$330 plus a review fee of $88 if you are becoming permanent after 4 years as a temporary resident.

Work Permit (permiso para trabajar) $203

Lost/stolen/damaged visas: $77

EXIT/RE-ENTRY PERMIT FEES

If you need to leave Mexico while a residency-related procedure is in process, you will need to apply and pay for an Exit/Re-entry permit, as you will not be in possession of your residency documents while the procedure is being completed. The fee for an Exit/Re-entry permit is $30 USD.

NOTE: if you are in the throes of a 'regularization' procedure (e.g., expired, or lost residency card), you **cannot** get this permit, and you **must** remain in Mexico until the regularization procedure is complete.

WHO MIGHT APPLY FOR A RESIDENT VISA

Retirees and Digital Nomads

If you do not earn money in Mexico, but are receiving it from abroad, like a pension, investments or another income source; In that case, you can apply for a Permanent Resident Visa if you have met the criteria financially.

Investors

Are you willing to invest your money in Mexico? Your investment can be directed at industry or services and must equal a minimum set amount.

Professionals

Are you a qualified professional? You must have your certificates validated by the Mexican Consulate in your home country and then apply for an immigration visa to live in Mexico.

Prominent Person

For this visa, the applicant must be a recognized national or international prestige or a prominent person, such as a scientist, researcher, humanist, artist, journalist or sportsman. This is left up to the Interior Ministry's discretion if your application will be accepted.

Technical or Scientific Professions

Are you a qualified technician or scientist? Mexico offers a category of visa which enables you to live and work in Mexico under sponsorship from a foreign company, which could be your own company. The company must cover all of your income and expenses while you are in Mexico.

YOU WANT TO LIVE AND WORK IN MEXICO

You should apply for the Permanent Resident Visa commensurate with the economic activity you want to undertake to work in Mexico.

Here are a few examples:

- A company-sponsored job

- Invitation to carry out academic or scientific research

- $130,000 USD to invest in a Mexican Company

You want to be a resident, but do NOT want to work in Mexico.

- If you have a regular source of income from abroad (investments, savings, pension)

- Apply for a permanent resident visa and satisfy one or more requirements (family connections, minimum income/investments, or political asylum).

- In the application, you must state what you intend to do in Mexico, like early retirement due to health.

VOLUNTEERING IN MEXICO

If you enter Mexico as a tourist to volunteer, the immigration official at the port of entry will usually grant you 180 days; this will also be written on the part of the form that's handed to you for safekeeping. Make sure you calculate your first day of arrival, then 179 days, and you must leave by that date. Remember that the FMM permit does not allow you to engage in any lucrative or paid activities while you're in Mexico.

If your volunteer work changes into a paid role for the organization you are employed by, they will need to sponsor you and change your immigration status and apply for a Temporary Resident visa with work privileges on your behalf

CHAPTER 18: QUICK SUMMARY

- As of January 2022, Mexico's passport ranks as the 24th most powerful passport in the world, with the ability to enter 159 countries across the world visa-free or visa on arrival.

- Mexican nationality is based on both the principle of jus soli (right of soil) and the principle of jus sanguinis (right of soil)

- Mexican law differentiates between nationality and citizenship as in most other countries in the Americas. Nationality is the attribute of the person in international law that describes their relationship to the State. In contrast, citizenship is given to those nationals (those who hold Mexican nationality) with certain rights and responsibilities before the State

- Birth Tourism is giving birth in a country that grants citizenship based on jus soli and provides benefits to all children born there

- There are several visa options for those visiting Mexico for an extended period or planning to make Mexico their permanent home

- Applying for legal residency is the start of a new adventure in Mexico If you want to live in Mexico for more than six months but not longer than four years, the temporary resident visa is what you want

- If you want to live for more than four years or permanently in Mexico, your best bet is to apply for a permanent residence visa

- After having a temporary visa for four consecutive years, you can apply to exchange it for a permanent residency visa. You can apply for this swap within Mexico. You usually don't need to show any more documents or prove economic solvency

- If you enter Mexico as a tourist to volunteer, the immigration official at the port of entry will usually grant you 180 days' leave to remain; this will also be written on the part of the form handed to you for safekeeping. Make sure you calculate your first day of arrival, then 179 days, and you must leave by that date

In the next chapter, we will discuss transportation getting to Mexico and, while you are in Mexico. Renting a car, taking an Uber or flying locally from one city to another in Mexico.

CHAPTER 19

TRANSPORTATION

TRANSPORTE

You can't understand a city without using its public transportation system.

EROL OZAN

DRIVING IN MEXICO

D riving in Mexico, even in Mexico City, is not as scary as many people make it out to be. If you can drive in Toronto, NYC, LA or Atlanta, then you can drive in Mexico City.

Since the early 1990s, Mexico has invested vast amounts of money in upgrading its interstate road network, working with the private sector to build and maintain high-quality interstate highways which connect Mexico's major towns and cities.

Most of Mexico's new interstate roads are tolled. The tolls are also relatively expensive compared to toll roads in the USA. However, the tolled roads are modern and well-maintained, usually four-lane roads (except in very rugged mountainous stretches where it is impossible to build a wide road), and provide a fast, safe and effective way to travel by land across Mexico.

You can travel on Mexico's non-tolled interstate roads, called libres, for free, but some are slower to travel on; most of these are two-lane highways, making it more likely that you will get stuck behind slow-moving traffic. They are also less well maintained than toll roads, so you'll need to look out for potholes and similar road surface hazards.

TIPS FOR DRIVING IN MEXICO FOR THE FIRST TIME

- Do not EVER drink and drive or do drugs and drive. If you are caught driving under the influence, no insurance will cover this, and you will get in big trouble (tickets/jail time/etc.) Please be safe!

- Lock your doors when you drive.

- If you get a flat tire (not covered in insurance), go to a mechanic or gas station to change it.

- If you are driving in a parking lot and you see a car in front of you backing out, note that they may not stop even if they see you. Local drivers don't really give the right of way to the car already driving.

- If you're on the highway and you're going to change lanes, your blinker will mean almost nothing to other drivers. Make sure to look three times before you do.

- If you are being tailgated, don't get annoyed or speed up. Let them do their thing. They will eventually pass you.

- Pedestrians are not used to cars stopping for them when crossing the road, so don't be scared if you see a pedestrian getting close to your car or if it looks like they are about to walk into your car.

- If you stop to let pedestrians cross the road, be aware of the cars behind you. They might not know someone is crossing, so they could pass you and hit the pedestrian. If you stop or brake suddenly, turn on your emergency lights to signal the driver behind you.

- If driving in the city at rush hour, be very careful at intersections or merge areas. Other drivers will completely ignore you and just try to jam themselves in front of you without using their blinker or checking.

CAR INSURANCE

Under Mexican law, you must have auto liability insurance from a Mexican insurer to drive your vehicle on Mexican roadways. Driving without adequate insurance for your vehicle is a risk, as police routinely ask to see insurance documentation when they stop road vehicles. Your US or Canadian policy will not suffice: you must have a policy underwritten by a Mexican insurance company.

Insurance can be purchased ahead of time online from any one of several different companies, including www.sanborns. com, www.mexpro.com, and www.mexicanautoinsurance. com. Do your due diligence to determine the coverage, price and company best suits your needs.

If you are involved in a serious accident in Mexico, where someone is hurt or killed, the police will detain you until the blame is assessed. Suppose it is deemed that you are to blame. In that case, you will be detained for longer until the other party (parties) are satisfied with any compensation you offer (or, more likely, your insurance company). At this point, they will sign the paperwork that will have you released from police custody.

Good insurance policies offer legal counsel and bail-bond services so that, in the worst-case scenario, you have the legal support and financial assistance you will need.

ACCIDENTS ON THE ROAD IN MEXICO

MINOR ACCIDENTS AND BUMPS

Mexicans will tend to walk away from minor accidents because many drivers will not have insured vehicles. If you are involved in a "fender bender" or other minor accident, don't be surprised if the other party drives off.

If the other driver does get out, you may need to wait until an insurance assessor arrives to resolve the matter. If you are renting a car and the other driver speeds off, you will be liable for the damage on the rental car (or the excess fee associated with any damage) if you are not travelling with "full cover" insurance.

SERIOUS ACCIDENTS

For more serious accidents, and where the police get actively involved, it is inevitable that you will be arrested and held until blame is assessed.

Police: 066 or 911

Fire: 066 or 911

Ambulance: 066 or 911

The emergency services number is 911 for all services, but you can call 066 for police, ambulance or fire.

HANDY PHRASES IN SPANISH:

- Give way - *Ceda el paso*

- Traffic lights - *Semaforas*

- Right of way – *Prioridad*

- Exit – *Salida*

- Danger – *Peligro*

- No parking - *Prohibido aparcar*

- Slow – *Despacio*

- Lane – *Un carril*

- City centre – *Centro ciudad*

- Local Highway – *Carretera*

- Roadworks – *Obras*

- Where is the nearest petrol station? – *¿Dónde está la gasolinera más cercana?*

- Excuse me, I'm lost – *Por favor, estoy perdido...*

- Go straight on – *'Siga todo recto'*

- Turn right – *'Toma el giro a la derecha'*

- Turn left – *'Toma el giro a la izquierda'*

- Detour - *Desviacion*

- Toll Road – *Carretera de Peaje*

- Road Closed – *Cerrado*

- Road Open – *Abierto*

- Motorway – *Una autopista*

- One-way street – *Dirección unica*

- Dual Carriageway - *Autovia*

HAVE YOUR DOCUMENTS WITH YOU

Have your driver and vehicle documentation on hand at all times when you are driving in Mexico. Suppose you are used to driving in a country where immediate documentation production is not required.

You may be accustomed to leaving your driver's license and/or other car documentation at home because if you get stopped, you can present it to the police later, or they will look up your record electronically from the squad car. This is not so in Mexico.

Traffic police are allowed to ask to see your license and your car registration card, known in Spanish as the "tarjeta de circulacion." It's also practical to keep your car insurance papers with you.

If You Get Pulled Over By The Police

You'll need to present your paperwork (as described above) to the officer who pulled you over.

If you don't speak Spanish, they may leave you alone unless your offence is serious or you are involved in a nasty accident; in such extreme circumstances, get your country's Consulate involved.

MILITARY ROAD CHECKS

If you drive long enough in Mexico, you will undoubtedly come across a Military road check. If you've lived in any country in Central America, you will be well accustomed to these. Often, they are temporary sites to check on vehicles coming and going. Usually, they stop every car that passes by; other times, it is random.

If you are the driver, don't panic. They want to look in your trunk, check inside the vehicle, and often they will look under the car. The best advice is to be compliant and do whatever they ask of you. They usually only take a few moments, and you'll be on your way.

These checkpoints are in place to monitor and prevent the illegal movement of goods on Mexico's roads, like precious woods, illegal firearms, ancient artifacts and illicit narcotics

.

RULES OF THE ROAD

Current speed limits are

- 10 km/h (6 mph) in parking lots and residential areas.

- 60 km/h (37 mph) in streets with no speed limit.

- 60–80 km/h (37–50 mph) on urban arterial roads (ejes, calzadas, beltways and freeways).

- 80 km/h (50 mph) in avenues with no speed limit.

- 70–90 km/h (43–56 mph) on rural two-lane roads.

- 90 km/h (56 mph) on two-lane highways.

- 90–100 km/h (56–62 mph) on major highways inside cities.

- 100 km/h (62 mph) on major highways leaving or approaching towns or cities.

- 110 km/h (68 mph) on major highways.

- No Mexican highway allows going beyond 110 km/h, but the speed limit is generally enforced above 130 km/h (81 mph) only.

Seat belts: The driver of a vehicle must wear a seat belt. Passengers are not required to do so.

Children and car seats: In modern taxis or cars, car seats may be able to be properly fitted. Unfortunately, older model cars may not have rear seat belts or the correct setup for attaching a car seat.

Children under seven years old: no matter what weight, and any child less than 60 pounds, must be in a suitable child seat, either rear or forward-facing or the booster seat for older children.

Alcohol: Passengers can drink alcohol; however, the driver of a vehicle is prohibited from drinking alcohol while driving a vehicle on public roads.

Drunk Driving: Drunk driving is punishable, and if caught, YOU WILL end up in a Mexican jail for an indeterminate period of time until you have sorted your mess out.

Cell phones: Unless you have a hands-free phone, it is illegal to use your mobile phone when driving in Mexico.

Toll roads: Mexico City has two electronic toll roads: a bridge called the Viaducto Elevado Bicentenario, and the other, Segundo Piso of Periferico Norte. You will see signs that read COUTA, meaning you will pay to travel on this road. Please keep your toll ticket as this is your insurance when travelling on the toll road.

Helmet Law: You must wear a helmet

Open Vehicles: You may travel in the back of an open vehicle, like a pick-up truck.

ROAD SIGNS

Here are some road signs that may be useful to know.

Stop	No Stopping	Do not Enter
No U Turn	Speed Limit	No Right Turn
No Left Turn	Stay Right	No Passing
Bicycles Prohibited	Pedestrians Prohibited	Trucks Prohibited
Horn Prohibited	These Vehicles Prohibited	Horsedrawn Prohibited

Maximum Weight	Maximum Height	Maximum Clearance
Inspection Area	Two way Traffic	No unloading
Farm Vehicles Prohibited	Centre Divide begins	One Way
Right Turn	Left Turn	Beach
Mechanic	Archaeological site	Craft Market

Parking	No Parking	Yield
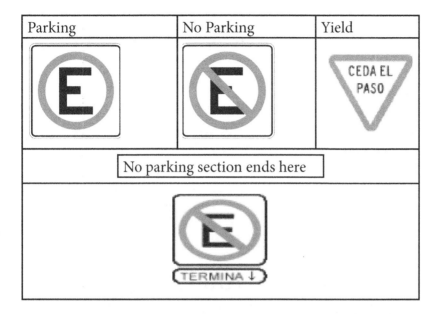		

No parking section ends here

SHIPPING A CAR

Importing a car to Mexico can be expensive and complicated. There are enough Mexican rules and regulations regarding license plates and vehicle registration (depending on the visa type) to give the most stalwart expat a migraine.

It is often advised that a better option if you are moving to Mexico permanently or for an extended stay would be to sell your car and purchase a new one in Mexico.

This can be the less complicated option, instead of attempting to legalize your vehicle after importation.

Driving a foreign-plated car in Mexico is illegal if you have obtained Permanent Resident status. While this may or may not be enforced by local police, it is enforced by the Federal

Police or 'Federales'.

If you are arriving in Mexico on a tourist visa, you must stop at the border and get your TIP or Temporary Import Permit. This permit is associated with your tourist/visitor permit and is only valid for 180 days.

The Mexican government offers information (in Spanish) on importing vehicles on their website: https://www.gob.mx/banjercito/articulos/sistema-de-importacion-temporal-de-vehiculos

BRINGING YOUR CAR TO MEXICO

DRIVING WITHIN THE "FREE ZONES"

If you drive a non-Mexican plated car across the border but remain within the "Free Zones," you do not need to apply for and obtain a temporary import permit for your vehicle. The Free Zones are

- within 16 miles (25 km) of the land border;

- the entire Baja California peninsula;

- a defined area in the northern state of Sonora; and,

- the southern state of Quintana Roo.

All roads leading into Mexico's interior have guarded checkpoints, where vehicles without Mexican license plates must show a temporary import permit.

Foreign vehicle import permits cannot be obtained at checkpoints in the interior of Mexico.

You must apply for and buy the permit ahead of time or at a Banjercito office near the border crossing.

BRINGING IN YOUR CAR ON A TEMPORARY RESIDENCE VISA

Temporary import permits (TIPs) are controlled by Aduana Mexico (customs) and are needed if you travel outside the Baja Peninsula or the border zones mentioned above.

Effective January 1, 2020, vehicle permits are digital, and windshield stickers are not issued. Applicants receive a digital copy via email. If you are entering from the south, there is also no need for a TIP in Quintana Roo, but you cannot drive from the north through the intervening states without a TIP.

For those entering as a pre-approved temporary resident from a Mexican consulate, vehicle permits are issued for the same length as your pre-approval visa - 30 days. You must start your visa process within 30 days of entering Mexico at your local INM office. Your next step as a pre-approved temporary resident is to extend your car permit (TIP).

Once you start your process in Mexico, Migracion (immigration) issues you a document indicating you have done so. That document has a NUT number starting with six zeros. Along with that document, you will need the original and copies of your passport, title or registration.

You will also need the document from which the holograph for your windshield (your TIP) was removed.

This document has a record of the TIP and information, so it's not something you would have disposed of after removing the sticker.

You also must complete a letter stating your request to extend your TIP, usually provided by Aduana (customs). Take these to the nearest Aduana office and request a TIP extension. Then repeat the trip when the visa is issued. Failure to do so will mean your vehicle deposit is forfeited.

It is the same process every time you renew your temporary resident visa. Your TIP must be attached to the new expiry date and extended for your visa duration.

In addition to the TIP fee ('T' does stand for temporary), you will need to leave a refundable deposit on a credit card according to the year of your vehicle:

- 2007 or newer: $400 USD (charged in MX pesos)

- 2001 - 2006: $300 USD (charged in MX pesos)

- 2000 or older: $200 USD (charged in MX pesos)

You may only request a permit for a vehicle registered in your name or that of your spouse, child or parent. You must show either a valid title or registration to obtain your TIP.

Recreational vehicles such as motor homes will often receive a 10-year TIP, and a deposit is not required.

Foreign residents (e.g. retirees) and those in Mexico on working permits holding Temporary visas/cards may bring in one car (their own) for the duration of their visas and subsequent extensions.

Tourists (using a tourist visa) may also bring in one car; if it's not their own, they must show documentation to demonstrate that they have permission to take the car to Mexico.

Trailers

A trailer does not count as a vehicle, but you need to show ownership of it, and it must be exported with the vehicle towing it when you leave Mexico.

Motorcycles, ATVs, etc.

If you are towing or carrying other single-passenger motorized vehicles, these may be registered with the car that is towing or carrying them.

You must show proof of ownership of all vehicles, and you can only bring up to three single-passenger vehicles—one each for up to three passengers travelling in the main vehicle. All vehicles must be exported together when you leave Mexico.

BUYING A CAR

You can breeze into a car dealership in any mid to large Mexican city and buy a car. Just don't expect the experience to be as simple as what you are accustomed to if you come from a developed country. However, you won't be too surprised if you come from a developing country. Most car dealerships in Mexico do not have a full inventory from which you can choose a vehicle. In the case of a new car, you will likely have to go into the dealership and select the particular vehicle you want from a book of options.

The dealership will have to get the car from the closest place with the model you selected. This often takes longer than anticipated. Most expats who buy new vehicles in Mexico pay cash for them, but even this can be a bit of a hassle. The dealership may want you to transfer the money from your bank account to theirs, so be prepared for this possibility.

Once the purchase is complete, getting tags for your new Mexican car can be another bureaucratic nightmare. There are many requirements and forms and proof of residence to be produced.

Visit the dealerships that you are interested in and ask questions about what will be required of you to get the tags and the car registration in your name.

Buying a used car is just as much of a dicey proposition in Mexico as anywhere else. Exercise great caution and, if possible, have someone mechanically inclined to assess the vehicle with you. There are many rules which vary from area to area about registering used vehicles.

GETTING A DRIVER'S LICENSE

A Mexican driver's license may require both a written test in Spanish and a behind-the-wheel test. Or it may not, depending on where you are applying for the license.

Many cities and tourist areas have expat consultant services to walk you through administrative issues like obtaining a driver's license or vehicle registration. It may be advisable to hire one of these experts to help with getting a driver's license, especially if you do not speak Spanish.

It is legal to drive in Mexico with your driver's license from your home country, although if you are buying a vehicle, you will have one year from the time you register a car in your name to get a Mexican driver's license. Getting a Mexican license is probably prudent if you plan to live in Mexico permanently or long-term,

You can get a driver's license through your tourist card, a pre-approved visa from a Mexican consulate, your temporary residency card, or your permanent residency card. In addition to your visa, you'll have to show the following:

- Birth certificate

- Valid passport

- Proof of address

- Medical forms

TAXI/UBER

Taxis are widely available in tourist areas and almost every city. To compete with Uber, some cities, such as Puerto Vallarta and Mexico City, have a Taxi app for your phone that makes getting a taxi super simple.

You can download the app from Google play. It gives you the official taxi rates, just enter your location and the location you want to go to. It requires you to sign in and create a password.

Even without an app, you should have no trouble finding a taxi in most cities and tourist areas.

Agree on the price before you get in. Sometimes fares are negotiable, but not always. Fares to and from the airport in larger cities may be higher and may not be negotiable. Taxis authorized to service the airport may have to pay expensive federal taxes and fees, which cause them to command higher fares.

Options other than taxis are available for airport transfers in most cities. Tourist areas will have car services and guide companies that do airport pick-ups and drop-offs.

These will be more expensive than taxis but offer a more comfortable and personalized service with larger, nicer vehicles available. Uber is not available in all areas due to conflicts with taxi companies but is an option in many, if not most, places.

Taxi drivers in larger cities like Mexico City complain that

Uber and other ride-sharing apps have cost them as much as 40% of their business and are unfair because ride-sharing drivers don't have to pay the taxes and fees that cab drivers do.

On the flip side, consumers argue that ride-sharing, such as Uber, is less expensive but more convenient, reliable, and safe than taxis. Sounds like Capitalism at work, doesn't it?!

MEXICAN BUS TRAVEL

Bus travel in Mexico is among the finest in the world. Bus stations, called centrales camioneras, are comparable to European train depots.

The quality and frequency of Mexican buses will delight any traveller, especially those who have experienced their counterparts in the United States.

No single website provides a one-stop guide to Mexican buses, so at first glance, finding information on the web may seem as chaotic as the bus terminals themselves! But if you know where you're going, the web offers great tools for novice and veteran travellers.

MEXICO BUS TRAVEL INFORMATION

Bus travel in Mexico is among the finest in the world. Bus stations, called *centrales camioneras*, are comparable to

European train depots. The quality and frequency of Mexican buses will delight any traveller, especially those who have experienced their counterparts in the United States.

No single website provides a one-stop guide to Mexican buses, so at first glance, finding information on the web may seem as chaotic as the bus terminals themselves! But if you know where you're going, there are many great tools to use.

Here is a quick list of bus companies that have been around a long time and have a good reputation;

ADO

ADO has the perfect bus service for you regardless of where you're headed in Mexico. With its extensive range of routes and ticket prices, they make it easy to get around the country comfortably and on budget.

These are the brands that make up the ADO family:

- ADO

- ADO GL

- ADO Platino

- Diamante

- Estrella de Oro Pluss

- Estrella de Oro www.estrelladeoro.com.mx/ This well-known bus line is more than 50 years old and provides service to Pacific-coast destinations like Acapulco and Ixtapa and inland towns like Taxco.

- Texcoco

- AU

- Cristobal Colon

- Cuenca

- ADO aeropuerto

- Ado Conecta

- OCC

Grupo Senda

One of the great things about Grupo Senda is that they have buses that cross over from Mexico to the USA plus a vast area of Mexico.

They have onboard wifi, complimentary food and drink, bathroom facilities, A/C and some buses come with an individual TV screen, extra legroom and reclinable seats, depending on your destination and level of service you pay for.

Omnibus de México

Omnibus de México operates one of the most extensive bus networks in the country and has routes in about two-thirds of Mexico's states, principally those north, west and east of the capital.

ACN Autobuses

ACN has routes crossing over both sides of the Mexico-United States border as well as nationwide routes.

ETN and Turistar Lujo

ETN is one of Mexico's best luxury bus companies. With only 24 seats and a configuration of three seats across (two on one side and one on the other side, rather than the usual four more commonly found on other bus lines), giving you the option of having an individual seat.

They have onboard WiFi, complimentary food and drink, bathrooms, A/C, power outlets, TV, individual TV screens, extra legroom, leg rest, reclinable seats, bed seats, all for a price.

Grupo AERS (Costaline, Futura, Turistar Ejecutivo)

Grupo AERS offers different bus lines depending on your budget and destination. They do offer complimentary food and drink, bathrooms, A/C, TV, individual TV screens, extra legroom, leg rest and reclinable seats, all depending on the line you pick and the price you pay.

DOMESTIC AIR TRAVEL IN MEXICO

Mexico has an extensive network of airports, and Mexico City has, for many years, been the "hub" for airline travel in Mexico. Recently, as more cities open up airports, you can travel from one airport to another and bypass Mexico City.

Domestic airfares in Mexico have ceased to be the bargain they once were. Occasionally airlines will run special offers but overall, "low-cost" airfares have been rising gradually as markets mature.

The four main domestic carriers: Aeromexico, VivaAerobus, Interjet, and Volaris, have all moved to provide what the airlines term "unbundled pricing" which means that the ticket price does not include things like baggage, seat assignment, or priority boarding—these once-included services are now optional extras, sold separately.

Airfares for transportation across less popular routes in Mexico, where only one domestic airline operates (or two, with one of the two offerings, a very limited schedule), can still be expensive—like the situation that existed before the market was opened up.

BUS STATION AT MEXICO CITY'S AIRPORT

Mexico City's airport has a bus station adjacent to it. You

can take a bus directly from Mexico City's airport to many cities, including Cuernavaca, Puebla, and Queretaro. Buses also depart to the airport in Toluca, where other low-cost flights operate. For a wider choice of destinations, you will need to travel from the airport to one of Mexico City's four bus stations.

FLIGHT TIMES IN MEXICO

Approximate Flying Times from Mexico City to:

- Acapulco – 55 minutes

- Aguascalientes – 45 minutes

- Cancun – 90 minutes

- Chihuahua City – 75 minutes

- Guadalajara – 60 minutes

- Huatulco – 85 minutes

- La Paz – 120 minutes

- Los Cabos – 120 minutes

- Los Mochis (for Copper Canyon) – 75 minutes

- Merida – 90 minutes

- Monterrey – 75 minutes

- Morelia – 45 minutes

- Oaxaca – 60 minutes

- Puerto Vallarta – 90 minutes

- Veracruz – 45 minutes

CHAPTER 19: QUICK SUMMARY

- Driving in Mexico, even in Mexico City, is not as scary as many people make it out to be. If you can drive in Toronto, NYC, LA or Atlanta, then you can drive in Mexico City.

- Under Mexican law, you must have auto liability insurance from a Mexican insurer to drive your vehicle on Mexican roadways.

- The emergency services number is 911 for all services, but you can call 066 for police, ambulance or fire.

- Have your driver and vehicle documentation on hand at all times when you are driving in Mexico.

- To drive in Mexico, you should be a minimum of 15 years old with adult supervision or 18.

- Importing a car to Mexico can be expensive and complicated.

- If you drive a non-Mexican plated car across the border but remain within the "Free Zones," you do not need to apply for and obtain a temporary import permit for your vehicle.

- Temporary import permits (TIPs) are controlled by Aduana Mexico (customs) and are needed if you travel outside the Baja Peninsula or the border zones, as mentioned above.

- A Mexican driver's license may require a written test in Spanish and/or a behind-the-wheel test.

- Taxis are widely available in tourist areas and almost every city. To compete with Uber, some cities, such as Puerto Vallarta, have a Taxi app for your phone that makes getting a taxi super simple.

- Bus travel in Mexico is among the finest in the world. Bus stations, called centrales camioneras, are comparable to European train depots.

- Mexico has an extensive network of airports, and Mexico City has, for many years, been the "hub" for airline travel in Mexico.

- Mexico City's airport has a bus station adjacent to it. You can take a bus directly from Mexico City's airport to many cities, including Cuernavaca, Puebla, and Queretaro.

In chapter 20, we discuss real estate in Mexico. The buying and selling of your property. How to rent and where.

REAL ESTATE IN MEXICO

BIENES RACIES EN MEXICO

Buy land, they're not making it anymore.

MARK TWAIN

Mexico is a country with nearly 1.2 million miles (2 million km) of land space; it's a vast place, and you will need to decide what area of Mexico you want to live in. Once you have decided where you want to live, you need to find accommodation that will suit your needs and budget.

Before we go any further in this chapter on real estate, I would highly recommend that you do 1 of 2 things.

1, come to Mexico for an exploratory few weeks to see what city or state most appeals to you. You can read about a city or state, but when you get your feet on the ground, you can either hate it or love it.

2, come with your bags packed and rent an Airbnb for a month. Rent a car and see the neighbourhoods. Maybe start in Mexico City, and then fly to the coast, the mountains or the island of Cozumel and rent a car there.

The initial outlay may be more than you want, but this will help you decide on a near-perfect town or city to spend the next few years.

This will only work if you are just coming with your suitcases; if you are shipping a container full of furniture, this will not be advisable. (See chapter 21: Your Home)

Honestly, if you sign a lease for one year and hate your chosen location, a year can go by quickly. Start looking for another home in another part of town or province and pack up your belongings and move when the time is right. It's just another adventure now, isn't it?

When we moved to Floripa, Brazil, we spent the first three months in one Airbnb. It was close to the hospital where my son was born.

Then, after renting a car, we drove around and found another fantastic area to spend a few months. My mom and daughter came in late July, so we needed a larger home and moved again. Yes, it takes some time and effort, but what a way to see a country or area.

FINDING AN APARTMENT

Many options are available for assistance in finding an apartment or house to rent, especially in tourist areas or larger cities.

Shopping for a rental online can be done through several different online property listing sites:

- https://www.metroscubicos.com

- https://www.inmuebles24.com

- https://www.homie.mx/h/

- https://www.vivanuncios.com.mx

Craigslist is available in several Mexican cities, such as Mexico City https://mexicocity.craigslist.org/, Guadalajara https://

guadalajara.craigslist.org/ etc. Go to Craigslist for Mexico, https://geo.craigslist.org/iso/mx, to find the city in which you are searching for a rental. Some say that Craigslist targets expats and non-natives and will cause you to pay more for a rental.

If you navigate securing a rental yourself, either online or directly with a landlord via a sign in the window, you are much more likely to be able to negotiate the most favourable terms if you speak Spanish. Otherwise, you might be better off having some assistance.

Having a trusted advisor familiar with local renter/landlord laws to help you through the rental process can be invaluable, especially if you are not fluent in Spanish.

Many realtors in Mexico handle home and apartment rentals. It relieves a lot of stress to obtain assistance with your transaction from a realtor familiar with the different areas in the city where you are planning to move. You may not know which areas are undesirable or prone to intolerable traffic conditions, but your realtor will. The services of a real estate agent should be free for you as the landlord pays their fees.

A 6 or 12-month lease would be a typical term with one or two months' rent as a deposit to be paid with your first month's rent. Rents can increase annually, and your contract may require one month's advance notice of when you plan to vacate.

All homes have propane tanks, as there are no natural gas lines like we have back in Canada. A gas tanker comes to your home to fill it. All your cooking will be done with gas, as is the hot water heating for the washer and dryer.

Power comes from CFE (Comision Federal de Electricidad) which is a federal institution in charge of the production and distribution of power in the country.

Power bills are based on a subsidized tier system. If you use a lot of power, you pay more per kilowatt, simple as that.

As for your water, many Mexican homes have a tinaco (water tank) on the roof to hold water, and the water system is fed by gravity. In addition, they will often have an underground cistern to hold water, which is pumped up to the tinaco as required.

While the city supplies water, it is not direct to residential faucets the way it is in Canada or the USA.

It comes to your cistern during the week, and you store it until you need it. And because it's not a pressurized system, no paper products go into the toilet. That's why you will always see a garbage can next to the toilet in Mexican bathrooms.

RENTING OUR APARTMENT

When we moved from Abu Dhabi, UAE, to Panama, my mother was in charge of finding a suitable location for us to live permanently. We didn't want the hassles of finding a place AFTER arriving here. It wasn't feasible for us to make an exploratory trip; the flights alone took two days and several thousand dollars.

It took us three months to decide that Panama was the place for us, so we decided to rent an apartment sight unseen.

My mother spent several hours reviewing listings of appropriate apartments, the prices, sizes, pool or gym, bedrooms and location. She put them all on a spreadsheet, and one by one, we either liked it, or we didn't. My wife and I were on the same page for the most part. Finally, we agreed on the apartment and reached out to the realtor who advertised the apartment. My mother worked with a lovely gal named Mahyn, a French expat turned Panamanian Real Estate agent who has since become our good friend. We asked lots of questions, and she took videos of the apartment, went outside and took pictures of the stores and what they looked like in our neighbourhood.

When all of us were in agreement, we wired half the money to the owners, and when we got to Panama, everything went well for the most part. We were in a hotel for three nights until the apartment was cleaned, but it was all good. Could we have lost everything? I don't think so. But saying that, if you can, make a trip to the country you are moving to and check out a few places, see where you would really like to spend the following year, and make the decision.

BUYING REAL ESTATE IN MEXICO

Buying a property is not easy, although it is more advantageous than renting. Several laws govern real estate transactions, and you need to pay attention to them so that you don't have any legal problems.

Technically, foreigners are not allowed to own property within 30 miles of any coastline or within 60 miles of a national border in Mexico. These are called 'restricted zones.'

A good example is buying real estate in Puerto Vallarta (or anywhere along the coast of Mexico). Foreigners do it day in and day out. They establish a "fideicomiso" or beneficial trust held with a Mexican Bank on your behalf and has worked well and with few problems for over 50 years.

One also needs to be aware that some properties listed for sale can be 'ejido' land, which means that the property may be communally owned or in some kind of dispute, title-wise.

Some realtors will proceed with negotiations and transactions on these properties, but this is strongly ill-advised, and they are best avoided.

In most places in Mexico, there is no MLS listing service, so obtaining the assistance of a good realtor familiar with your area of choice is essential.

Some cities, like Puerto Vallarta, for example, have an MLS. Still, a real estate agent will be invaluable in guiding your search for a home and then lining up any attorneys, translators or notaries you may need to complete your purchase.

Google 'realtors in ____, Mexico' for your city of choice, and you will find plenty of knowledgeable real estate professionals in almost every city and tourist area. Facebook groups are also good places to get recommendations on realtors.

The real estate market in Mexico for Americans and Canadians is a cash market, for the most part.

It is possible to get a mortgage in Mexico under certain conditions, but interest rates will not be as favourable as you are accustomed to in the US or Europe.

An expat-owned mortgage company in Mexico caters to foreigners looking to secure a mortgage for their home purchase: http://mexlend.com.

Mexlend can facilitate mortgages anywhere in Mexico from their offices in Puerto Vallarta.

There is sometimes the opportunity to obtain developer financing on new properties. And occasionally, homeowners are willing to finance the property they are selling at least partially.

Inform your realtor if you are particularly interested in finding a property with some financing available.

WHAT'S THE APPROXIMATE COST OF DIFFERENT PROPERTIES IN MEXICO?

While prices vary from place to place, the cost of properties on the beach and in major cities is roughly the same.

This table will give you an idea of some average property prices around Mexico.

LOCATION	PROPERTY TYPE	COST
Playa Del Carmen	1 BR 1 Bath Apartment	$2,695,000 MXN $ 135,749 USD
Polanco, Mexico City	2 BR 1 Bath Apartment	$4,500,000 MXN $ 226,669 USD
Ecatepec, Mexico City	3 BR 2 Bath House	$980,000 MXN $ 49,367 USD
Guadalajara	2 BR 1 Bath Apartment	$1,255,000 MXN $ 61,711 USD
Puerto Vallarta	3 BR 4 Bath House	$5,831,000 MXN $ 293,746 USD
Monterrey	3 BR 4 Bath House	$5,385,000 MXN $ 271,278 USD

USING A NOTARY

Suppose you are interested in living, opening a business or buying property in Mexico. In that case, the first thing you need to do is hire a notary to guide you through the legal process.

A Notary (or Notario) in Mexico has very similar functions to an American notary, but the importance and power in Mexico is much more significant.

A Notary provides legal advice, gives authority to transactions and is usually appointed by the Governor. All notaries are lawyers, but very few lawyers achieve the status of a notary.

This is different from the US where anyone can take a test and become a notary.

In Mexico, as in all countries in Latin America using the same notary system, their function is to advise clients, interpret wills, and write, read, explain and authorize all relevant documents.

The Notary assists in various acts such as powers of attorney, incorporation of companies, purchases, donations, mortgages, trusts, and inheritance.

The Notary also attests to facts, makes notifications, requirements, existence and capacity of people, recognizes signatures, and gives faith to legal protocols and facts.

A NOTARY IN REAL ESTATE

A Mexican notary plays a vital role when buying real estate in Mexico; their main task is to identify the buyer and seller, explain the contract's content, and resolve issues.

He/She determines the characteristics of the property you are about to purchase, the amount of time it will take to complete the operation, and arranges your different payment methods.

They will review and perform the paperwork needed for

the deed, evaluate the property's value, and determine the corresponding taxes. All of this will allow him to check and correct any misunderstandings.

Once the established requirements that the buyer needs to comply with to buy real estate have been met; the taxes have been paid, the documents signed and sent to the public registry, the transmission of the property and the testimony that corresponds to the buyer will be delivered so that it is registered in the Public Registry of the Property and the change of ownership is made.

Finally, consider that the buyer pays the expenses of the Notary's fees.

Remember that resolving doubts involving the purchase of the real estate in Mexico does not generate any cost since advice and consultancy are offered free of charge throughout the country.

The expenses on the services performed by the Notario depend on the state where he is located, but only one-sixth of the costs correspond to purchasing fees. The rest is applied for different reasons:

• Procedures for obtaining different certificates,

• Taxes for acquisition, and

• Expenses generated by the appraised and the new house scriptures.

USEFUL TERMS

- Lawyer or solicitor - *Abogada o abogado*

- Estate Agent - *Agente inmobiliario*

- Apartment - *Apartamento*

- Architect - *Arquitecto*

- Tax Consultant - *Consultor de impuestos*

- Bathroom - *Cuarto de baño*

- Kitchen - *Cocina*

- Community of owners - *Residents Association Condomínio*

- Purchase/Buying and selling - *Compra/Compra y Venta*

- Purchase Contract - *Contrato de Compra*

- Address - *Dirección*

- Bedroom - *Cuarto*

- Title Deeds - *Títulos de propiedad*

- Mortgage - *Hipoteca*

- Tax - *Impuesto*

- Value Added Tax - *Impuesto al valor agregado*

- Key - *Llave*

- License - Licenca

- Light - *Luz*

- Furniture - *Muebles*

- Notary Public - *Notario público*

- Swimming Pool - *Piscina*

- Property - *Propriedad*

- Resident - *Residente*

- Company - *Empresa*

- Insurance - *Seguro*

- Terrace - *Terraza*

OBTAINING BASIC SERVICES: ELECTRICITY, WATER

You'll need to arrange for utilities before you move into a house. If you're renting, these will already be installed–but new construction will require new connections.

Electricity — To be connected to the central electrical grid, your home must be within 114 feet (35m) of an electrical post. You will need to hire an electrician to set up the wiring and install the meter and energy cable.

Water Supply — Most urban areas receive their water through the main water supply running through Mexico. Some people also choose to hire water trucks to supply water. You may want to install a purification system because tap water is of questionable quality in many places.

It is your responsibility to pay these bills on time, do not expect a statement to come in the mail like back home.

HOW DO I PAY FOR MY PROPERTY?

Unlike in your home country, where you can get a mortgage from the bank or mortgage company at 1% for 25 years, foreign countries do not like to offer this service to expats. If they do, the interest rate can be 6-8%. You must show proof of income and employment if you're a permanent resident or married to a Mexican national who can act as your guarantor.

Keep in mind that different banks can require additional documents. Make sure you do your due diligence when applying for loans outside Mexico or your home country. Again, without seeming repetitive, ask your lawyer and never attempt these things yourself. It is just not worth it.

HERE ARE 8 OPTIONS TO CONSIDER FOR FINANCING YOUR INTERNATIONAL PURCHASE

Pay Cash

If you have the cash to buy outright, this is an option. Sellers love the hassle-free, quick close of a cash transaction. Cash can make you a desirable buyer, and you might negotiate a better price or win a bidding war as the trouble-free buyer.

However, you also need to consider what else you could do with that money and whether or not you want that much of your cash tied up in one deal.

Seller Financing Or Owner Financing

Look at developments where the builder offers some financing. Even some standalone properties will have owners willing to provide financing. However, the deals can still require a significant amount of cash (50% or more down), and interest rates can be very high, in the 8-12% range, so financing doesn't provide much more flexibility than paying all cash.

Get A Mortgage From A Bank

As mentioned earlier, it's challenging and costly for foreigners to get a mortgage from a bank. Interest rates are high, borrowing limits are low, and options are limited.

Find A Money Partner To Fund The Deal

If you can't get funding from a bank, the builder or the owner/ seller, you might still get financing from a money partner willing to fund the deal in exchange for profits.

You will likely need a good track record or specialized knowledge to obtain this type of funding, and if this is your first home, you don't want to have to split the profits of the sale years down the road.

Private Loan

You can get a money partner to fund the deal for profit, a private lender. This is not a great option, as interest rates can be very high.

Line Of Credit On Your Business

If you have a large enough line of credit, this is an excellent means to obtain money at a very low-interest rate. And depending on the size of the line of credit, it might be high enough to cover your Mexican purchase.

Use A HELOC

A Home Equity Line of Credit can let homeowners borrow money against the equity they've built in their homes. HELOCs can offer flexibility in borrowing, but they have limitations. They also carry the risk of foreclosure and can require considerable discipline.

This will only work if you keep your existing home in the USA; otherwise, this will not be feasible.

Do A Cash-out Refinance

If you have rental income back home, here is a great way to leverage them. Refinance and take the available funds to purchase your home in Mexico.

If you want property in Mexico to diversify your investments internationally but only want a property to use but not necessarily own, you could consider buying a US rental investment that provides sufficient cash flow to pay for your rental in Mexico.

This way, you're making a real estate investment, and still getting abroad, but it's a domestic investment that doesn't come with the hassles of international ownership.

CURRENCY

Buying any property generally involves a significant amount of money.

When converting from one currency to another, the difference between one exchange rate and another can make a difference of thousands of dollars on your purchase.

Do not underestimate the difference a good exchange rate can make, especially concerning pesos and dollars. We know people who have sold properties and have made more money on the exchange rate difference than they have to sell their property.

I recommend you investigate the best and safest ways of sending your money abroad. As currency dealers have increasingly sophisticated products, you can agree on rates for the future. They can advise you when to buy or agree to buy for you when the rate hits a certain level. You can even agree to a fixed rate for longer periods if you make regular payments abroad (for example, for a mortgage or moving your pension money). We work with currency dealers we have known for years, who can give you a good exchange rate for your purchase.

SELLING YOUR HOME

The most important thing when selling your home, and before you sign an agreement with the realtor who will be selling your home, is to find out how much Capital Gains Tax (IRS) you will have to pay as this amount will be deducted from the sale price of your home. Hire a good tax attorney to make sure you get the very lowest amount to be paid, a good attorney can usually figure out what kind of deductions can be used to bring this cost down, in some cases, way down.

The Capital Gains Tax is calculated by taking the sale of the house, minus the cost you paid, minus all deductions, and that is the Capital Gains. From there, you will apply a tax rate of between 1.92% to 35%, depending on how much the Capital Gains are. This is why it is important to hire a good attorney and a good realtor to ensure the price you sell for reflects the price you will pay in Capital Gains.

Capital gains exemptions are only available to temporary residents, permanent residents and Mexican citizens. If you hold a tourist visa, you don't qualify for the capital gains exemption,

To qualify, you must have an RFC (Registro Federal de Contribuyentes - a Mexican tax ID), and you need to attach it to a utility bill for your home. This will prove that you have lived there for the required three years as your principal residence.

I would suggest you get a good realtor, one you trust and who knows his/her job inside out. Their fees are 6-8% of the selling price and can be as high as 10%. You will also need to pay the Mexican Value Added Tax IVA (16%) onto the agent's commission cost, and the seller is responsible for making this payment.

Again, you will need your notary; it's a must. If you liked the first one you used when you purchased the home, just keep them. Suppose you hold your title inside a fideicomiso - within 62 miles (100 km) of an international border or within 31 miles (50 km) of the ocean. In that case, you will also need to budget for the 'trust cancellation fee', which is about $1,000 USD.

THE ROLE OF THE REALTOR IN REAL ESTATE TRANSACTIONS

The real estate broker can be considered a negotiator whose role is to facilitate the buying and selling of real estate between the developer and the consumer. When a real estate negotiation takes place, you always want to get the best deal, and it is the broker who will present the various options that may suit your needs.

The broker must also inform you about the main aspects of the property. They must act not only as a negotiator but as a professional in consultation, showing the characteristics of the place and the neighbourhood, such as services offered in the region, businesses and if the region tends to appreciate in value.

In addition, the broker greatly assists you in searching for the documents needed to carry out the business, facilitating and comprehensively explaining how all the legal procedures in the purchase of property work, causing future headaches to be generated during the entire process of real estate transactions. Be sure to do research and find a reliable real estate broker that can offer a complete and high-quality service, in addition to being on top of everything.

If you have a good broker and pay attention to the primary laws that govern real estate transactions, buying your property will become more straightforward, and your dream of owning your own home will be more tangible.

BEFORE YOU BUY, WHAT TO CONSIDER

As I've already mentioned and will mention again, buying property in Mexico is a lot different than buying property back home. Buying real estate is one of the most significant investments you can make.

It can also be one of the most stressful. And any stress can be compounded when buying abroad, with additional complications such as language barriers and unfamiliarity with local laws and procedures. That said, you can legally and successfully purchase property in Mexico, but you must approach it differently than what you might be accustomed to.

SO, HOW ARE THINGS DIFFERENT?

More **due diligence** is needed. Due to less regulation and oversight, a greater degree of due diligence is required to ensure no issues with the property. And the principle of

more due diligence is better, never hurts.

Pick a reliable and honest realtor who has a good work ethic. Back home, the only differences between realtors may be their work ethic, how many years of experience they've had and whether their personality or style matches yours. However, in Mexico, other critical differences exist in Mexico, such as reputation, honesty and trustworthiness. As a result, only work with an agent who comes highly regarded and recommended from more than one source. Ask the realtor for references and check them.

Carefully Inspect, Verify And Scrutinize The Property Before You Buy

Get a home inspection. Don't skip the survey. Make sure the property or development has an adequate water supply. And determine if the water source is municipal water or water coming from a private well on the property.

Check out the water quality and pressure levels. How about sanitation – how will wastewater be processed? How will the garbage from the development be disposed of?

Also, check out the neighbours. Who are they? What do they do on their property? Make sure they don't burn garbage daily or have dogs barking all night, and learn what they do on their land. Spend lots of time on property due diligence. Check to verify who owns the property is the person who is selling it. And, don't buy property you haven't personally seen at least twice. If you're building, visit often.

Before you purchase,

- Visit the property several times.

- Interview multiple realtors and attorneys.

- Visit numerous property developments.

- Do your homework and look far and wide for a great deal.

You will be happy you did.

If You Don't Get The Best Deal, Be Prepared To Walk Away

A massive contributor to financial success is ensuring you have purchased your property at a great price. By great, I mean fantastic, and not just good. Also, other factors are essential, such as ensuring the property is of high quality, that there are no such problems as liens or title defects, and the development and the local community are safe and of high quality. But your final price will likely make or break your long-term financial success with the property.

Use Legal Documents With Robust Buyer Protection Built In

Since realtors and lawyers don't use one standardized set of legal documents sanctioned by some type of oversight entity that governs real estate purchases, work with someone who uses a set of tested, tried-and-true documents.

They should have multiple buyer protections built-in (or review multiple document sets from many different attorneys and realtors to create your own).

MLS IN MEXICO

The MLS system in Mexico has been slow to catch on, although numerous attempts have been made to create a national network.

The first MLS system originated in Puerto Vallarta as www. MLSVallarta.com in 1988 and existed for a short period in the Los Cabos region as MLSCabo.com in the early 90s. They originated in these two markets as the majority of buyers are American or Canadian and familiar with the benefits of an MLS real estate system in their home markets. MLS systems have not had as much success in other parts of Mexico. The Cabo system underwent a few structural changes before contracting with FLEX MLS software in 2010.

Today, it represents over 90 brokers in the State of Baja California Sur. It is now called MLS BCS (www.mlsinbajasur. com), which operates as a corporation in which each subscriber Broker is permitted to own one voting share.

Brokers and agents subscribe through MLS BCS upon meeting requirements and committing to following a strict set of Operating Policies and Procedures, requiring each listing to be Exclusive and the broker to have a complete property records file in his office on each listing.

The MLS BCS has been invited to participate in the oversight council of the new Real Estate Agent License Registry, helping to write the Code of Ethics for the 2017 State License law.

MLS BCS is generally recognized as the country's model for MLS operation. In Puerto Vallarta and Riviera Nayarit,

MLSVallarta.com still serves the region as Mexico's oldest and longest-running MLS system.

MLS Vallarta is a private, independent MLS system with membership for qualifying brokers and developers. The Puerto Vallarta and Riviera Nayarit real estate associations formed their own MLS system in 2012, known as www.VallartaNayaritMLS.com, adopting the same FLEX system used in the Los Cabos region.

Membership rules exist for both systems in Vallarta systems, and only legal, existing real estate businesses can apply for membership. Both are well used by local brokers, developers and the buying/selling public.

Think Ahead To Ownership – Choose Partners Now That You'll Need After The Purchase

Once you purchase your property, you'll want to use it, rent it, improve it or maybe even build a new structure.

These activities will require finding reputable, honest, trustworthy property managers, remodelling companies, interior designers, builders, and the like.

This task isn't easy. Similar to finding a good realtor and attorney, it will take some work.

So, before the purchase, start the search for reputable post-purchase partners to ensure you'll be able to find them in your local area.

Some properties in Mexico are extremely remote, which

can make the task of finding solid post-purchase resources challenging. Figure out if this is going to be an issue before you buy instead of realizing it afterwards.

Don't Rush It, But Rush It When You Need To

As a general rule, don't delay making an offer once you find the property you want to buy, as truly exceptional properties are hard to find anywhere in the world. However, don't buy property you haven't visited. No matter how much research you do – talking with knowledgeable friends, looking at pictures, getting information from the internet – never buy unless you've visited the condo, house, or land. And be sure to do your due diligence to ensure the property and title are clean. So, if you find a great property at an exceptional price, do your homework, but move fast.

Due To These Differences, Be An Engaged Buyer

You, as the buyer, must drive and understand the process. You must own your property process search in earnest. So, get educated. Owning property in Mexico can be a satisfying, enjoyable and rewarding experience, but you must approach purchasing differently than buying property at home.

EXPECTED RETURNS ON YOUR REAL ESTATE INVESTMENT

As a basic rule of thumb for vacation rental properties in recent years, you can expect an annual net return of 4 – 6% on your investment. According to local property managers, on average, a good rental property will rent for about 65% of the year. But these figures can climb as high as netting an 8 – 10% on investment if you build or buy the right kind of rental for the growing premium rental market.

Depending on the features of the property, the average rental home can expect occupancy rates of

- 75 – 100% occupancy rate December – April,

- 25 – 50% May – July

- 10 – 25% August – September, and November

- 0 – 10% October

WHAT TO LOOK FOR WHEN PURCHASING A POTENTIAL RENTAL PROPERTY

Purchasing a property within walking distance to the beach or one with great ocean views will typically see a better return than homes with a jungle view or ones that are far from tourist destinations.

Qualities for a vacation rental:

- Close proximity to the beach

- Close proximity to amenities

- Security and or gate

- Clean and comfortable

- Private

To be a great income property in Mexico, property managers will advise that you have some or all the following features:

- At least three bedrooms for families; or a small, separate, private villa on your property for couples

- En suite bathrooms in the main bedrooms

- Oceanview

- Pool

- A/C (at least in the bedrooms)

- Internet

- Cell service capability

- TV/Satellite

- Wildlife and birdlife sightings

Additional features that will add to the success of a rental property are:

- Microwave

- Toaster

- Beach chairs

- Guest information book with preferred tour companies, local eateries, etc

- Pool/lounge chairs

- Blow dryer for each bathroom

- Blender for smoothies/drinks

- Kitchenware, like a strainer, cooking knives, serving spoons, etc.

- Board games or playing cards

- Books

- Candles, flashlights

- Flower vases, preferably the tall square variety made of thick glass

- A large selection of good quality bath and beach towels

- 2+ sheet sets and a comforter/shams for each bed

- 2 sets of zippered covers for all pillows

- 2 mattress covers for each bed

LOCAL PROPERTY MANAGERS CAN HELP MARKET YOUR PROPERTY

Many local property management companies can market, rent and manage your property and clients. They promote locally and internationally and address questions and concerns, taking care of clients before and while renting. They handle billing and taking records for you and generally take a 20% commission for all of the above work.

Often, rental properties in Mexico will be featured on VRBO and Airbnb, as these are the top sources for acquiring vacation rental bookings worldwide.

Positive reviews on any online rental platform are the most helpful tool for positioning your property as a great rental in Mexico and receiving more bookings.

Professional photos with great hospitality staging are standard tools used by some of your area's most frequented property rentals.

If you want to manage your rental property, especially if you live locally, it is easy to do when using the right tools for the job.

Typical Vacation Rental Property Ownership Costs

- Property insurance

- HOA fees (if applicable to your development)

- Utilities (water, electric, gas, cable)

- Property insurance (weather damage, vandalism)

- Pool maintenance

- Cleaning services

- Repairs and maintenance

- Exterior landscaping

REAL LIFE STORY FROM THE HAPPY HUATULCAN!

Part 1: April 2021

I got our realtor's name from a friend who was pleased with her. When we arrived in Huatulco, she showed us six places based on our preferences. There was one that stood out in terms of value for the money. It was a new build, so we met with the architects to discuss timelines and options.

They were/are surprisingly flexible about our modifications - and here's the more shocking part - they did not charge us more for extras than builders here in Canada would certainly have done.

My husband has been a contractor for years, so he was very surprised when we asked for under-cupboard lighting in the kitchen, extra shower accessories in each shower, lighting and finish per the model unit, and a different choice of granite and floor colour than their palate.

It occurred to me that they priced upgrades into the asking price, but we were prepared to pay 240K USD for a 2 bed, 2.5 bath condo anyway. Where we live in Ontario, Canada, where $400K won't buy a trailer park model 1-bed on a leased lot, so 240K USD feels like a bargain for 24 hr security, a rooftop 22m pool, BBQ with pizza oven, and common area loungers/tables.

One of the nuances of our condo is that it is a mere block from the ocean, and therefore as foreigners, we needed to create a Land Trust (Fideicomiso) through a local lawyer. Again, our agent set that up for us; it cost 150 USD, and the lawyer was completely fluent in English and was a lovely fellow. We will use him again for VISAs.

The one thing we knew about but still was a bit shocking is the 7% purchase price fee – Purchaser's Acquisition Tax. It's a big hit up front, but our annual property tax will be around $1200 yr. Given that we pay nearly that per month in Canada, again, it feels like a deal.

A few other things we learned are that these costs can be deducted from the capital gains on selling, i.e. notary/legal fees, real estate commission, furniture allowance, and if you have residency, you can apply for a 5-year capital gains credit.

So there you have it - easy peasy - the key message is to employ a trusted local to help navigate their system. Hopefully, our move there in October this year will be as seamless!

Part 2: January 2022

Since the story left off in April 2021, and covid continued to make both travel and supply chain issues a challenge, we did not get to Huatulco until early December 2021 as opposed to the Oct 2021 goal.

But let me step back and comment on the fiasco associated with getting an appointment with one of the Mexican Consulates in Canada. After a year of cancelled or unavailable appointments in Ontario, I called every consulate in Canada. I was surprised at the differences in process...and wait times or unwillingness to offer appointments, such as the one in Montreal that only sees residents of QC.

After many emails and phone calls, I finally got a returned call from Vancouver for an interview in 2 weeks! I took the appointment and booked a flight, and it worked out fine (great way to use all of those WestJet cancelled flight credits!). Not only was the lady there very helpful, but I was also granted the first part of permanent residency in 1 day.

Once I got to Mexico, they did their part within a week. The total cost of using a Mexican lawyer was about $500 USD and very straightforward once the Canada-end of the gauntlet was run!

Our condo was delivered as promised and surpassed our quality expectations. We love the 180-degree view with floor-to-ceiling patio doors, amenities and access to everything within 5-15 minutes of walking, including a block from the beach.

This particular area of Mexico is interesting in that it is only a 35-year-old "planned community" that is really only just starting to mature, so it doesn't feel crowded, dirty and "Americanized" like Cancun. As a matter of fact, there are no "name brand" chain stores here - locals and expats prefer the "small community feel." The town of Crucecita is as charming as Mexico gets, with little shops and a huge "el Centro" to sit and people watch.

Another fabulous aspect of Huatulco (total population 50K) is that it is made up of a cluster of smaller towns, each tucked into conservation areas and with building height restrictions of no more than 4 floors. The sidewalks are wide, shaded and very well-groomed. The number of city employees here is impressive. Every day they are out in full force watering boulevards, sweeping sidewalks and managing gardens.

Everyone here says "Buenos Dias" or "hola" to every passerby. Kids help their families in stores or as street vendors, and there certainly aren't any elderly without the arm of a teenager to lean on. The frolic at the beaches is wild and loud and exactly the way a beach should be enjoyed!

The locals are warm, welcoming and kind. It truly feels like a step back in time to when family and community were the priority. And I'll comment here on something that is mentioned repeatedly – safety in Mexico. I had a conversation with a Mexicana who is raising 2 children herself, and she specifically moved to Huatulco because of the safety aspect. This topic seems to be a point of pride in this area, and perhaps we can boast a high level of safety simply because people all seem to make a living here.

There are countable (on one hand) street people and all known to the locals who help out by offering water and food. On a similar topic, there are relatively few street animals thanks to several active organizations that raise money for pet and stray sterilization, as well as several that arrange international pet adoption services. This has been the one consistent blemish across all Latin American countries we have travelled to over the years...but gratefully not here.

Let's talk about houses since we just bought our second! It is sticker shock in reverse here!

Since house prices in Canada have gone stratospheric, most homeowners could capitalize on location arbitrage. That $1 million Cdn end-town home in Milton, Ontario, could be exchanged for a penthouse condo overlooking the ocean that comes with 4 pools, 4 tennis courts, 9 hole golf course, a gym, restaurants etc. Or check out this 3 bedroom, ocean view, 3000 sq ft villa for $1 million Cdn.

The sensible thing to do would be to get a modern 1000 ft condo for $300K and bank the $700K because it would take a long time to burn through that here! If buying locally, the food costs are a similar happy shock as houses. So how much would a dozen eggs, 1 kg of flour, 1 kg sugar, granola, cream, 4 bananas and 2 avocados cost in Canada? The cost here is $6 Cdn.

When we are "splurging" at our favourite Thai restaurant, we have a hard time spending more than 300 pesos (15 USD) which includes beer or a cocktail. A typical "street food" meal such as tacos or tluydas for 2 people plus a beverage is $7 USD. And it's tasty, healthy food - free-range meat, homemade shells and often homemade cheese.

There is the social/political consideration which during this covid situation is glaringly different in Mexico. In essence, the federal government advised each province to manage covid the way that worked best for them. Our particular area experiences a lot of domestic tourism as many people from Mexico and Oaxaca Cities vacation here, so most businesses were open for most of the pandemic.

Unlike Canada, which forced certain businesses to close, then doled out welfare, Mexico does not have the same resources... And from the expat's view, life is just carrying on as usual here in contrast to Canada, where many provinces are still in various levels of "lockdown" a full 2-years after the start of covid.

So are we happy about moving to Huatulco, Mexico? You bet! After years of research and visiting, this meets and exceeds the vast majority of our requirements.

Signed the Happy Huatulcan!

Thank you, my friend, for your great stories. It's nice to hear how happy you are in Mexico and that buying real estate was considerably easier than expected. It's always nice when that happens.

CHAPTER 20: QUICK SUMMARY

- Mexico is a country with nearly 1.2 million miles (2 million km) of land space; it's a vast place, and you will need to decide what area of Mexico you want to live in.

- Many options are available for assistance in finding an apartment or house to rent, especially in tourist areas or larger cities.

- Many realtors in Mexico handle home and apartment rentals. It relieves a lot of stress to obtain assistance with your transaction from a realtor familiar with the different areas in the city you are planning to move to.

- You cannot drink water in Mexico. You must either purchase your water or put in an under-the-sink filter to provide potable drinking water.

- Technically, foreigners are not allowed to own property within 30 miles of any coastline or within 60 miles of a national border in Mexico. These are called 'restricted zones'.

- A Mexican notary plays a vital role when buying real estate in Mexico. Their main task is to identify the buyer and seller, explain the contract's content, and resolve issues.

- You'll need to arrange for utilities before you move into a house. If you're renting, these will already be installed– but new construction will require new connections.

- As a basic rule of thumb for vacation rental properties in recent years, you can expect an annual net return of 4 –

6% on your investment.

• Many local property management companies can market, rent and manage your property and clients.

Chapter 21 discusses your home and how you will move everything you have to Mexico. There are many choices, and when you finish the chapter, you will better understand which method you would like to use.

CHAPTER 21

YOUR HOME

TU HOGAR

Change is a great and horrible thing, and people love it or hate it at the same time. Without change, however, you just don't move.

MARC JACOBS

In 2019 we shipped our household contents from Dubai to Panama in a cargo container; however, I had several boxes of stuff I had stored at my father's house over the years, and he was moving, so he asked me nicely to get rid of all my stuff! After leaving Abu Dhabi for the last time, we went back to Canada to see my father and some old friends before moving permanently to Panama; plus, I needed to get documents authenticated for my residency process.

We spent a week in Canada, and during that time, I went through the boxes, trying to decide what to do with them all. My mother, who had come from Abu Dhabi with us back to Canada on our way to Panama, also had several containers that she could not bring when she moved to Abu Dhabi in 2017.

There were 11 boxes/crates in total. After assessing what we had and what we wanted to keep, we decided to ship it by air freight with Copa Air. I must say, shipping a container load was more straightforward than shipping 11 boxes.

Firstly, we didn't have a vehicle that would fit that many boxes. For the drive, we had to rent a truck, pay the insurance and drive to Toronto. We had to find the shipping company's location (which took a better part of an hour) and unload our boxes. That was about $150 CAD, and the cost to ship 11 boxes was $450.00 CAD. So $600 CAD in total. I probably should have just thrown it all away, but there was a big box of Legos for my daughter, books that I had had since I was her age, and my mother had stuff from when she a child.

The skid arrived in Panama a few days later, and we were unprepared for what happened next. As a Canadian, I assumed I would go to the airport, prove the shipment was mine, pick it up, and go home. Nope, that was not the case.

It took over two weeks to get our stuff and probably another $100 in Ubers and taxis. It indeed was a nightmare. I didn't realize what a headache this would be.

At one point, my mother and my assistant Eli went to the airport, and my mother was asked to open all the containers so they could see what was in them. Then, they got in a car, went outside the facility and sat in the car for almost an hour while the immigration officer tried to decide how much tax she would pay for this stuff. Talk about stress. After an hour, they drove back and said he couldn't figure it out, and they were closing as it was noon, and they would try and figure something out tomorrow. Back home by Uber, again.

On the next visit, my assistant was so pissed he got into an argument and punched the guy in the nose for being such an idiot and spent the night in jail. Still, no stuff.

After five trips to the airport, finally we got it all (2 weeks later). My mother cried when it arrived. She was sure we would never get our things, but we did, and there were no extra charges attached to the shipment. I'm still not sure why this took so long. Knowing what I know now, I would suggest you use DHL. It's door-to-door pickup and drop-off. Yes, it costs more, but you will have fewer headaches.

CUSTOMS IN MEXICO

To move household goods into Mexico, you must have an immigration status of a permanent resident or a temporary resident.

To be excluded from the Mexican IVA tax, your items must enter Mexico no later than six months from the time your visa is fully issued in Mexico.

Here are some documents you must provide to bring household goods into Mexico:

- Resident Card - official document of temporary or permanent resident status

- Bill of Lading (B/L or BoL) - required for transporting goods by sea. If shipping by air, this document is known as the air waybill (AWB)

- Packing list - Detailed catalogue of your goods, including a description and shipping box number for each item

- Proof of last entry date - may be an airline ticket or reservation.

- Proof of address - may be a utility bill dated within three months of your last entry.

- Passport

- Letter of declaration to customs - including your Mexico address, a description of your goods, and acknowledgement of the requirements to bring your goods with you when you move to Mexico.

- Letter of empowerment - authorizes a customs broker you work with to handle and transport your goods.

- Declaration of household goods - required only for permanent residents and Mexican citizens - is optional but also recommended for temporary residents.

WHAT IS ALLOWED INTO MEXICO

Article 90 of the Mexican customs law states that the items you take across the border must be used as personal items (never new) and furniture of a house, for example, clothes, books, furniture, appliances and electronics, linens and outside furniture, and lawn equipment.

Tools and implements are also allowed if required for your profession or used for a hobby. Medical equipment, such as a wheelchair, blood pressure or sugar monitors and oxygen generators, are allowed duty-free. New and unused items and those in unopened packaging may be permitted into Mexico but will likely be subject to duty and other requirements.

Passengers over 18 may bring in up to 10 packs of cigarettes, 25 cigars (not Cuban) or 200 grams of tobacco, and up to 3 litres of liquor or 6 litres of wine.

It is possible to drive into Mexico with your household goods and furnishings, which may or may not require the payment of a modest tax or duty.

WHAT IS NOT ALLOWED INTO MEXICO

If you are flying into Mexico, you can bring up to $500 USD per person in personal items and other permitted goods duty-free. If you enter Mexico by land, $300 USD of goods per person is allowed.

Travellers cannot bring in more than $10,000 USD in currency without declaring the total amount. You can bring in $9,999 USD without any questions, and no need to declare. Please keep in mind that it is the equivalent in other currencies, in cash, cheques, money orders or any other monetary instrument, or a combination of them. You must declare the amount exceeding $10,000 USD. You will not have to pay duties or taxes, but you must declare it on the Customs Declaration form.

No fresh or frozen food, plants, spices, or seeds are allowed. While personal medication, supplements, perfumes or other cosmetics are allowed when carried with your luggage, it is not recommended to ship these items with your household goods. Vehicles, including cars, boats, recreational vehicles and trailers, are not considered household goods and must be declared and approved separately.

Menaje de casa is a permit for moving household and personal items to Mexico. It is available from Mexican consulates and is granted to expats with a temporary or permanent resident card.

At the consulate, you will need a valid photo and a temporary or permanent resident card; you must provide proof of address outside and inside Mexico and four copies listing the household items in your shipment.

Your list must contain a detailed description and the quantity of the goods. You must indicate the brand, model, and the serial number of electronic items. The fee for the menaje de casa permit is $6.35 USD. The tax exemption is only valid for the first six months after you receive your residency card.

And don't forget to get your birth certificate and bring it with you. In Mexico, it is a document that is often required.

NARCOTICS

The prohibition of narcotics and marijuana is serious. There is no such thing as 'medical marijuana in Mexico, and attempting to enter the country with marijuana in any form will likely land you in jail.

FIREARMS WHEN MOVING TO MEXICO

Firearms are heavily restricted, and very specific permits and permissions must be obtained to import weapons and ammunition, such as for hunting. Attempting to enter Mexico with even one shotgun cartridge forgotten in the bed of your pick-up truck can result in a trip to a Mexican jail. This is not a trifling matter. Likewise, pocket knives or other knives on your person are prohibited.

The US Department of State warns US citizens against taking any firearm or ammunition into Mexico without prior written authorization from the Mexican authorities.

Citizens can own up to 10 registered firearms (one handgun and nine long guns) per household. Businesses cannot keep a firearm on the premises unless this business is also their residence. Any lost or stolen firearms have to be reported immediately to the La Secretaria de la Defensa Nacional, often referred to as 'la Sedena.'

TRANSPORTING YOUR FIREARMS

It is essential to recognize that owning and carrying a firearm are two different things in Mexico. The only place your firearm is permitted is in your primary residence. To have it at another residence or to transport it anywhere—even to go hunting or target shooting—you must have another permit, including proof that you are an active member of a shooting or hunting club. The permit must be renewed every year.

CARRY FIREARMS LICENSE IN MEXICO

Carry Firearms Licenses in Mexico are extremely rare. "La Sedena" has issued roughly 3,000 of these permits in a country of over 120 million residents, including those who carry firearms for work.

However, in some cases, the army, navy, private security, police officers, rural landowners, politicians, affluent citizens, and other citizens or residents who think that they are in danger can apply for a Carry Firearms License, provided that they have:

- Proof of employment

- No criminal record with the use of a firearm

- Served in the military

- Can pass a drug test

- Prove they are mentally and physically capable

- Can demonstrate a need to carry firearms because of the nature of their employment or occupation, circumstances in how they live, or any other legitimate reason.

There are two main types of Carry Firearm Licenses: official use and private citizens. Private citizens must renew their licenses every two years, whereas officials can hold their license as long as they work in a job that requires a firearms license. These licenses only apply to a particular individual— and not to a company, for example—for their exclusive use.

THERE ARE 3 BASIC TYPES OF PERMITS AVAILABLE TO RESIDENTS

Each type of permit is outlined in the Mexican constitution:

- Home Protection

- Hunting and Sporting

- Gun Collecting

TRANSFERRING A FIREARM IN MEXICO

Regarding transfers of firearms or private sale of weapons, both the buyer and seller must appear at La Sedena along with the weapon to legally process the transaction.

IT'S TIME TO MAKE A DECISION TO SELL YOUR HOME OR RENT IT OUT

You've made the choice to move to Mexico. You've picked the city in which you want to live. And now you have to decide if you want to sell your home and everything in it, or keep the furniture and rent out your home.

This can be an exciting time for everyone in the house, or it could be full of tears. If your children grew up in the family home, it would be tough to put that 'For Sale' sign up.

I would give them the first option. They know the home, and if they don't want to part with it, they might want to purchase it. No real estate commission; everyone wins!

If you have no children, or your children are coming with you, then selling your home is a good option.

You might also want to keep your home, furnishings and all, and rent it out long-term or short-term using Airbnb or VRBO. You will have to set everything up before moving, but it certainly can be done, and if you want to return to visit family and friends, you have a familiar place to stay.

There are also rental companies in many cities that, for a fee, take care of everything for you. If your home is paid off, you could enjoy a few thousand dollars monthly in rental fees minus maintenance, etc. It's an option that needs consideration.

Only you know the right decision to make. If you get to Mexico and hate it, you can always return to your hometown and purchase another home or try another state, one lower in state taxes.

TIME FOR THE MOVE

So then the next big decision you must make is which of these five are you going to make:

- **Cargo Ship** - everything you can fit in goes

- **Shipping** partially using air freight or shipping containers – Sell some, bring some.

- **Rail**

- A **moving company** from your current home to your new home in Mexico.

- **Two suitcases** each and a carry-on - sell everything and start fresh.

No matter your choice, there is no one right way to accomplish your goals. If you ask your friends and family for advice on what to do - 'should I take absolutely everything OR should I scale down, sell it all here, and buy new what I need in Mexico' you will likely have a split decision. 50/50.

All five concepts are perfect. It depends on how you feel about starting all over again. If you have furniture that has been passed down through your family, or you have spent a lot of money and time finding the most beautiful bedroom suite in the world, you need to decide if you would be happier taking everything or starting all over again

Do you love to shop? Is that your idea of fun? (it's not mine) Just remember that you'll be in a new city and a new country, and if you don't have a good command of Spanish, maybe trying to shop for everything brand new might be a little daunting.

You can also go on Facebook and look through second-hand groups. They sell everything on these sites.

My mother bought her bedroom suite from one of these sites. She looked at it, seemed okay, gave them a deposit, and hired a moving truck to pick it up. So, 2 hours to find the product she wanted, 1 hour to get to the location and back, and 2 hours for the moving truck to pack it all up and bring it back to our home. She paid half the price in the store, as it was a little banged up, but she saved herself about $600 USD.

She was so happy with her find that when we needed a bedroom suite for our spare room, she returned to her trusty Facebook group and found another suite identical to hers, only in a queen size. My mothers was a King Size (called matrimonial in Spanish). It wasn't quite ½ the price, but it was in better condition.

You can find absolutely everything on these sites. Just use the F search function and type in your item. I would suggest doing that before you sell everything, or vice versa, bring everything with you. Although our Facebook group is not a buy/sell group, there is still a lot there to help you with moving to a new country. Check it out here: https://www.facebook.com/groups/expatmoneyforum

1. CARGO SHIP

LET'S TALK LOGISTICS OF USING A SHIPPING CONTAINER FOR YOUR HOUSEHOLD GOODS

Let's see how much work getting ready for a shipping container can be. Will it be worth all of the aggravation and work to have all of your items in your new home? What will this cost you?

Questions you need to answer are:

How far from a port city are you, and what will the cost be to get your stuff there? (If you live in Toronto, Vancouver, Los Angeles or Miami, it will be much less expensive than if you live in Ottawa or Salt Lake City.) (This price is usually the breaking point.

I would move on to the next category if this price is high. It's probably not worth it, but keep reading; it may all work out). If you are anywhere inland in the USA, it will be more complicated, but hundreds of cities are coastal and will reduce the cost of shipping.

- What is the cost of the shipping container to go from your port city to the Port in Mexico?

- What are the extra charges that this freight company doesn't cover?

- How much is the insurance for making the trip? (usually a % of the retail value)

- What are the broker fees in Mexico, and what don't they cover?

- The cost to bring your items to your front door from the port (could be prohibitive)

- The cost of hiring a moving company to bring your items into your house or apartment

- The cost of damaged items (it can happen)

- Import or customs fees (depending on your visa)

- Other unforeseen expenses that no one can predict

Your first call will be to either a broker or a freight forwarder who will work with you to coordinate your shipping needs or the shipping company itself. A freight forwarder does not move your freight itself.

The freight forwarder acts as an intermediary between a shipper and various transportation services such as ocean shipping on cargo ships, trucking, expedited shipping by air freight, and moving goods by rail.

Compare prices with brokers, the same as you would a

moving company.

The Port of Los Angeles' website has a list of freight forwarders http://www.portoflosangeles.org/maritime/freight_forwarders.asp, and here are a few privately operated forwarder listing services that Export.gov lists:

- **Directory of Freight Forwarding Services** http://www.forwarders.com

- **Freight Gate** https://freightgate.net

- **Freight Net** https://www.freightnet.com

You may find that a few ships are leaving and arriving in Mexico from your port city. Check different ports. If you are in the middle of the USA, look at Los Angeles, Seattle, or New Orleans. It's most likely the cheapest port in North America for shipping to Mexico.

A freight forwarding company is meant to take on some of the responsibilities of moving your goods from your home to the port in Mexico.

If you bypass the freight forwarding company and go directly to the shipping company, you must coordinate with them. They may deal with you, and they may not. They may also give you the names of the freight forwarding companies they deal with in your area.

When deciding on the cost, you won't have to sell your appliances, big or small, as Mexico's electrical grid is the same frequency as Canada and the USA, so you can pack that beautiful new fridge and matching stove you just bought.

The only thing to remember is that if you live near the coast (which is hard not to do), the sea air can cause havoc with your appliances. But if you have to buy new ones once you get to Mexico, there is no difference.

First: Prices

1.	Packers at your home	$
2.	Moving Company from home to 1st port	$
3.	Freight forwarding company from port to port (shipping fee)	$
4.	Insurance	$
5.	Broker fees/transportation in Mexico	$
6.	Unloading and delivering to your home in Mexico	$
7.	Additional 10% for unknown costs (damage, etc)	$
Total		$

Add up these costs and fees. Is the end cost feasible?

Will this make you happy? You are the only one who can decide this. People can tell you their stories, but you are the only one who can decide. Maybe the price is $15,000 USD, can you live with that?

Let's go with that price and see how we fare with the other three options.

COMPARE SELLING EVERYTHING TO SHIPPING EVERYTHING

Add up what you think you will get from selling all of your furniture, and be realistic. Not everything will sell; some you will end up giving away or donating to your favourite charity.

Go through your house with a pen and paper and list everything. Many businesses buy used items, or you could have a garage sale or sell them to family & friends. Get a rough estimate of what you would make and how long it would take to sell everything.

See #4 in this list to finish this task.

2. PARTIAL SHIPPING

Another option is shipping some of your belongings by air or freight. The nice thing about coming from either Canada or the USA is that you can find cheap flights for cargo. Let's say you spend $1000 USD on a few boxes of tools, your mother's favourite dishes and some clothes you can't leave behind.

The other option is still to ship via ocean freight but share the container and the costs with someone else who is going to the same port. As long as you are flexible with the dates, this is an excellent option if you just have ½ a container. Check with the shipping company.

3. RAIL

Using rail may be the best option for those living inland. The containers for rail and ship are the same, so use the metrics outlined. Use the same freight forwarders and figure out how long the process will take, the closest city to unload, and if they have a moving company that can bring your container to your home.

I know many people who have used this method and are very satisfied.

4. MOVING COMPANY

Depending on where you live in the States or Canada, like rail, it may be feasible to ship via land. Check with several companies that take freight into Mexico. It could take up to a few months and be expensive, but they come and pick up everything and drop it off in your new home.

This is a viable option, even at a hefty price, considering the hassles entailed with the other methods. Later in this chapter, we discuss moving companies and the laws enforced when using them; when you talk with them about their services, see if this is one they will do and the cost. The moving company may or may not load and unload in your cities, but check with them. It could be a service they provide.

5. ARRIVING IN MEXICO WITH 2 SUITCASES COMPARED TO SHIPPING EVERYTHING

Add up the cost to repurchase the items you will need here in Mexico. The time it will take to purchase, find the best stores, and converse only in Spanish. Sometimes the purchase price can include the delivery, but that is not always the case.

You will have to hire a moving company or truck to bring items from the store to your home, all while trying to speak Spanish! And honestly, I found many great stores while I was in Mexico; however, every country has its style of furniture and clothing. In a few countries I've lived in, the furniture style was atrocious, so just beware of the trends in Mexico. The other thing to remember is the city you'll be moving to. Mexico City is quite different from Cancun or a small mountain town.

One thing to keep in mind, and personally, I'm not sure what is worse. If you bring everything that will fit into a 40' cargo container (or possibly 2-40' containers), you just have to box it up and have it moved here once. The movers will bring it up in the elevator or your new home and help you set it up. It's done, and you never have to worry about finding good quality furniture, tools, or clothes.

If you decide to sell everything, you must schedule garage sales, decide how much $$ you want for your items, and possibly cry when your favourite sofa is carted away at 10% of what you paid.

The other thing to remember is that if you have some cumbersome items, like hand tools, or gym equipment, you might have trouble finding them in Mexico and will have to buy them, which are extremely expensive due to their weight. Okay, so you can figure out selling everything and moving with two suitcases. You don't need guidance; let's move on to using a cargo ship and sending your household to Mexico.

USING A CARGO SHIP

There are many, many things to consider when moving. Moving can either be front-loaded (pack everything up and move to your destination) or backloaded (sell everything and repurchase it in your new destination). Both are a ton of work, and as we've discussed, it depends on how badly you want your stuff or how much you like to shop.

I would only recommend shipping if you have purchased a new home or rented an apartment and know and understand the size and dimensions of the building. With the measurement in hand, decide what will be sold, given away, trashed or taken with you.

Envision your new home and try to picture each piece of furniture in its proper spot. Will that wall unit work? Is this chair just too big? Or do you need a smaller bedroom suite? Make a coded inventory sheet with everything you own and go one by one and either check it off or give it an appropriate symbol K-keep, T-trash, S-Sell, G-give away. Then, take your inventory sheet, re-do the list with each category and make sure it's exactly what you want. This may seem arduous, but it works.

If you're trying to decide which items to bring, here are the main ones people wish they had brought; carpets, bookshelves, bedroom suites with mattresses, coffee tables, dining room tables, children's toys, lawn chairs, curtains, clothes (for all seasons), good linens, bed pillows, kitchen appliances of all types (including a can opener), their good knife set, tools in every size and shape, and lamps.

Depending if you have grass or a backyard, bring everything to do with gardening with you. Again, this depends on your location. If you are in a big city with a Walmart (or equivalent), then all of these items can be purchased, but if you are in a small town, nowhere close to big box stores that you are accustomed to, then be selective on the items you pack.

DETAILED LIST

For customs purposes, this is where a very detailed list of all of your items will come in handy. Make sure you have the original purchase price (close estimation will do) and what you think it's worth at this time.

When considering the furniture to bring with you, please remember how long your items will be wrapped up and in the shipping container before getting to your new home in Mexico. You can expect some damage, especially if Customs decides to go through all of your things.

Also, remember to wrap your delicate items well. Make sure that all screws and instructions are taped to the backside. Keep all warranties and pertinent documents together and note where they are.

DO NOT put your good jewellery, coins, money, or anything of value in the shipping container. No meat, herbs or alcohol are allowed through customs. Coming by boat is very different than coming by air.

ARE YOU READY?

We measured a 20' container with masking tape in our apartment to determine if it would be big enough. I mentioned earlier that our home in Abu Dhabi came partially furnished, so we didn't require the 40' container, but if we had to bring beds, dining tables and living room furniture, we would have needed a 40' container.

It seems enormous when you think about it, but once everything gets loaded, it looks relatively minor.

Here are the dimensions of the container for shipping by sea. If you are using rail, find out what the measurements are and use the same concept.

20-Foot Container:

- Dimensions: 19 feet, 10 1/2 inches long x 8 feet wide x 8 feet, 6 inches high (579.12 cm x 243.84 x 268.22)

- Volume/usable space: 1,169 cubic feet (33.10 cubic meters)

- Typically moves one to two bedrooms or one car plus some boxes

40-Foot Container:

- Dimensions: 40 feet long x 8 feet wide x 8 feet, six inches high (1219.2 cm x 243.84 x 268.22)

- Volume/usable space: 2,385 cubic feet (67.53 cubic meters)

- Typically moves three to five bedrooms or one car and two bedrooms

You could also possibly have the option of a partial container. Maybe someone else is also going to Mexico, and you can share the container. The chances are not very high, but it's worth asking.

The containers are not packed full; please keep this in mind. You will have professional movers; however, we all know that time is more important than saving space.

When Does Ocean Freight Make Financial Sense?

There is no exact volume or weight at which ocean freight becomes profitable; however, after talking with several shipping companies, they generally notice that sea freight starts to make sense from 2 cubic meters or 200 kg.

For smaller volumes, air freight will be more competitive and much faster.

Maritime Groupage (Lcl) Or Full Container Load (Fcl), Which Option To Choose?

Considering only the financial factor, a full container load (FCL) becomes profitable from about 15 cubic meters. Note that this volume is less than half the capacity of a 20-foot container (33 cubic meters). The entire container also has an advantage in terms of security: the container is sealed from departure to arrival.

Remember that you have to tell your supplier or forwarder that you want to insure your cargo. Thus the insurance cost is fixed according to the value of your cargo. In this case, about 0.5 to 0.6% of its value.

GLOSSARY OF TERMS FOR INTERNATIONAL SHIPPING

Bill of Lading: Original contract/customer receipt for belongings. This document is related to ocean shipments and should include the dates, services and charges involved in the international relocation.

Cargo: Goods being transported – by air, sea or land.

Certificate of Origin: A document determining the country where shipped goods were manufactured or produced. It must be signed and sealed by a Chamber of Commerce to certify the true origin and may also require legalization by proper officials in the destination country.

Consular Invoice: A special invoice that some countries require to control and identify imported goods.

Containerization: The use of boxes, cartons, drums, barrels, etc., to transport a shipment.

Currency Adjustment: An added fee on charges for ocean freight to compensate for currency fluctuation between countries.

Customs: The place in every country where physical examination of imports and exports is done. It can also refer to fees placed on these imports and exports.

Customs Clearance: The process where the customer obtains the release of goods from customs. This process includes documentation handling but excludes the physical handling of cargo.

Demurrage: A fee charged to the customer for keeping a container beyond a particular length of time.

Destination Agent: The point of contact for the customer shipping goods. This person is the authorized receiving agent for a shipment if it is going into storage.

Duties: Taxes imposed on the importation and exportation of goods.

Freight Forwarders: A licensed company that handles the formalities regarding foreign or domestic shipments. Freight forwarders will assemble and dispatch these shipments on behalf of others.

Household Goods Shipment: Personal property/goods being shipped for use or intended use in the home.

Import Permit: A special permit allowing certain items into a foreign country. A government agency must issue this permit before shipping the specified goods.

Origin Agent: The agent handling the estimating, scheduling, surveying, packing and loading of an international shipment at the origin.

PBO: "Packed by Owner" – the owner/customer packs his or her goods at the origin. This method is not always acceptable in certain countries.

Okay, the next step is

Call 2 or 3 moving companies in your area for a price to help you box everything up and move to your new location: I've moved dozens of times in my life, and truthfully, the sanest way is to hire someone to help you pack everything up and load it onto the truck. D I Y moving is not for everyone; it certainly is not for me.

OR

Pack it yourself: then call your moving company to load it into the truck. If you are lucky enough to have a relocation package, you will have none of this. You will find the above the way to go. Your company will hire another company to ensure that all your belongings are safe, secure and packed properly inside the truck.

Hire a moving company to take your belongings to your local port so your household goods can be shipped to your new country. If you are lucky enough to live in a port city like Seattle or Toronto, it will be much easier to make the move. If you live inland, the moving company will take your belongings to your closest port and unload your contents into another container that will be lifted onto the ship.

Also, if you work with the cargo shipping company, there is a possibility that they can bring the 20' or 40' container to you, drop it in your driveway (if it will fit), and load it from there. Once it is fully loaded, they come back and pick it up and slot it for your overseas travel.

If you are thinking of moving this way, here is my suggestion. Try to bypass the middle person in all of these scenarios. You might not be able to, but I would suggest talking directly with the shipping company, like Twill, which is owned by the largest cargo shipping company in the world. They deal primarily with logistics companies, but they take a bite out of your money, and it's not that hard to do. You will have two choices, a 20' or a 40' shipping container dedicated solely to you.

Here are my thoughts on keeping or selling. It's how I've done it and will likely do it in the future, but the cool thing is that we're all different, and moving for a different reason. Find what works for you, and just go for it.

When we moved from the UAE to Latin America, I sold all of our electrical appliances. The middle east uses a plug different from Latin America, so I sold everything. If you come from the States or Canada, the plugs are identical in Mexico.

That included our hairdryer, crockpot, kettle, iron, lamps, TV, and anything plugged into the wall. I had the most beautiful red KitchenAid blender. I had to almost give it away, it was heartbreaking, but I couldn't take it with me.

We also sold anything that would not make the voyage intact, including the initial move from our apartment to the port, then the journey across the ocean. We had an awesome set of closets that we paid a pretty penny for and absolutely loved them. We only had them for about six months.

We sold them for ¼ of their retail value to our next-door neighbour, who was so pleased. I knew they would never make the voyage, so what was the point? Had I known that we would be making this move six months later, I wouldn't have bought them either. Oh well, not much we could do about it.

We also had a few cabinets in our bedroom that we sold. We didn't think they'd make the voyage, but in retrospect, they would have done just fine, and lasted in this humidity. We did bring the four IKEA bookshelves I mentioned earlier that, after several years in this humidity, are just fine. But again, we didn't know how the voyage would be.

In retrospect, I would bring everything I could possibly bring. Selling everything, we only got about 15-20% of the retail value of our appliances, but we couldn't take them with us, but with the furniture, we knew that we would need all of that in our new house. We knew how big our new apartment was and that we would have to fill all the rooms.

We brought 20 boxes of books, all of our clothes (winter and summer), kitchenware (amazingly, 20 boxes from a small kitchen), a desk, computer monitors, all of our carpets, toys (tons and tons of toys), a sewing machine that my mom moved in her car from Toronto to Dubai, two years prior, which is still sitting in one of our spare bedrooms. Other than that, just odds and ends, and that took up a 20' cargo container.

Here are a few questions to ask yourself when deciding what to bring:

- The weather in your new country

- Will you be working, or are you retiring and living off a pension?

- Will you be active in your new country

- Is your old home too big to fit into your new home?

- Are your children coming with you, or are they staying behind?

- Is your new home furnished? Or partially furnished?

- Does your new home have an outside kitchen? With an outdoor oven?

- Can you purchase most of your things in Mexico for a reasonable price?

- Do you want to sell everything you own at a fraction of what you paid and then pay retail prices for everything you just sold?

IT'S NOW TIME TO GET AN ESTIMATE FROM A MOVING COMPANY

A mover can provide two moving estimates or price quotes: a binding and a non-binding estimate. While non-binding estimates are more common, especially for long-distance moves, we'll look at both.

What Is a Binding Estimate?

A binding estimate means that the price quoted in an estimate is the amount you pay—even if there are unforeseen extra costs. A non-binding estimate means that the price you pay will probably be different than the estimated price movers tell you.

Mover Estimate

When the movers visit your home to assess the household goods that you'll be moving, they will provide you with a copy of the moving estimate. It will either be a binding or non-binding agreement. Ask any questions at this time.

Questions to Ask During The Estimate

1. Find out their registration number, write it down, and keep it. All moving companies should have a number called a USDOT number.

2. Ask the company what their rate is. Most companies will provide a rate per pound and a distance rate, especially if you are moving long distances. They will give you a written quote and provide you with a copy. The estimate will include all charges, and you both must sign to make it a legally binding contract.

3. Ask if there will be any additional charges or fees associated with the move. Oversized furniture, heavy items and your estimate will be based on how your home is set up and if the movers can move in and out quickly. If you live on the 2nd floor of a walk-up apartment, it will be

more expensive to move your items than if the truck can pull up to the front door and be taken out that way.

4. Will your moving company use a subcontractor? If the move is from state to state, they may hire a subcontractor to cross different states. Find out all of these companies' names, addresses and phone numbers and keep you updated on the times as they cross the states.

5. Find out if the moving company offers insurance. How does a claim happen if your items do not arrive in the condition they left your old home?

6. When moving day arrives, how do they protect your furniture? Do they use shrinkwrap, provide a free blanket wrap, or do they charge extra for this service? You don't want surprises after your household items are loaded on the truck.

7. Are there any hidden fees?

Is Taking All of Your Stuff Really Worth It?

You've had several moving companies give you their quotes; it's now time to sit down and go through them all. As I've mentioned, do you live in the middle of the country and is getting a moving van to the coast going to cost you thousands of dollars?

Hire the Movers

You've now decided that the price is right to make the move to Mexico. Once you've agreed to the estimate, you'll receive the official contract between you and the mover. Everything you need to know about your move will be on the contract, including the date of pick-up, the estimated delivery date, the estimated amount, and any insurance you have included in the estimate.

You will also see the cancellation policy, type of truck to be used, goods the movers will not move, and any extra charges that may be applicable for your move.

This contract will allow the movers to move your items, so make sure you read it carefully and negotiate any terms you do not agree with or understand.

Bill of Lading

This is one of the most important documents you will receive from your movers. You will receive this on moving day, outlining your agreement with the moving company.

The mover must have this to move your things. You must sign this document stating that you agree with the terms and conditions and the total cost of the move. The mover will also sign the contract, giving you a copy, which you need to retain as this is your official contract and service receipt.

Inventory Sheet

I would suggest that you keep excellent records of all packed boxes. Label them, number them and then record them on an inventory sheet. As they leave the house, mark them off and when you arrive at your new home, mark them off again. This inventory sheet will be your official document on the items the movers are moving. I would also suggest that you take pictures of all of your items.

If you are moving high-value items, please ensure they are insured and that the insurance company knows you are moving to Mexico.

Rules

The following rules come from the Federal Motor Carrier Safety Association (FMCSA) and must be observed by your moving company when preparing and implementing a binding estimate:

Description of Shipment and Services

The binding estimate must accurately describe the shipment and all the services the company will provide. If you asked the moving company to provide additional services, such as long carry charges, shuttle service or flight charges, the company must bill you separately for these charges following your move. At the time of delivery on your moving day, the moving company cannot charge you more than the amount of the binding estimate. A binding estimate must be in writing, and they must give you a copy before you move.

Payment

Payment is due at the time of delivery. If you agree to a binding estimate, you must pay the amount owed by cash, certified cheque, money order, cashier's cheque or wire transfer (with a fee) due at delivery.

Your mover can agree to payment before moving, extend credit, or accept a credit card. This is up to the moving company. If you can't pay the mover upon delivery, the company will place your belongings in storage until you can pay the binding estimate. The storage fees are your responsibility, and you will be charged.

Recordkeeping

Your mover must retain a copy of the binding estimate and attach it to the bill of lading.

Clarity of the Contract

The moving company must clearly state that the estimate is binding to you and your mover. Each binding estimate must also clearly state that the charges are only for services outlined in the estimate.

Right to Refuse

Before loading your household goods, if the moving company thinks you have additional belongings not stated in the estimate, the mover can refuse service. Make sure everything you need to move is clearly outlined in the estimate. If you need to add items, tell your mover so you can work out an agreement before they start to load your shipment.

Accepting the Contract

Once the moving company agrees to move your belongings, they must either confirm the binding estimate, negotiate a revised written binding estimate listing the additional household goods or services or add an attachment to the contract. This must be in writing, stating you both will consider the original binding estimate as a non-binding estimate. Again, avoid any "add-ons" if you can. It can lead to a higher-priced move and result in not having a mover on moving day.

Additional Charges

Once your mover loads all your household belongings, they have agreed to the binding estimate. No changes can be made, or additional costs added, except for agreed-upon services and charges. As stated earlier, these additional charges must be billed after delivery. Only the binding estimate can be charged upon delivery.

Not-To-Exceed Estimates

The best option for all binding and non-binding estimates is the binding not-to-Exceed estimate. It means that if the actual weight of your shipment is more than the written estimate, you still pay the amount quoted. However, if the exact weight is less than the written estimate, you pay the lesser amount. If you ask for a binding not-to-exceed estimate, you'll never pay a higher price than the estimate. Your cost can only go lower. Whenever you get an estimate, always ask for a binding not-to-exceed.

BRINGING IN A DUMPSTER FOR THE REST OF YOUR STUFF

If you've been in your home since you or your spouse was born, I assume you have a lot of stuff that will not make the transition. Sometimes your standard garbage bags and roadside pick-up just won't cut it. It's time to rent a bin, put it in your driveway and throw out what you don't need.

You've had three weekends of garage or home sales, if this happens during the winter months. You're left with a lot of stuff you neither want nor need.

You can box up much of the unwanted stuff and donate it to The Salvation Army or the Goodwill. You can also put an ad in CraigsList for items that didn't sell; however, sometimes, the time involved outweighs the price you will recoup. It just depends on the items. Now you're left with trash and lots of trash. Ask your kids to come for the day, put work gloves on, toss everything into the bin and say 'goodbye.' You will be relieved when it is done, and your move to Mexico will be a much better experience.

TIMELINE FOR YOUR MOVE TO MEXICO

2-3 Months Before Moving

- Decide what to do with your current housing: sublet, sell or terminate your lease

- Arrange for housing in your host country

- If you are moving for work, figure out when you'll need to report and if your family will have to arrive after you

- Research storage costs for leftover personal possessions

- Choose your international moving company and make arrangements for your international move

- Apply for visas, work permits and other documentation

- Perform more research on your host country

- Give notice to your child's school and request school reports and documentation

- Find a new international school for your children, or even better, schedule a call with us at https://ExpatSchool.io to look at schooling options with us

- Obtain original copies of your birth certificate, passport, marriage license, driver's license, work references and medical files

- Check quarantine laws

- Research international health insurance coverage; for this, I recommend visiting this link: http://insuredexpats. com

- Book flights

- Start the immigration process with your lawyer

- Review the list of prohibited items that are not allowed in Mexico

- Meet with your Financial Advisor

- Ensure your Social Security and pensions are on direct deposit

- Renew your Driver's License so that it doesn't expire while you're gone

- Ensure your Voter Registration is current

One month before moving

Notify the post office of your change of address

Change the address on your credit card accounts, bank accounts and other billing accounts

- Verify whether your bank has an international branch in your host country

- Cancel your car insurance policies and begin coverage on your new insurance

- Make changes to your banking information with your employer for your salary to be deposited into the correct account

- Host a garage sale to downsize the number of items you have and will bring with you on your move

- Order any prescriptions you may need to get: contact lenses, medications, etc.

- Find out generic names of your medications so you can find them abroad

- Consider sending a smaller shipment of essential items ahead of your move so they will be there before you arrive

- Ensure all documents for immigration have been done

- Cancel your memberships

Three weeks before moving

- Separate items that will be staying behind during the move

- Send out change of address notifications to friends and family

- Schedule the date for your utility services to be shut off in your old home

- Enjoy your time with friends and family before you leave

- Sell your firearms

Two weeks before moving

- Take your pets to be immunized and obtain travel documents for them

- Make sure any bills are up to date

- Continue downsizing your items

- Begin packing your belongings

- Move items that will be left behind to the storage facility

One week before moving

- Continue to pack and purchase last-minute items

- Make an inventory of your items that will be moved, including the value for each item.

- Empty your safe deposit box and consider moving these items offshore

Two days before moving

- Continue packing last-minute items

- Clean your home

- Withdraw cash needed for your trip and your first week.

- Pick up and drop off any last-minute things: books to the library, pick up dry cleaning, etc.

Documents to bring with you:

No matter where you are moving, overseas or locally, the following documents will be necessary for you to bring on your journey. Locate and obtain these documents as far ahead of your move as possible so you are not scrambling at the last minute.

- Passports

- Travel documents

- Birth certificate

- Marriage certificate

- Divorce papers

- Child custody papers

- Adoption papers

- Drivers licenses

- Medical records

- School/university transcripts

- Insurance policies

- Legal documents: tax records, power of attorney, last will and testament, bank statements

- Immunization certificates

- Dental records

- Tax records

- School records

- Social Security cards

- Veterinary International Health certificate (for pets)

- Pet vaccination records

- Customs documents (customs forms, power of attorney, valued inventory list, receipts and invoices, special permits for certain items)

CHAPTER 21: QUICK SUMMARY

- Moving to a new country is a considerable expense and one that should not be taken lightly. Over the past years, I have talked with many expats about their moves. What did they take? Do they wish they had done things differently? And each answer is different. One size does not fit all. I wish it did, but it doesn't.

- I've mentioned earlier, our family loaded everything into a cargo container and had it shipped. That worked for my family and me, but it might not work for you and yours. Put the time and effort into this section of moving. Make sure you are happy with your specific outcome; that's all I can advise.

- To move household goods into Mexico, you must have an immigration status of a permanent resident or a temporary resident. To be excluded from the Mexican IVA tax, your items must enter Mexico no later than six months from the time your visa is fully issued in Mexico.

- Article 90 of the Mexican customs law states that the items you take across the border must be used as personal items (never new) and furniture of a house, for example, clothes, books, furniture, appliances and electronics, linens and outside furniture, and lawn equipment.

- No fresh or frozen food, plants, spices, or seeds are allowed.

- Firearms are heavily restricted, and specific permits and permissions (such as for hunting) must be obtained to import firearms and ammunition.

- There are five ways to move to Mexico. Cargo Ship, partial container, rail, moving company and two suitcases.

- Get quotes from moving companies and sign a contract.

- Bring in a dumpster to get rid of the items from your home that are unsaleable or not able to make the trip with you to Mexico.

- A three-month timeline for your move to Mexico.

Chapter 22 is about becoming a digital nomad, leaving your old life behind and what needs to happen so you can live a good life overseas.

WORKING ABROAD

TRABAJANDO EN EL EXTRANJERO

Twenty years from now you will be more disappointed by the things you didn't do than by the ones you did do. So throw off the bowlines. Sail away from the safe harbour. Catch the trade winds in your sails. Explore. Dream. Discover.

MARK TWAIN

Definition: Digital Nomad, Wikipedia

Digital Nomads are people who use telecommunications technologies to earn a living and conduct their life in a nomadic manner. Such workers often work remotely from foreign countries, coffee shops, public libraries, co-working spaces, or recreational vehicles.

It is usually accomplished through devices with wireless internet capabilities, such as smartphones or mobile hotspots. Successful digital nomads typically have a financial cushion or need to develop high self-reliance and self-discipline.

The digital nomad community has had various events established to host members of it. The most common digital nomads include retired or semi-retired persons (including snowbirds), independently wealthy or entrepreneurs, and (often younger) remote workers.

People typically become digital nomads for many reasons, including the quest for financial independence and a career that allows location independence. Although digital nomads enjoy the advantages of freedom and flexibility, they report loneliness as their biggest struggle, followed by burnout.

The lifestyle also presents other challenges, such as maintaining international health insurance with global coverage, abiding by local laws, obtaining work visas, and paying taxes following home and local laws.

If you are at the beginning stages of the idea of working remotely, there are many decisions you must make and plans that must be made before actually making that first step out the door.

1. GET RID OF YOUR DEBT (AND STAY OUT OF DEBT)

This is a crucial step in making your reality come to life. Eliminate all of the small stuff you used to buy. Don't add things like new golf clubs, more makeup or a fancy new chair in your living room to watch Netflix. Stop buying, and sell what you already have.

If you plan on travelling from country to country, you will need only a few small items. You can store sentimental things and items you might want years later. You can always come home at any point, pick up where you left off, or sell everything you kept and keep going.

Just because you made the decision today doesn't mean you can't change your mind a year down the road and come home. No one will think less of you if you find that the digital lifestyle is not for you. Maybe the white picket fence is what you want, and that's okay. The worst thing would be to wake up at 70 years old and wish you had taken that chance when you were younger.

2. HOW WILL YOU PAY THE BILLS

Start now, and figure out what works for you. If you have a job, will your employer grant you a leave of absence, and can you try working remotely? Maybe your employer is gung ho for you to continue working the job you already have, just from the beaches of Mexico.

Maybe your boss is sitting on the fence, thinking, hey, she gets to work from the beaches of Mexico, and I'm stuck here in this awful office. Here's an idea you can pitch to him. Figure out the minimum salary you would need to live off of for a month.

Double that figure and then tell your boss you'd be willing to take a pay cut for the 1st year to show you that you can still do the job that you've always done, maybe better, because now you're not commuting 40 minutes each way to work. That figure may well be 20% less than he is paying you now, but for you, there is no need for a car, gas, insurance and wasting 80 minutes of daily commuting. You can decide if a 20% decrease in pay worth it. Maybe it is.

And maybe you want to quit your 9-5 for something new and exciting, something you've created for yourself.

There are a ton of ways to make money online. Figure out what you do best. Is there a job for that? Are you a Veterinarian? Start an online business for expats that have pets that travel with them. Are you an SEO expert? Set up a profile with Upwork and look for remote jobs.

3. SMALL IMPORTANT STUFF

You've decided to become a digital entrepreneur; your boss has said, 'okay, let's give it a try,' and you're selling your items.

Here are some essential items to take care of before you go:

- Get your phone unlocked

- Everywhere you go, join a digital nomad community

- Get travel insurance

HERE ARE THE TOP 20 JOBS FOR REMOTE WORKERS

Teacher, Writer, Website Developer, App Developer, Affiliate Marketing, Consulting, Translator, Computer Programmer, E-commerce, Illustrator/Graphic Designer, UI/UX Designer, Videographer/Photographer, Social Media Manager, Freelancer (SEO, Photog), Digital Entrepreneur, Blogger/Vlogger, Video Creators, Virtual Assistant, Start a YouTube Channel, Data Entry

FREELANCING WEBSITES

- https://www.fiverr.com/

- https://www.freelancer.com/

- https://www.guru.com/

- https://www.upwork.com/

The above is for anyone wishing to travel abroad and work. One thing to keep in mind is to apply for as many jobs in your field as possible, but don't expect to be hired right away.

Just keep applying for jobs.

Prospective employers will want to see that you have done work and people are happy with your performance. As time goes on, you will be hired for jobs more often.

CHAPTER 22: QUICK SUMMARY

If you are at the beginning stages with the idea of working remotely, there are many decisions you must make and plans that must be made before actually making that first step out the door.

Here are some important items to take care of before you go:

- Get your phone unlocked

- Everywhere you go, join a digital nomad community

- Get travel insurance

- Get rid of your debt (and stay out of debt)

- Decide on the type of work you want to do

CHAPTER 23

DOING BUSINESS IN MEXICO

HACIENDO NEGICIOS EN MÉXICO

Your time is limited, so don't waste it living someone else's life.

STEVE JOBS

By 2050, many believe Mexico will be the 7th largest economy in the World. Projected to grow at a 3.5% annual average rate over the next three decades, a growth rate superior to other developed economies.

My good friend and Mexican lawyer, David Galindo, from RVG Abogados, wrote this out for me. I hope you get great value from it:

CHOOSING A LEGAL ENTITY

Representative Office: It is helpful to establish a RO only when the main goal is to promote a service or show a product since it is not allowed to generate any income.

Sociedad Anónima: It is similar to a US Corporation, therefore may not be able to be treated as a branch for US. tax purposes, and it doesn't require minimum equity to be incorporated.

Sociedad de Responsabilidad Limitada: Provides most of the organizational elements of an SA but is different in its ownership structure and the fact that it is limited to 50 owners referred to as partners. US parent companies often choose the use of an SRL because it may provide significant US tax benefits by being eligible in the US to Check the Box.

LABOUR

An employer is required to withhold and submit to the tax authorities the following contributions:

Social security: The employer must contribute an amount equal to 30-35% of the employee's salary to Social Security.

Housing fund: Additional amount equal to 5% of the employee's salary paid to a Housing Fund known as INFONAVIT.

Retirement fund: Employers must contribute an amount equal to 2% of the employee's salary to a retirement fund known as an Individual Savings Account.

Profit-Sharing: Mexican law requires sharing 10% of taxable income among workers. This expense is mandatory for all companies. Also, consider paying a Workers Union fee.

GENERAL TAXATION

Corporate Tax: (ISR), a rate of 30%, is applied to the net profits generated from a Mexican territory's income. No State within Mexico has an income tax.

VAT: consists of a 16% tax (reduced to 8% in the borders and certain States) applied to most transactions involving goods or services taking place within Mexican territory, including importing of goods and services. Other significant taxes could apply depending on the activities to be performed in Mexico, such as the IEPS, a tax on the manufacturing of oil combustibles, tobacco and alcoholic beverages, and local taxes.

TRANSFER PRICING

Following the recommendations of the Organization for Cooperation and Economic Development (OCED), Mexico has adopted the Income Tax Law, the Arm's Length Principle.

This fundamentally considers that commercial transactions entered by a related party should set prices and amounts of considerations that would have been used between independent parties. Hence, to comply with the "Arm's Length Principle," gain or loss on transactions carried out by related parties may be determined by using any of the following methods:

- Comparable Uncontrolled Price Method (CUP);

- Resale Price Method (RPM);

- Cost Plus Method (CP);

- Profit Split Method (PS) and

- Residual Profit Split (RPS) Method;

- Transactional Net Margin Method (TNM)

CUSTOMS DUTIES

The applicable customs duties can vary depending on a variety of factors, and not just the nature of the goods being imported. Specific customs duty treatment exists for countries with which Mexico has entered a free trade agreement. Customs duty treatment is also different for companies that operate under one of Mexico's export incentive programs.

Canada, Mexico, and the US have entered the United States–Mexico–Canada Agreement (USMCA). Under this agreement, goods deemed to have originated in any of these countries are subject to preferential customs treatment when entering any of the other two.

Mexico has also entered into free trade agreements with the European Union, Japan, Israel, Chile, Colombia, Costa Rica, Bolivia, Nicaragua, Guatemala, Honduras, El Salvador, Switzerland, Norway and Liechtenstein.

IMMEX

The main advantage of this program is to allow legal entities to manufacture products and maquil activities in Mexico without creating a Permanent Establishment (if so desired), also regarding VAT, the importation of the equipment and the raw material to be transformed won't cause such tax. A tax exemption significantly reduces manufacturing cost is: that is why many foreign companies are choosing to set up in Mexico and enjoy all the benefits they get by making this decision.

DOUBLE TAXATION TREATIES

Mexico has entered into Agreements to avoid double taxation with:

Argentina	Iceland	Estonia
New Zealand	Korea	Switzerland
Romania	Chile	Australia
India	Finland	Norway
Kuwait	Turkey	Russia
China	Austria	Indonesia
France	Panama	Latvia
Ukraine	Singapore	Columbia
Bahrain	Ireland	Germany
Peru	Lithunia	United Arab Emirates
Slovakia	Barbados	Czech Republic
Greece	Israel	Luzemborg
Poland	South Africa	United Kingdom
Belgium	Denmark	Hong Kong
Italy	Malta	Portugal
Spain	USA	Brazil
Hungary	Ecuador	Netherlands
Japan	Qatar	Uruguay
Costa Rica		

This network allows Mexican companies to interact globally with partners and third parties.

LAND ACQUISITION AND REAL ESTATE TAXATION

Foreign companies and individuals can acquire real estate properties within Mexico; however, some requirements apply in each case. Mexican entities with foreign shareholders are entitled to acquire land whenever the incorporation of foreign shareholders is allowed by the company's articles of incorporation.

Real estate located within 100 km from any frontier line or within 50 km from the coast (restricted zone) can be acquired only by foreign companies or companies with foreign shares. Individuals are entitled to acquire land within the restricted zone for residential purposes if the Ministry of Economy authorizes a special trust. Land acquisition is generally taxed locally with a rate varying from 1 to 3% of the value of the land.

MIGRATION COMPLIANCE

It is common for representatives of a foreign parent company to act as managers or advisors to a Mexican subsidiary, thus being required to spend extended periods in Mexico. There are, generally speaking, two types of visas available:

Short-term business visa FM-3 (Non-migrant): A short-term business visa grants the recipient the right to enter and leave Mexico and conduct business therein but not to reside in Mexico permanently. The FM3 visa may be processed at any Mexican Consulate located abroad or the FMN business or directly processed upon arrival at a Mexican point of entry.

Long-term business or permanent visa: A long-term business or FM-2 (Migrant) visa grants the recipient the right to live and conduct business within Mexico indefinitely and be employed by a Mexican company.

LOCAL TAX INCENTIVES

Foreign investment is a field where the 32 states of Mexico always compete. Local governments have established a variety of tax and economic incentives for those who can invest in Mexico. Generally, such incentives consist of the following:

- Exemption from the Local Payroll Tax (3%) during the first year of activities and 50% during the second year.

- Estate co-investment to be used in the training of technical or professional employees.

- Estate co-investment is to be used in the creation of water, energy and roads required for the company's installment.

- Sale of industry equipment, land, and assets at competitive prices.

CHAPTER 23: QUICK SUMMARY

- By 2050, many believe Mexico will be the 7th largest economy in the World.

- Projected to grow at a 3.5% annual average rate over the next three decades, a growth rate superior to other developed economies.

- Doing business in Mexico is an excellent idea for many reasons. Here's what you should be looking at,

  - Choosing a Legal Entity

  - Labour

  - General Taxation

  - Transfer Pricing

  - Customs Duties

  - IMMEX

  - Double Taxation Treaties

  - Land Acquisition and Real Estate

  - Migration Compliance

  - Local Tax Incentives

In Chapter 24, we talk about Mexican taxes and how you pay yours.

MEXICAN TAXES

IMPUESTOS MEXICANOS

The best things in life are free, but sooner or later the government will find a way to tax them.

ANONYMOUS.

If you are an expat in Mexico, you will pay property taxes if you own your home in Mexico. You'll owe income tax if you collect rent, own a business or have a job.

The least you'll pay is VAT (Value Added Tax) on almost everything you buy at the store.

INCOME TAX IN MEXICO

If you are a US citizen, the United States taxes its citizens and permanent residents on worldwide income based on residency and citizenship.

Canada taxes citizens on worldwide income unless they have moved their legal residence outside of Canada. If you earn income in Mexico, it must be declared on your US tax return. You can get credit on your home-country return for taxes paid in Mexico.

The Federal Tax Code establishes that a foreigner will be considered a resident of Mexico for tax purposes when his domicile has been established in Mexico.

This is unless he has been physically present in a foreign country for more than 183 days, consecutive or not, in a calendar year and can demonstrate residency for tax purposes in that other country.

WORLDWIDE TAXATION FOR AMERICANS

If you are an American, you will pay taxes on your worldwide income, regardless of where it's earned or where you live, and it is your responsibility to pay taxes to the US government.

For the scope of this book, it is impossible to cover American or Canadian taxation properly. This book is a guide to help you to move to Mexico.

If you require more in-depth information and wish to work with me to reduce your taxes, regardless of your home country, you can apply here to work with me: https://expatmoney.com

You Have To Pay Taxes Regardles Of Nationality

Mexico, unfortunately, has a taxation system that leaves much to be desired for expats.

The taxation laws in Mexico are different for foreigners compared to the residents, and you might want to enter the country after formulating a proper tax minimization strategy.

Some things that you should keep in mind when you go to Mexico include,

QUALIFYING AS A RESIDENT FOR TAX PURPOSES

There are two conditions under which the Mexican government will classify you as a resident for tax purposes. These are:

- Mexico is your primary home, and you spend over 183 days in the country yearly.

- If the Mexican Tax Administration Service concludes that your vital interests lie in Mexico–this happens if:

    - More than 50% of your income is derived from Mexican sources.

    - When the main center of your professional activities is in Mexico.

    - If you've lived and worked in Mexico for one full year

The country taxes all foreign residents based on their worldwide income. If you're classified as a resident for tax purposes, you'll pay taxes on all your income to the Mexican government. You'll have to pay taxes on all capital gains and passive income.

The personal income tax bracket in Mexico is as follows:

- If you make 1MXN—5953MXN, the rate is 1.92%

- 5954MXN—50,525MXN is 6.4%

- 50,526MXN—88,793MXN is 10.88%

- 88794MXN—103,218 MXN is 16%

- 103,219MXN—123,580MXN is 17.92%

- 123,581MXN—249,243MXN is 21.36%

- 249,244MXN—392,842MXN is 23.52%

- 392,843MXN—750,000MXN is 30%

- 750,001MXN—1,000,000MXN is 32%

- 1,000,001MXN—3,000,000MXN is 34%

- 3,000,000MXN and above is taxed at 35%

The country charges a flat 30% corporate tax rate.

Many retirees, expats and working foreign nationals in Mexico satisfy their tax obligations to their home country without paying Mexican taxes.

How this is possible is a question for a tax professional well versed in international tax law.

POSSIBLE TAX INCENTIVES IN MEXICO

In the interest of improving the investment environment in Mexico, the government has also introduced a few corporate tax incentives that you could utilize.

I think everyone should read up on all the possible ways to

minimize their tax liabilities before setting off to Mexico–it helps to have a plan in place that can help you sustain your wealth.

Some incentives include:

- Taxpayers in the border zones can apply for a tax credit valued at 30% of their total tax liabilities. This can reduce the corporate tax liability to 20% and individuals to 23%.

- VAT reductions from 16% to 8%.

- No income taxes on temporarily imported raw materials assuming they are exported

These temporarily imported raw materials will also not be subjected to any VAT.

- 30% tax credit for R&D expenses

- 25% tax credits if you hire employees with disabilities

- 10% income tax credit for movie productions

This is not the entire list of tax credits the Mexican government offers.

Given the profit potentials apparent in the Mexican economy and the tax minimization possibilities available under President Obrador's regime, the ease of doing business in the country is near incomparable.

REAL ESTATE TAXES

There are three types of residential property tax,

- A 2% acquisition tax when you buy the property

- Annual property taxes (known as predial)

- Capital gains tax when you sell the property.

Property taxes (predial) in Mexico are very low. It is common to have annual property taxes of $100 or less.

If you sell the property, you'll owe capital gains tax. Capital gains tax can be figured in two ways, You can pay 25% of the declared value of the transaction, or

You can pay 30% of the net value—the difference between the assessed values at the time you bought the property and when you sold it, taking into consideration how long you held the property, any improvements made, any commissions paid, and other allowable expenses. (If there is a significant difference between the assessed value recorded for the property when you bought it and the value you claim when you sell it, you could be in for a big tax bite.) You should calculate your capital gains tax both ways with the help of an accountant or notary and pay the lower one.

Value-Added Tax

In Mexico, a Value-Added Tax is applied to the selling of most retail goods and services. This tax is 16% in most of the country and 11% in border areas.

EASE OF DOING BUSINESS

Recently, Deloitte published a report summarizing all the characteristics that would showcase the potential of Mexico's business environment. The results of the report were quite impressive. Some of the key highlights include:

- 46th in competitiveness across all major economies

- 54th in the ease of doing business rankings

- Has access to 61% of all the global trade

- 13 FTAs with over 45 countries across the world

Each of these factors speaks volumes about the advantages of working in Mexico. It's clear that the economy has restructured over the past few decades to become increasingly export-oriented, and this approach has cleared the path for many interested investors.

To improve their economic conditions, the people of Mexico have understandably turned their sights outward. They have leveraged their position on the greater North American continent to serve the markets of Canada and the US. Using these markets as a conduit, the Mexicans have reached out to the rest of the world to take advantage of their competitiveness.

The Mexican economy offers lower production costs and more benefits to economies than all of Asia. In recent years, we have witnessed a shift in production from Asian economies to closer Latin American economies for this very reason.

The language barrier and time differences in further-flung Asian countries often lead to supply chain disruptions in the global economy that require an instantaneous response to market changes. Therefore, creating your business base in Mexico, with its convenience to American, South American, and Canadian business hubs, offers your business an immediate and obvious advantage.

FOREIGN INVESTMENT LAWS

All of the foreign investment in Mexico is governed through the Foreign Investment Law enacted initially in 1993 but amended over the years.

The investment environment is friendly for foreign investors, and the law is pretty straightforward. https://www.economia. gob.mx/files/comunidad_negocios/ied/foreign_investment_law.pdf.

All foreign investors can make investments in any economic sector with some exceptions. You can work in any sector that you like, except for certain reserved economic activities that include:

- Exploration and extraction of oil and other hydrocarbons

- Planning and control of national electrical systems

- Nuclear energy generation

- Telegraph services

- Radiotelegraph services

- Postal services

- Issuing any form of currency

- Controlling, supervising or surveilling ports, airports, and heliports

The sectors mentioned above are strictly under the control of the government, and you can only participate in these activities after the state's prior approval. The law also makes it clear that Mexican nationals or the state can only own some businesses–these include

- Domestic land transportation for passengers, tourism, and freight

- Development banking institutions

- Rendering specific professional and technical services as highlighted by law

There is also a set of injunctions that specify investments in companies concerning the amount of ownership you can hold. These are

- 10% of cooperative companies for production

- 25% shares in domestic air transport, air taxi transport, and specialized air transport services

- Up to 49% share in

  - Manufacturing and distributing firearms, explosives, and other similar products. This does not include explosives used for industrial, extraction, and construction purposes.

  - Printing and publishing newspapers that are to be

distributed solely within Mexican territory

- Series "T" shares in Mexican companies operating in agriculture, ranching and forestry lands

- Freshwater, coastal and exclusive economic zone fishing–this does not include fisheries.

- Port administration services

- Port pilot services

- Shipping companies working in inland and coastal navigation. This does not include tourism, port construction machines, machines used for environmental conservation and operations.

- Fuel and lubrication supplying companies for ships, airplanes, and railway equipment

- Broadcasting

However, the government still gives you room to negotiate for higher shares in some of these ventures. If you're willing to, you can still maintain majority holdings in these ventures.

INVESTING IN THE COUNTRY

Right now, the Mexican economy needs willing investors who can inject capital into the market. The administration has also responded to these needs by minimizing barriers to entering the market and introducing new incentives to garner the Mexican economy's attention. Many investors are cautious about moving in, but the fact is that this export-oriented economy and low production costs provide an unprecedented opportunity.

The law also highlights the regulations that dictate how people can use real estate for mining and fishing purposes. The relevant injunctions include

- You can acquire property for commercial purposes in non-restricted zones and must provide the Ministry of Foreign Affairs a notice within 60 days of acquisition.

- You must get prior approval from the Ministry of Foreign Affairs to acquire property as part of a trust; the trust's beneficiaries must include:

  - Mexican companies without a foreign exclusion clause

  - All foreign individuals and corporations

Incidentally, these clauses apply to real estate acquired for both commercial and residential purposes. These trusts are valid for 50 years and can be renewed upon expiration.

CHAPTER 24: QUICK SUMMARY

- Mexican tax laws are not that favourable for expats as they differ when you are a national

- A good tax structure is essential before moving to Mexico because if Mexico is your primary home, and you spend over 183 days in the country yearly, you are a tax resident.

- The US taxes its citizens and permanent residents on worldwide income based on residency and citizenship

- The Mexican government has introduced a few corporate tax incentives that you could utilize

- Value Added Tax is 16% in Mexico

CHAPTER 25

CONCLUSION

CONCLUSIÓN

You've asked yourself so many questions as you've gone through this book, You won't know these answers until you make the move.

The biggest thing to get out of the way right off the bat is that this new country of yours, Mexico, is not the USA or Canada or wherever you are coming from. It never was and never will be. But it can be your new home. For however long you want it to be.

If you go into this adventure with the idea that you are the one that will be making the changes, that you will be adapting, I think that's half the battle. Or maybe more than half.

I would suggest one of the most important concepts is to put yourself out there and find new friends. Spanish-speaking friends AND English-speaking friends. It will help you adapt to the changes that await you. It will help when you feel lonely and you miss your best friend from back home or your family members who are not moving with you. If you've made some new acquaintances, then life will be much easier.

There are many ways to make new friends. You will find yourself in a new apartment or villa on the beach, and you will need to get out and see what your new town or city has to offer right away.

Don't wait until you have that pang of loneliness because that can quickly become a regret. Regret for packing up your entire life and moving to Mexico.

Do you dance? Join a dance club. Do you like to hike? Join a local group that gets together once a week and goes on an adventure.

Have dinner out once a week, sit outside and make friends with people that are near your table. Strike up a conversation; I doubt anyone will turn you away. Start by asking them a question. "We're new here; what would you suggest doing on a Saturday night"?

Maybe you will become friends, or maybe you won't, but it's worth the small effort to put yourself out there.

Know that living abroad requires patience. Your life will not look like it did when you lived in Edmonton or Seattle; it will be different and take time. And make friends where you can. If you meet someone from the US or Canada, make friends with them; they might need you as much as you need them.

From there, as your Spanish becomes better, you can do the same thing with the locals in Spanish. Ask them where they like to shop. The best gym in the city? What are the best schools for your children? They will be thrilled that you speak their language and that you have at least tried to communicate with them. You may not understand everything they say, but that's okay. Smile, nod your head and then say warmingly, 'Gracias, muchas gracias.'

Every situation is unique. However, it's important to take the time to define your intentions. Doing so will help you to make some important choices in relation to your move, especially the things which will underpin your move to Mexico, for example, the type of immigration permit you will apply for, the type of location you want to live in, your work situation (if that exists), and how you organize your accommodations.

Before leaving home and moving to Mexico, here are some important things you need to take care of:

- Find, pay and talk with an immigration lawyer or at least a Mexican service provider. Someone that knows and understands the process that is required, especially if you don't speak Spanish.

- Create a plan to receive your mail and tax documents.

- Renew any bank cards that will be expiring soon, as it may be challenging to have replacements sent to you abroad.

- Find suitable short-term accommodations before getting on the plane. You can always move after a few weeks, but don't lock yourself in for a year. My friends got an Airbnb for four months but found out once they were there that it wasn't close to anything, and they had to Uber everywhere. They had paid in advance, so they were kind of stuck. You can always extend your stay if you really like where you've picked.

- Unlock your cell phone and purchase a local SIM card to save money on roaming fees as an expat.

- Make sure you understand the visa requirements and double-check that all the paperwork is in order. If you have to fly home just to get something done, it can waste a lot of money and time.

- Get a multi-country adapter if you are not from the Americas.

- If you have a favourite snack food, and you're pretty sure you will never be able to get it again, stock up. Take it with you; you'll at least get to enjoy it for a little while.

- Tell your bank you are leaving. Then, tell them again. Write to all of your credit card companies and give them your new address.

- Make sure you have a bank card with no foreign transaction fees. It really does suck when you have to pay $5 to take your money out at a bank machine and another

$5 from your home branch.

- Leave a photocopy of your passport, insurance documents, credit card and ID with someone back home.

- Carry your vaccination health card with you.

- Make sure you have adequate health care coverage for emergency use. Make sure you are covered fully for anything that might happen along the way. I always recommend private international health insurance, here is an excellent company to work with https://ExpatMoneyShow.com/insurance

- If you have pets, contact your airline to figure out what needs to be done before moving day. Check with the government in Mexico to find out what is required for your pets to enter the country and stay there.

- Cancel subscriptions to anything that comes in the mail. There is no mail service in Mexico, so you won't be able to do a redirect.

- Last but certainly not least, throw a big huge party to say goodbye to all of your friends and family. Tell them they are welcome to visit whenever they like; they just need to bring you one of your favourite treats from your hometown.

When my mom's friends came from Canada in January 2020, she asked them to bring her 4 lbs of lard (which can't be found in Panama) and a bottle of Aleve from Shoppers Drug Mart. Almost everything else we can find close to where we live.

Parties are important for closure. Yes, I am going through with this. No, I am not insane. Yes, I can't wait to get there and start my new life! And Yes, you are welcome, all of you!

Moving to Mexico offers many advantages that you won't find elsewhere. Making a living in the country is quite easy, especially as a digital nomad, and, as many people have already discovered, Mexico is a perfect retirement destination.

If you are considering an escape from the political turmoil and ever-increasing government encroachment in the U.S, Mexico is well-deserving of a place at the top of your list of possible alternatives. Once you make the move to Mexico, you may well find that your money generates more value in your life. With the low exchange rates, stable inflation, low cost of living, and massive investment potential–Mexico is simply the place to be right now.

But to be clear, Mexico should not be regarded as a cheaper version of the United States or Canada, one with better winter weather and fresher tortillas. It is not a country where the stack of dollars that delivered you solidly into the middle class back home will now make you look rather upscale and posh, with a bit of staff now and then, both in the house and in the garden.

Mexico will not change for you, although it will require you to change for it in order to discover a rewarding place there. A good way to look at this is that growth and change is the reason you came. We all could have stayed just the same back at home and always known what to expect. This is not a place for people who can't handle surprises or have lost their knack for improvisation. People in Mexico are accustomed to doing things as they have always done them. In this context, they feel that no explanation for this is required, and to ask for one evokes a reaction of startled surprise.

One Last Thing I'd Like To Share With You Before Signing Off.

HERE ARE A FEW THINGS YOU NEED TO DO:

Before you apply for a Mexican immigration visa, you'll need to have a number of documents apostilled in your home country. This typically takes about 2-3 months to process, so it's best to be prepared. These documents include:

- Marriage and birth certificates

- Passport, naturalization document, green card, proof of citizenship, etc.

- Social security cards

- Vaccinations, dental and medical records

- Insurance policies

- Academic records and diplomas

- Employment records

- Proof of residency (utility bills with your name and address)

- Driver's licenses

- Original reference letter from your bank (two banks would be better) addressed to a specific Mexican bank and signed by a bank official.

An Apostille is an internationally recognized method of authenticating government-issued documents such as birth and marriage certificates and driver's licenses. In the U.S., a state's Secretary of State can do the Apostille.

Life in Mexico: Never a Dull Moment!

SOURCES

- https://kids.nationalgeographic.com/geography/countries/article/mexico

- https://www.britannica.com/place/Mexico¡

- https://everything-everywhere.com/unesco-world-heritage-sites-mexico/

- http://microsite.smithsonianmag.com/ads/mexico/Heritage/historical.html

- https://travelmexicosolo.com/best-places-to-visit-in-mexico/

- https://www.mexican-clothing-co.com/traditional-mexican-dress.html

- https://sportsaspire.com/popular-sports-in-mexico

- https://www.chimuadventures.com/blog/2017/02/mexico-geography-blog/

- https://en.wikipedia.org/wiki/Tourism_in_Mexico

- https://althistory.fandom.com/wiki/Mexico_

- https://www.mexperience.com/lifestyle/history-of-mexico/pre-columbian-era/

- https://www.myrouteapp.com/en/motor-and-car-routes/mx

- https://kidworldcitizen.org/the-story-of-the-mexican-flag/

- https://theculturetrip.com/north-america/mexico/articles/the-story-behind-the-mexican-flag/

- https://www.lonelyplanet.com/articles/best-time-to-visit-mexico

- https://talkbaja.com/understanding-bajas-climate-zones/

- https://www.detailedpedia.com/wiki-Mexico_City

- https://www.mexperience.com/mexico-essentials/getting-married-in-mexico/

- https://www.timeanddate.com/holidays/mexico/benito-juarez &q=benito+juarez+birthday&ei=EJmuT4qMF-nDoQWRtPmL CQ&sa=X&ct=res&resnum=8&ved=0CEgQFjAH

- https://www.timeanddate.com/holidays/mexico/cinco-de-mayo

- https://ich.unesco.org/en/RL/indigenous-festivity-dedicated-to-the-dead-00054

- https://www.timeanddate.com/holidays/mexico/revolution-day

- https://www.holidayscalendar.com/event/august-bank-holiday-in-ireland/

- https://www.travel.com/cities/1002640-mexico-city

- https://en.wikipedia.org/wiki/Mexico_City

- https://www.detailedpedia.com/wiki-Mexico_City

- https://www.atlasobscura.com/places/the-great-pyramid-of-cholula-san-andres-cholula-mexico

- https://en.wikipedia.org/wiki/Condesa

- https://www.bondicentral.com/post/four-days-in-vibrant-mexico-city

- https://en.wikipedia.org/wiki/Puerto_Vallarta

- https://en.wikipedia.org/wiki/San_Miguel_de_Allende

- https://learn.iwillteachyoualanguage.com/spanish-beginner?affiliate_id=1764132

- https://learn.iwillteachyoualanguage.com/grammar-hero-spanishjp9hueb4?affiliate_id=1764132

- https://amzn.to/2OFr3ko

- https://learn.iwillteachyoualanguage.com/spanish-conversations-sales-pagevfdb8oq8?affiliate_id=1764132

- https://learn.iwillteachyoualanguage.com/spanish-conversations-sales-pagevfdb8oq8?affiliate_id=1764132

- https://expatmoneyshow.com/italki

- https://learn.iwillteachyoualanguage.com/grammar-hero-spanishjp9hueb4?affiliate_id=1764132

- https://amzn.to/2SdlbAV

- https://amzn.to/2UH8AHV

- https://amzn.to/2UDKcXR

- https://www.swedishnomad.com/mexico-fruits/

- https://blog.amigofoods.com/index.php/mexican-foods/mexican-drinks/

- https://www.numbeo.com/cost-of-living/cpi_explained.jsp

- https://www.statista.com/topics/5761/supermarkets-in-mexico/

- https://www.pointsandtravel.com/grocery-stores-in-mexico/

- Comparisons made on https://www.numbeo.com/cost-of-living/

- https://www.gob.mx/banjercito/articulos/sistema-de-importacion-temporal-de-vehiculos

- https://www.mexconnect.com/articles/164-living-healthy-in-mexico-insurance-health-care-and-mexico-s-medical-tourism-a-resource-page/

- https://www.mexconnect.com/articles/1821-know-the-law-in-mexico-medical-coverage-and-hospitals/

- https://expatmoney.com/blog/panama-health-care

- https://en.wikipedia.org/wiki/Homeschooling

- https://www.worldschoolingcentral.com/what-is-worldschooling/

- https://expatschool.io/novice-program

- https://expatschool.io/high-school-program

- https://en.wikipedia.org/wiki/Mexican_nationality_law

- https://infogalactic.com/info/Mexican_nationality_law

- https://expatmoney.com/blog/top-countries-for-birth-tourism

- https://www.passportindex.org/visa.php

- https://iaea2022.org/index.php/conference/travel-information

- https://funnyinterestingcool.com/viewtopic.php?t=312

- https://www.mexperience.com/your-mexican-tourist-permit-fmm/

- https://thisismodernaging.com/mexico-retirement-visas-101/

- https://themazatlanpost.com/2018/09/08/types-of-visas-available-for-those-wishing-to-reside-in-mexico/

- https://k9h2z2w9.stackpathcdn.com/wp-content/uploads/Guide-to-Driving-in-Mexico-Mexperience.pdf

- https://en.wikipedia.org/wiki/Speed_limits_in_Mexico

- https://overlandsphere.com/overland-forum/threads/entering-mexico-with-your-foreign-vehicle.4535/

- https://www.mexperience.com/temporary-import-permit-tip-vehicles-mexico/

- https://www.mexconnect.com/articles/561-mexican-bus-travel-in-all-its-adventure-and-glory/

- https://www.mexperience.com/transport/flights-in-mexico/

- https://www.creditkarma.com/advice/i/what-is-a-heloc

- https://micasarec.com/en/mexico/san-miguel-de-allende

- https://en.wikipedia.org/wiki/Canc%C3%BAn

- https://retirementandgoodliving.com/whats-it-like-to-live-and-retire-in-cancun-mexico/

- https://www.oyster.com/articles/11-things-you-need-to-know-before-traveling-to-cozumel/

- https://cozumelmycozumel.com/cozumel-island-living/

- https://www.mexicoonmymind.com/campeche-2/

- https://en.wikipedia.org/wiki/Mazatl%C3%A1n

- https://focusonmexico.com/moving-stuff-mexico-household-effects/

- https://siam-shipping.com/shipping-tips/how-lcl-freight-work/

- https://internationalmoving.com/glossary-of-terms-for-international-shipping/

- https://www.thespruce.com/binding-estimate-hiring-movers-2435985

- http://www.ishipitright.com/guide-to-international-moving/

- https://careerforfreshers.com/articles/a-bright-future-for-digital-nomads-in-2021/

- https://devrim.im/digital-nomads

ABOUT THE AUTHOR

FOUNDER & CEO - EXPAT MONEY™

Mikkel Thorup is the world's most sought-after expat consultant. He focuses on helping high-net-worth private clients to legally mitigate tax liabilities, obtain a second residency and citizenship, and assemble a portfolio of foreign investments including international real estate, timber plantations, agricultural land and other hard-money tangible assets.

Mikkel is the Founder and CEO at Expat Money™, a private consulting firm started in 2017. He hosts the popular weekly podcast, the Expat Money Show, and wrote the definitive #1-Best Selling book Expat Secrets - How To Pay Zero Taxes, Live Overseas And Make Giant Piles Of Money.

A world traveller since his teens, Mikkel Thorup has learned his craft in three unique and unconventional ways; first, by living it himself, continuously pushing the boundaries testing new ideas around the globe; next, from diligent and intense study consuming over 2000 books and courses on the subject; and finally, by apprenticing and learning directly from the world's top legal experts in the field.

Mikkel has dedicated himself for over two decades to building this mountain of knowledge, one that is not constrained by languages, cultures, or borders.

He now works one-on-one with private clients utilizing thiscombination of hard-won experience and in-depth knowledge and has helpedhundreds of people to build their dream lives abroad.

As an autodidact, Mikkel stopped attending school at 12 years old before officially dropping out at the age of 15. Both his own experiences growing up, and those of his children as expats in an increasingly remote world, have inspired Mikkel to innovate in the field of education.

In 2021 he co-founded the Expat International School of Freedom & Entrepreneurship. This revolutionary online learning program focuses on encouraging children and teenagers to develop their skills and abilities in a purpose-driven and responsible way and how to apply them in the real world.

Since leaving Canada as a teenager, Mikkel has been an avid traveller. He has circumnavigated the globe over 400 times, visiting more than 100 countries and has called 9 different countries home in his 20+ years of non-stop continual travel around the world.

Mikkel Thorup has inspired countless individuals through his podcast, books, and appearances on hundreds of radio and podcast interviews.

A respected and sought-after keynote speaker has seen him invited to present at events inChina, the UAE, Belize, Costa Rica, the USA, Panama, Liberland, Ukraine and many more. He speaks on immigration, maximizing international investments and how to move offshore for more freedom, privacy and protection. He is a powerful speaker with a rich and inspiring story.

Mikkel Thorup is the Free Cities Ambassador with The Free Cities Foundation, and sits on the Board of Directors for multiple construction and community development companies that are focused on freedom and self-sustainably in Latin America.

As a passionate philanthropist, Mikkel Thorup sits on the Board of Directors for 10 Eighteen Uganda, a non-profit organization dedicated to providing resources and opportunities for teen mothers in the Namuwongo slums of Uganda.

Mikkel Thorup is a dedicated husband and father of two. When not helping clients or growing his 7-figure consulting firm, he enjoys travelling and spending time with his wife and children.

To learn more about Mikkel Thorup, you can join his daily email correspondence, EMS Pulse - an invaluable resource for planning your new life abroad that is currently enjoyed by over 37,000 expats and expat hopefuls worldwide or you can email support@expatmoney.com

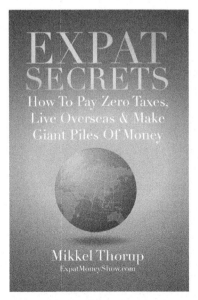

"It will open your mind about expat opportunities - Mikkel explained and debunked many myths associated with expats lifestyle. By reading this book, I was encouraged and motivated to persue a lifestyle that I always dreamed of! He showed that you can create wealth, raise family, travel the world and make impact to the world while living outside your place of birth!" Filip Stankovski. **Available on Amazon.**

Made in the USA
Las Vegas, NV
29 August 2023

76819003R00262